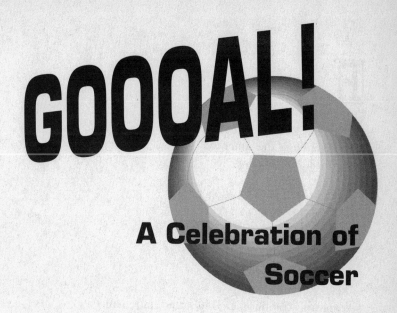

GOOOAL!

A Celebration of Soccer

Andrés Cantor
with Daniel Arcucci

A Fireside Book
Published by Simon & Schuster

FIRESIDE
Rockefeller Center
1230 Avenue of the Americas
New York, NY 10020

First Fireside edition 1997

FIRESIDE and colophon are registered trademarks
of Simon & Schuster Inc.

Photos courtesy of *El Gráfico* magazine and the author's
personal collection.

Designed by Irving Perkins Associates

English translation: D. W., R.P.P.

Manufactured in the United States of America

10 9 8 7 6 5 4 3 2 1

Library of Congress Cataloging-in-Publication Data is available.

ISBN 0-684-81440-4
      0-684-83340-9 (pbk)

Contents

Prologue
by Carlos Salvador Bilardo

This is a different kind of soccer book. It talks not only about team histories and participants, about statistics and individual names, but also about the evolution of soccer from a technical and tactical point of view, and also from the perspective of its organizational and political context. As a history of the World Cup, this book covers it all.

From the start, it becomes clear how soccer has always been inextricably linked with politics. The book summons up images from the thirties of *Il Duce,* Mussolini, watching from his honorary box, to our own time, with countries fighting over the venue of a World Cup tournament as if it were an affair of state. That's what the modern World Cup competitions have become after all: a national event, in which everybody participates. And when I say everybody, I mean not only those spectators present in the stadiums, but also those in front their television sets across the world, another symbol of our time.

At the center of this story—although not always, as will be seen—is the tactical evolution: how soccer was played, how it is played now, and how it will be played. Before, it was played purely and exclusively for love of country, as we will see from the words of Francisco Varallo, hero of the first World Cup. Now—and I got to hear it myself in Italy 1990—many players have a different attitude, as expressed by comments such as: "Oh well, we lost, so at least now we get to go home." The motivation is different now—money rules—and some of those who have it made are content to sit back and relax as the games pass them by. Those who are not in this situation, dream of one day getting there by way of the World Cup: It is the showcase, the screen, and the podium for their international marketability. Many things are at stake: money, contracts, corporations, the governments themselves. . . . Now, players are even paid to celebrate their victories a certain way, as occurred with the Brazilian players in 1994. There are still some romantics left, but not many. Fortunately, I had the kind of players on my national team who played for the pride of wearing the colors of their country. I can assure you that not one of us was there for the money: We made thirty thousand dollars in the first championship (Mexico 1986) and fifty thousand dollars in the second (Italy 1990). We spent almost all of it on tickets that we gave away to friends: Maradona spent twenty thousand dollars, Caniggia fifteen thousand, and I spent eleven thousand dollars. There are plenty of other players, some famous, some not, who hate to lose, and I am sure their pain is not motivated by economics. Otherwise, how can we explain Maradona's tears after the final in Italy 1990 or Baresi's after missing his penalty kick in USA 1994?

Among the many revelations in this book, there is a very important one for me, because it verifies what I have always believed: The soccer world is getting more and more uniform. With every passing World Cup, there are more potential candidates. That is to say that things are getting more and more even across the board. More and more teams are participating, from every corner of the planet, with no continent excluded. It isn't just Europe against South America any more; Africa, Asia, Oceania, and North America recently jumped on the bandwagon. . . . But parity cannot be measured definitively, so I'll leave that debate for another book.

What I can ascertain, from this story of the World Cup and from my own personal observations, is that soccer has stagnated tactically: In this aspect, it has fallen behind by a decade. And FIFA is responsible for it. It did much at the promotional level, but little at the technical-tactical level. Consequently, soccer's influence is widespread, but its technical and tactical features have not evolved along with its popularity. So here we are with a super-sophisticated World Cup like USA 1994 with stupendous TV coverage and technological advances, but we've lost the fundamentals: great players, great skill, the action taking place on the field, which should be what's most important.

This should be our main concern: otherwise, everything else is useless. We are out of business. And soccer is a business-show or show business, as I once said in 1960. At that time it was very hard for me to accept, but time has finally demonstrated that it is true.

That's why we have to take care of soccer, keep it up to date. Otherwise we will have games that are not good business for anybody and even less for the fans, as was the case with some games of the USA tournament. And that's not good.

Soccer should evolve the same as other disciplines. If science, medicine, and communications evolve, why not soccer? One could prove that in 1994, for example, the same strategies were used as in 1986 and 1990. What does this mean? It means that there was no evolution.

Another thing I always wanted to see—and this book has done it for me—is some sort of record of the main protagonists of the different World Cups. How do they remember the times in which they were at the center of the soccer world, and how do they experience it now, from the outside?

In the end, it is evident that soccer is like life itself. As in life, not everything has been invented yet; it is still possible to grow. In the past, it was enough to know how to read and write just as it was possible for a soccer player to specialize in one position within the tactical plan. Now, one needs to know languages and computers and, in soccer, it is necessary to know the secrets of all the positions. The player who knows how to play only one position is not going to advance. With this change, in which the players would become even more technically skilled and capable of being positioned in different parts of the field, strategy would have to be modified. Ideally everybody would be able to play every position. The best yardstick for measuring this ideal is the following: The day when pregame shows disappear, it will be a step forward. What I mean is, the day when absolutely nothing of what will happen on the field will be predictable, beginning with the positions of the players . . . that's what soccer should aspire to and that is what future World Cup events should reflect.

Over a span of so many years it is difficult to make comparisons. Was the game played better before or now? It's the same as asking: Is life better now or before? Well, life has evolved, just like everything else . . . medicine, engineering, aeronautics, computer science. It is logical, therefore, for soccer to follow the same road.

To achieve this we have to search for innovations, such as the new rule forbidding the goalkeeper to handle the ball after a teammate has passed it to him. Now, I, myself, am fighting for some things: For example, that there be no substitutions allowed after eighty-five minutes, because their main purpose after that point is to waste time. Another possibility is to implement kick-ins instead of throw-ins, because it would provide more scoring opportunities.

First, one has to test and then change—everything helps.

Even the players' transportation isn't the same. Years ago, all the teams traveled on one ship, to Europe or to America. Now, it's almost impossible for two teams to get on the same plane during a World Cup. Before, the press were almost unnoticeable; now, they set attendance records at each event.

All the nuances, all the elements that make up a good history. And have no doubt that the World Cup will continue to be great as long as great soccer players continue to appear on the scene. I always enjoyed being asked before a World Cup: Who will be the star? Before Mexico 1986, I had the opportunity to answer with an enormous list of names: Platini, Zico, Hugo Sanchez, Rummenigge, Maradona. Before USA 1994, faced with the same question, it was hard for me to answer because I wanted to talk about real stars, those whose names will go down in history as the truly great players of the World Cup.

The equation is always the same: If one has good soccer players, one is able to develop a good strategy. It's the same as in life, exactly the same: In a competitive world you've got to stay one step ahead.

For now, the balance sheet says we are stuck. The tendency has to be reversed, and the technical as well as tactical levels have to be raised. To achieve this, there is no other way but to instill from the very beginning more technique and less strategy. This is what today's soccer calls for. It is necessary to stop the ball with your chest as if your life depended on it, because if it gets away from you by a few inches too many, your opponent is right there on top of you to take it away; it is necessary to learn to kick with both feet, dribble, and head the ball. In short, today's soccer player must be a technical, tactical, and physical phenomenon, able to play with speed, as well as precision.

In the Mexico 1970 tournament, one of the most beautiful in history, the game was still played at a slower pace. The final, Brazil against Italy, one of the great games of its time (in my opinion), proves it. Today, that's no longer possible: The objective is to be able to play the ball with the same virtuosity but greater speed.

That's the great challenge of the World Cup competitions to come, in which players will have less room to move.

I was often asked: "Bilardo, how would you like to be remembered in the history of the World Cup?" And I always gave the same answer. . . . As a man who defended the technical player, but who demanded from him the maximum effort so as to make him useful tactically; as a man who, in the face of the worst imaginable criticism and pressure, defended a style that was subsequently proven effective and implemented throughout the world. So, I would be thrilled if, after reading this magnificent tour through soccer's most sublime moments, it were said: "Yes, Mr. Bilardo, you were quite right when in 1965 you championed the kind of soccer that is played today."

Introduction

I always had to fight for soccer, always: in Argentina, my country—where soccer is in the blood—I fought for the chance to enjoy it to the utmost; in the United States, my adopted country—where it was necessary to reestablish soccer—I've fought to help others discover it and, in doing so, to continue enjoying it myself.

As I begin this history—which is in part my own—an early image comes to mind: I am urging my parents to stop buying *La Opinión,* an Argentine newspaper that dedicated almost as little space to my favorite sport as an American newspaper, and to bring home *La Nación* with its giant sports page filled with soccer news. I consumed it all because for me, the pleasure consisted not only in going to the stadium and seeing my favorite team; soccer was life itself. That must be the reason that it was—and is—filled with such great joys and such deep sorrows. Among the latter, I remember one clearly, and coincidentally it deals with the World Cup tournament. It occurred in 1969, during the qualifying rounds for the first World Cup that Mexico was going to host in 1970. It was a gloomy, cold, and restless afternoon. Early that day, my father and his friends had left the villa on the outskirts of Buenos Aires, where we were spending the weekend, and headed toward the legendary La Bombonera stadium, where the Argentine national team was to face Peru for its chance at the biggest international event imaginable. My father left me behind that day, just as the national team was also left behind—the 2–2 tie with Peru eliminated Argentina from Mexico 1970. It was the last major disappointment suffered by Argentine soccer, which from that time on has never been absent from the big show.

My passion for my team, Boca Juniors, knew no limits, but any match in any division appealed to me. For someone who felt about soccer the way I did, moving to a country like the United States—where *fútbol* did not even go by the same name—was a hard blow, too difficult to absorb. But my parents' decision was final, and I landed in California. Soccer withdrawal forced me to make an extreme decision: I would separate from my family, return to my country, and finish my studies there, even at the risk of knowing that I would not be together with them until I stabilized my situation. When I finally returned, some good news improved my mood: The Los Angeles Aztecs had signed Johan Cruyff. To my delight, that Dutch great, one of the most recognizable names in the entire history of the World Cup, lived in my own neighborhood, only a few miles from Pasadena's Rose Bowl. One morning, I waited for him to take his Dobermans out for a walk, and I accosted him. I spoke to him so much, threw so many details at him, and was so passionate about making him see that I did not miss a single Aztec game that Johan ended up believing there was a nut in the neighborhood who felt about soccer the same way he did. It was the era of the Cosmos, of Pele and Beckenbauer. But I was soon left with a bitter aftertaste since soon thereafter, all signs indicated that the most wonderful game on Earth would never catch on in this country.

Disenchanted, I set my goal on making a very special journey: to Argentina, to attend, in any way possible, the 1978 World Cup. I remember it today and still feel the cold of that harsh winter cutting into my bones, but I also remember the special warmth of a World Cup being played in my own country. I was staying in Buenos Aires, but I went three times by train to the city of Rosario in the country's heartland, a four-hour journey, to follow Menotti's national team. I saw the finals in River Plate's Monumental stadium from an unusual and auspicious place: the highest row of bleachers right behind the goal, right next to a . . . television camera. Color television had arrived in Argentina as had instant replay. Many years later, a similar contraption would film me as well as the game, so that I could share this passion of mine with millions of viewers.

All of that would begin after my first efforts as a reporter. After college and my first appearances on Spanish-language radio programs, at last an offer came from the Univision television network. They kept me informed of every soccer event that took place. When the sports director arranged to meet me, he advised me to bring two shirts, two ties, and two jackets. "For one audition? How strange . . . ," I thought. Then, Jorge Berry told me: "You're doing the first game today . . . and the next one next Sunday."

I did the color commentary for that initial match between the Chivas Rayadas of Guadalajara and Rosario Central of Argentina. "Very good, very good," they told me. "But what we need is a play-by-play man . . . are you game for the next one?" I was willing to do anything. The next match was the Mexican club America against AS Roma of Italy, and it was then that I shouted "Goooalll" really loudly, for the first time. It came from my soul, from my heart. It had the power that comes only from things that spring from one's essence. I put my dreams, my childhood, my life into that scream, one that I had been hearing forever from listening to Jose Maria Muñoz, the legendary Argentine sportscaster, on the radio at home . . . it was my starting point.

First from Laguna Niguel and later from Miami, where Univision moved its headquarters, I had the opportunity to broadcast soccer—which was the same as broadcasting my deepest passion—to everyone in the United States. I no longer had to travel six hours by car to Mexicali as I did during the Latin American "Little World Cup" of Uruguay in 1981 to watch soccer on television in a room at the Holiday Inn. It was now in my hands to take soccer everywhere.

Perhaps because of that, when I announced on July 4, 1988, that the United States of America would be the site of the 1994 World Cup, I was filled with mixed emotions: on one hand, the anger of feeling that it was a country that for so long had not appreciated something so beautiful and therefore did not deserve it; on the other hand, the inevitable hope that someday *fútbol,* or soccer—whatever one wishes to call it—could be appreciated by everyone.

That's what I was thinking when I assumed the responsibility—not to mention the effort—of broadcasting that World Cup's fifty-two games. And I shouted—from the heart—that word that sums up soccer: "Gooooooooal!!!"

This work attempts to summarize the spirit of the most beautiful sport in the world, through all aspects of its evolution and development. Every World Cup has its own story, written by men whose images grow with the passage of time until they are transformed into legends. A reporter's appreciation of soccer is a subjective act, not an exact science. Throughout the history of soccer, reporters have attempted to capture with utmost honesty their memory of a game and its impact on the public. A thousand different interpretations may be offered for a play or a feat without any of them being wrong. In this book, I pour out the passion and fascination that soccer has always aroused in me and, through the unique perspective of its protagonists and witnesses, I offer you this reporter's interpretation of the history of the World Cup.

The Birth of the World Cup

Today, with the World Cup having been established as the biggest and most spectacular sporting event in the world, one cannot help but admire the fabulous vision of the leader who, more than sixty years ago, conceived and planned it.

Let's go back in time to when the hero of our story, the Frenchman Jules Rimet, at the age of forty-eight, assumed the presidency of the International Soccer Federation (FIFA)—founded on May 21, 1904. The birth of FIFA, of course, created the possibility of organizing an international soccer tournament, but because of soccer's participation in the Olympic Games, this dream had to be delayed until 1921 when the great Frenchman got it back on track.

Jules Rimet understood even then that the amateur players, which the International Olympic Committee was insisting on, were not the only great representatives of his sport, which was rushing headlong toward professionalism. Therefore, in 1926, with a statement that seems bold even by today's standards—"that soccer could reinforce the ideals of a permanent and real peace"—he proclaimed the need for organizing, within a period of no more than three or four years, the first world tournament open to all the federations, without distinction between professionals and amateurs.

The opposition of powerful England, defender of amateurism till the end, was not sufficient. With Rimet—a man who combined diplomacy and leadership—another Frenchman, Henri Delaunay (accompanied by a special commission composed of four additional members, the leaders Bonnet, Meisl, Linneman, and Ferretti)—a man who put words into action—remarked almost prophetically: "The best soccer players cannot participate in the

Olympic Games. We must implement a tournament which represents us. . . ." To top it all off he made the commission's work official: "This Assembly has decided to organize in 1930 a competition open to the national teams of all the associated federations."

In three successive congresses of FIFA (Barcelona, Zurich, and Geneva), the system of the competition—the cup, by elimination—and the period of time between each competition—every four years, alternating with the Olympic Games—were established. And so, on May 26, 1928, in Amsterdam, just as Uruguay was retaining its Olympic title after a final with Argentina, the World Cup was born.

The congress had just won their biggest battle, when they were confronted with another: Where would the first tournament be held? The Europeans—Italy, Holland, Spain, Hungary, and Sweden—were quick to volunteer; Uruguay, in South America, did the same, and the war of political interest, a constant factor in this story, was on.

Rimet once again gave proof of his amazing vision: He saw that the doors of the faraway New World, across the Atlantic, were opening in order to make soccer a universal show. To reinforce his opinion, he used an almost irrefutable argument: the record. Uruguay—with the other great team of South America, Argentina—had just dominated and won two spectacular Olympic finals, in Paris 1924 and Amsterdam 1928. After the 1924 final, the Europeans understood that there was another way of playing: with more ball-control skill and the ability to carry it. And after the 1928 final, there were those who were now totally convinced, like the British correspondent of the *Daily Express,* who declared: "There is no team in my country that could put on a show as great as the one Uruguay and Argentina have."

Not even the regional rallying around Italy's candidacy could change the obstinate and skillful Frenchman's mind: On May 18, 1929, at the Congress of Barcelona, Uruguay was proclaimed host of the first World Cup.

A prominent Uruguayan, Viera, found the perfect words to justify the decision: "Other countries have history, we have soccer." Immediately, the French sculptor Abel Lafleur was hired to design the trophy that was to trouble the sleep of soccer players the world over for years to come: a *Winged Victory* made of eighteen hundred grams of solid gold, which survived several harrowing episodes—thefts, disappearances, kidnappings—until it was eventually left in the hands of the Brazilians in 1970, when they won it for the third time. But that was still a long way off. . . .

Uruguay 1930

The fight to host the 1930 World Cup had left a good deal of bad blood, and in those days there was one surefire way for the losers to retaliate: by staying home. Italy, Holland, Sweden, Spain, and Hungary, having lost out on the opportunity to organize the tournament, were the first to turn their backs on it. The British (England, Scotland, Wales, and Northern Ireland) followed suit, stubbornly adhering to the tradition in the British Isles of placing amateur events before professional ones. Along with the British, the majority of the European national teams—including Austria, Czechoslovakia, Switzerland, and Germany—excused themselves from participating in this first World Cup, arguing that Uruguay was too far away, especially given the difficulties of a long journey in those days. To persuade them, the organizers tried to be accommodating, offering to pay for their transportation and lodging. But that wasn't enough.

The only ones who agreed to the journey, which entailed a fifteen-day-long crossing of the Atlantic, had reasons other than mere economics.

France went because it was the home of FIFA's president and the founder of the tournament, Jules Rimet. Still, even Rimet's influence couldn't compel the greatest Gallic striker of the period, Racing Club of Paris's Manuel Anatol, to come along. Also left behind was national team coach Gaston Barreau, because of prior commitments to his students at the Paris Conservatory. Belgium also made the trek to Uruguay. The "Red Devils" had been persuaded to make the trip by their compatriot Rodolphe William Seeldrayers, vice president of FIFA.

Romania's King Carol, an enthusiastic sports fan, had pledged his country's presence during FIFA's Amsterdam Convention in 1928, and a king's word was law. Yugoslavia could not turn down the opportunity to sail to South America on the cruise ship *Florida*. It was a ship created exclusively for the entertainment, pleasure, and relaxation of the rich and, therefore, the Yugoslavs set sail ready to enjoy two weeks of the *dolce far niente* (doing nothing).

The rest boarded the *Conte Verde,* which gave them a chance to do some training: swimming, weights, and even Ping-Pong. They gave up on practicing after some of the few balls brought on the ship went overboard, casualties of the first bizarre attempts to play soccer at sea.

That's how Diego Lucero—pen name of Luis Sciutto, a Uruguayan journalist who had settled in Argentina and the only person to attend the first fifteen World Cups—remembered it not long ago, before his much lamented death in 1995:

> I remember it as if it were yesterday. In the first days of July, the ocean liner *Conte Verde,* converted into the floating embassy of soccer, entered the port of Montevideo. The delegations from Romania and Belgium had embarked in Genoa. There had been problems with the Romanians. Most of their players worked for the British companies that exploited Ploesti's rich oil deposits, and the English refused them the three-month leave that a World Cup adventure entailed. A woman came to their rescue. The witty and beautiful Madame Magda Lupescu, who, according to rumors, was King Carol of Romania's mistress. The aggrieved players went to Magda with their plight. The lady wanted to help the young players and asked the king to intervene on their behalf. In response to the royal intercession, the English gave in. The golden World Cup trophy borne by Jules Rimet and FIFA vice president Maurice Flischer had come aboard at Villefranche, near Nice, where the *Conte Verde* had made a stop to pick up the French delegation. The arrival of the *Conte Verde* marked a milestone in the history of Montevideo.

From the Americas, after a far less arduous voyage, came neighboring Argentina as well as Paraguay, Peru, Bolivia, Chile, Brazil (which went aboard the *Conte Verde* for the last leg of its voyage), and Mexico. Also, the United States arrived, thoroughly prepared and ready for anything. In those years, American clubs customarily used foreign players, especially Scots. The almost immediate naturalization process allowed the United States to use these players on its national team. As we'll soon see, the results they obtained that time around may be surprising.

So, here they were: thirteen teams. Not all of which came willingly. Sixty-four years later, no pressure would be necessary: 144 participants would hurl themselves into the fray for a place among the final 24, which would play USA 1994.

But let's go back to the Uruguay of 1930 and see what kind of country the thirteen pioneering teams found.

Uruguay had 1,900,000 inhabitants all sharing an obsession called soccer. A journalist of the time, Osvaldo Heber Lorenzo, summed it up better than anyone else: "A Uruguayan who does not like soccer is not a Uruguayan." Perhaps for that reason, the financial difficulties suffered in the aftermath of the Wall Street crash were set aside and the positive energy of the people was channeled into the single-minded desire to be on the world's center stage—at least the center of the soccer world—which, to them, meant practically the same thing. Before achieving this, however, they had to overcome some minor technicalities.

First, a stadium worthy of the big event needed to be built. The stadiums of the country's two big clubs, Peñarol and Nacional, were neither large enough nor modern enough. Peñarol's stadium was in Pocitos, while Nacional's was in the Parque Central, at the corner of 8 de Octubre and Cibeles Street. The government chose Parque Battle and Ordoñez as the location for the new, giant stadium in the city of Montevideo. Designed by architect Juan Scasso, the new stadium was christened the Centenario, a name that commemorated the hundred-year anniversary of Uruguay's National Constitution. Work on the stadium started in February of 1930 and continued uninterrupted until the stadium's inauguration midway through the tournament. Workers labored day and night, illuminated by projection lights. Finally, after consuming 160,000 cubic meters of soil, 14,000 cubic meters of cement, and 1,000,000 pesos, the big ring of cement was completed. Montevideo could now proudly boast of a stadium with a capacity of 90,000 and two stands carrying the names of the greatest achievements in Uruguayan soccer up to that point: Colombes, in Paris, and Amsterdam, the sites of Uruguay's two Olympic titles.

Montevideo was a beautiful city, but the Europeans, thinking they were destined for the middle of nowhere, were surprised to find Ford and Chevrolet automobiles cruising the streets and a President, Juan Campisteguy, who welcomed them in French. Besides, everyone breathed soccer, and, after all, that was what it was all about.

The tournament started on July 13, 1930, at two o'clock in the afternoon. The inaugural match was not played in Centenario stadium, where work was still in progress, but in Peñarol's stadium at Pocitos Station. Before a crowd of no more than five hundred people, France beat Mexico. The first game and the first result: 4–1. Also the first injury, suffered by French goalkeeper Thepot, ten minutes into the game. At that time, substitutions were not yet allowed, so the French were forced to play with ten men, and the defender Chantrell had to put on a different shirt and become the team's goalie.

And, of course, there was the first goal in World Cup history. It was the work of Frenchman Lucien Laurent, nineteen minutes into the game. He later remembered it like this: "Our goalkeeper Thepot gave the ball to our center-half Pinel, who passed the ball to me. I beat a Mexican defender with a short dribble and gave the ball to my left wing, Langiller. I sprinted toward the penalty area and, after getting the ball back, I shot from fifteen meters to the right of the goalkeeper Bonfiglio, scoring the first goal."

The next day, the same stadium hosted a Group 3 competition. By a score of 3–1, Romania defeated Peru, which exhibited a skillful and refined style that would be sustained throughout the years. It was the game in which Romanian back Steiner established quite an unpleasant precedent: He became the first player to break a bone in World Cup play. The style of play was very tough and, perhaps for that reason, the Centenario would later include a surgery room, making it unique in the soccer world . . . not only for that reason, I might add.

The tournament proceeded without many surprising results, but it did have some notable high points. On July 15, France and Argentina matched up in a high-level encounter. Goalkeeper Thepot had already recovered from his injury, and the confrontation between two great midfields (Suarez–Monti–Juan Evaristo for the Argentines and Villaplane–Pine–Chantrel for the French) promised to bring out the best in each. This promise was fulfilled in a tough and even game. The scales were finally tipped in favor of the South Americans when, at eighty minutes, Pinel left Monti a slight opening on a free kick. The Argentine beat Thepot with a precise, powerful shot. The French rushed to the attack but stood in disbelief when, at eighty-four minutes, they heard the three whistles ending the game.

The whole French team surrounded Brazilian referee Almeida Rego in protest. The Uruguayan public—who had been rooting for the French from the first minute—poured onto the field and all hell broke loose until Almeida Rego, after consulting the linesmen, acknowledged his error and ordered play to resume. But the delay had taken the French off their game, allowing the Argentines to continue their march to the final. No sooner had they overcome the last obstacles of their Group—Mexico and Chile—when coach Pedro Olazar surprised everybody by pulling his two strikers. Out went Perinetti and Cherro, in came Carlos Peucelle and Guillermo Stabile. The gamble paid off as the "Infiltrator," Stabile, went on an incredible scoring spree, scoring three goals against Mexico and two against Chile, and earning himself a place at the top of the goal-scorers list.

Things were starting to fall into place, and those who should have won, did. In Group 2, Brazil fielded a weak team because a dispute between the Sports Confederation and the Paulista Federation left the best players at home. Among those left behind was Friedenreich, a great scorer. To put it in perspective, it would be as if Brazil had come to World Cup 1994 with Flamengo, Fluminese, and Vasco da Gama players but without Sao Paulo, Palmeiras, or Corinthians. There they faced a better Yugoslavia, sustained by goalkeeper Jaksic, whose style was elegant both in play and dress, down to his immaculate white gloves. Joining him were midfielder Stefanovic and strikers Sekulic and Bek. They eliminated Brazil and also beat the Cinderella of the group, Bolivia.

As for Group 3, it had Uruguay, and so attracted the most attention, as would be the case with every host team. On July 18, the centennial of Uruguay's National Constitution, the home team, La Celeste, made its debut, inaugurating Centenario stadium. It was an all-out party, with eighty thousand spectators full of patriotic fervor. However, a difficult game cast a shadow over the festivities, temporarily, at least. Peru refused to be overlooked, and their tiny but tough goalkeeper Pardon saved almost everything, making no apologies for almost spoiling the festive mood in the stadium. I say almost because fifteen minutes into the second half, "Manco" Castro—Hector Scarone's backup—scored, giving Uruguay victory (1–0) but not peace of mind. As with Argentina, the home team started out confidently but ended with doubts. Like his Argentine colleague Olazar, Uruguayan coach Alberto Supicci changed his attackers: out went Urdinaran, Petrone, and Castro and in came Dorado, Scarone, and Anselmo. In the long run, however, this move paid off. In the decisive match against Romania, the veteran thirty-two-year-old Scarone masterfully led La Celeste to a 4–0 score before the first half was even over.

In Group 4 the United States whizzed by without problems, eliminating Belgium and Paraguay by an identical score of 3–0. The North Americans were known as the "shot-putters," and they were, well . . . mostly Scottish. With their big physiques and impressive strength, men like Alec Wood, James Gallagher, Andrew Auld, James Brown, Bart McGhee (Scottish), and George Moorhouse (English) reached the semifinal, where the luck of the draw gave them a difficult opponent: Argentina. Questioned by journalists about the upcoming match, American official Wilfried R. Cummings responded, perhaps innocently: "We're not concerned about this semifinal game against Argentina. Our mind is already on the final, against Uruguay."

In the other group, the fates had determined that either Yugoslavia or Uruguay would be the finalist.

For the two South American teams, the semifinals were perfunctory exercises. Both teams won their respective games by an identical score: 6–1.

On July 26, on a playing field almost totally flooded by the previous night's rain, Argentina's Monti opened the score against the United States, and Peucelle and Stabile, who reappeared in the starting lineup, scored two and three goals respectively, ending the American dream.

On July 27, in front of the largest crowd of the tournament (the game grossed 35,057 pesos, almost 14 percent of the total), Uruguay overcame an early goal by Yugoslavia's Sekulic and mercilessly responded with six goals of their own. Three goals by Cea, two by Anselmo, and one by Iriarte gave the victory to Uruguay.

The story was playing itself out without any surprises; the final was as everyone had expected: Uruguay against Argentina, a classic rivalry.

This was just the first World Cup, but over the years it would be more and more evident that this most special tournament would come to define the best of soccer, in every aspect, particularly the tactical.

So how did Uruguay and Argentina play? To answer this question we need to go back a few more years to 1925, when the international board decided to change the offside rule. Until that time, Rule 11 required three defenders between the goal and an attacker without the ball. It therefore sufficed for one of the defensive backs to move forward when a pass came to the lead striker, leaving him offside. The rule change allowed for one less defender than previously necessary to leave an attacker offside. Therefore, the center-forward who had been the line of attack's playmaker, positioned behind the line of strikers, now took a more advanced position on the field, pushing against the rival defenders like a thorn in their side.

That is how Argentina's "Infiltrator" Guillermo Stabile, leading goal-scorer of that World Cup, rose to stardom, at the expense of his own teammate "the Olympic Pilot" Nolo Ferreira, playmaker of his country's fanned-out attack in the 1928 Olympics.

Uruguay and Argentina played the 1930 final with that same style. What stood out in the home team was its deep defense, with one of the backs playing behind and covering the holes left by the other. The insiders played near the center-half, narrowing the spaces that he had to cover and helping him support the forwards.

Moreover, the statements from that period draw a clear picture of the importance of tactics in that era's game. As Argentine striker Carlos Peucelle stated: "We had never trained harder than we had for that competition. They made us do twenty laps around the field. As far as tactics, they were never discussed. We went out on the field and we knew what we had to do." Uruguayan coach Alberto Suppici recounted: "In those days we didn't have any chalkboards and we didn't devise any strategies. Practice was purely recreational. On the field, before ideas about this changed, the one that guided the team was the captain."

The Argentine delegation had chosen Hotel La Barra of Santa Lucia, in the outskirts of Montevideo, as their training camp. The Argentine officials were trying to shield the players from being distracted by the ten or fifteen thousand Argentines who crossed the River Plate to follow each of their team's games. They achieved that goal, but the players could not be protected from the pressure that was starting to build.

The favorite target was Luis Monti, the "double wide," a typical center-half of the time and Argentina's tough leader. In the final of the South American Cup the year before, he had clashed with a tough guy from the other side of the River Plate, Lorenzo Fernandez, and that was another reason to keep an eye on him. He began to get anonymous threats directed not at him, but his mother. "Her life depends on the result," they read.

As for Roberto Cherro, he just couldn't handle the stress. This great star, who had already suffered a nervous breakdown after the game against France, backed out of the final.

Nolo Ferreira wanted to replace him, but Stabile, with his goals, had beaten him to it, and "the Olympic Pilot" would not agree to play in any other position.

In goal, there were no guarantees. The team had started with Bossio as goalkeeper and then replaced him with Botasso.

It was a chaotic situation for Argentina, at least as far as morale was concerned. Things seemed to stabilize when a great star with the most infectious smile of the River Plate region came to visit. The legendary Carlos Gardel sang "For the Boys" and repeated his performance for the other side, even though Uruguay's situation wasn't much different. They were isolated in a place filled with green and silence, the Parque del Prado. There they awaited the final game, with an early to bed and early to rise regimen. The only one who broke the rules was goalkeeper Mazali, who insisted on acting off the field as he did on: His style was modern. He liked to leave his goal-line to intercept crosses, and he generally succeeded. One night, he silently left the training camp and was surprised—as he furtively returned—by the coach. He left again, but this time he didn't come back.

That's how the two rival teams, who knew each other all too well, got to the final match. It was clear that the game wouldn't settle any score, but it was so important to the history of both that it inspired some good stories, even before the start of the game as the players entered the stadium.

In the Uruguayan locker room, Peregrino Anselmo, who had scored two goals in the semifinal against Yugoslavia, asked the captain of his team to exclude him from the starting eleven. When Jose Nasazzi, the "great leader," asked him why, Anselmo could only lower his head. . . .

In the Argentine locker room, Luis Monti, who had been receiving threats, begged not to play. Two executives from his club, San Lorenzo, made an urgent trip to Montevideo. The officials, Bidegain and Larrandart, finally persuaded him to suit up for the game. Of course, they could do nothing to solve another problem: "Pancho" Varallo, the youngest player on the team at nineteen and substitute for Cherro, had suffered a sprain. They tested him by making him kick a wall. "He can play," said Coach Olazar, "if he puts on a thigh brace."

He put it on and went onto the field with his teammates, who were all elegantly dressed with gray coats covering their traditional jerseys. On the other side, the Uruguayans appeared in their traditional uniforms, ready to play.

More than half of the Argentine fans, who had crossed the River Plate in ten boats to root for their national team, were left outside the walls of Centenario stadium. For security reasons, the number of fans allowed to enter the stadium had been reduced to sixty thousand. Also because of security, the referee had been chosen only three hours before the match. This responsibility fell to Belgian John Langenus, who quickly demanded special protection for himself and his assistants, security guards for his family, and a boat ready to depart one hour after the end of the game. From early that morning, mounted police and soldiers armed with bayonets guarded the stadium, which stood out in all its splendor. At 2:10 P.M. on that historic July 30, the teams went onto the field to play the first World Cup final, with more than four hundred members of the press there to record it for posterity.

"They sent me anonymous threats. I couldn't sleep the night before because they serenaded me with insults. When we came back to play the second half, there were about three hundred soldiers with sawed-off bayonets. I knew that they weren't going to defend us. I realized that if I touched someone, the fuse would be lit. So I told my teammates, 'I'm a marked man, you guys play your best, because I can't.' What did they expect? For me to become a martyr over a soccer game?"

The dramatic testimony of Luis Monti reflects the tension he and his teammates experienced at the end of the first half. Argentina was ahead 2–1. At the game's start, Pablo Dorado—Uruguay's right wing and the tournament's youngest player—had opened the scoring when, after getting the ball from Castro, his running shot beat Botasso. At twenty minutes, Carlos Peucelle was fed by Varallo, and his high shot got past Ballestrero, deadlocking the game. At thirty-seven minutes, a cross by Monti was received by Guillermo Stabile, who beat Ballestrero from close range, giving the Argentines the lead. During the play, Uruguay's Nasazzi had stayed back raising his arm, demanding an offside that neither the official Langenus nor his linesman Christophe called.

"An anxious wind filled the stadium," wrote a Montevidean journalist. In that atmosphere, they went to the locker rooms. There, "el Negrito" Andrade, bordering on a nervous breakdown, fell to the floor and screamed, "We can't lose! They are Argentine and we are Uruguayan!" His outburst motivated the home team, which came out for second half ready to do anything to win. That's how one of their players, Ernesto Mascheroni, remembered it: "In the first half, we played very soft because the officials had told us if there was any rough play, the organizing committee would suspend the game. Our game was by nature a physical one, but we had no bad intentions. We were blocked for those first forty-five minutes. When we went out to play the second half, Nasazzi told us: 'Well, we have to defend hard, because if not, we're dead.' The Argentines had a great squad. Players with great ball-handling skills and a formidable passing game. We had to guard them before they got the ball. Any other way, we were screwed."

At least that's how it seemed until at fifty-seven minutes, Castro and Scarone got together, the ball found the feet of Pedro Cea, and his low shot got past Botasso.

At sixty-eight minutes, Mascheroni stopped an Argentine advance and gave the ball to Santos Iriarte, who tried a shot from thirty meters out. Botasso's late reaction helped the ball go in the net, putting the home team ahead.

Finally, at eighty-nine minutes, one minute from the final whistle, Dorado's high cross from the right side was met by a Castro header. Game over.

With that indisputable 4–2 win, Uruguay was crowned the first World Champion in history.

Their leader, captain, and star remembered it like this: "We put vigor, character, and courage together on the field, and we made history with what is still known as, and will be known as, 'charrúa (plough) blood.'"

On the other side of the river, there were two schools of thought. The newspaper *Crítica* dramatized: "We shouldn't play the Uruguayans anymore. . . . They had to win by hook or by crook and so they did." The magazine *El Gráfico* titled its article "Dotting the '*I*s' and Crossing the '*T*s'" and delved into the heart of the matter: "The Argentine team was not cowardly. It was not the penalties that caused our defeat. The truth is that Uruguay presented a midfield line superior to ours, frustrating most of the Argentine attacks and supporting its forwards well. You can say that Argentina did not perform well, but do not say that it was afraid, because that would be slanderous."

The first title was in Uruguayan hands. They had gone undefeated in the tournament, with fifteen goals for and only three against. The first title was theirs and they had certainly earned it.

FRANCISCO VARALLO
(Argentina)
Uruguay 1930

At eighty-five years of age, Francisco "Pancho" Varallo still lives in the same La Plata house he began building in 1931. He was the first big-money, star transfer of the brand-new Argentine professional league. In front of that solid construction, which stands on the outskirts of the city of La Plata, sixty kilometers from Buenos Aires, a gold plaque reminds him every day, when he wakes up in the morning to attend to his sports betting and lottery agency, that he is a living legend: one of the men who kicked off this fantastic story called the World Cup.

When he was only eighteen years old, he was a member of the Argentine national team which played—and lost—the final against Uruguay in Centenario stadium. The images are so vivid in his mind, so stuck in his heart, so clear in his words that—out of respect for such greatness—one can only ask and listen so as not to squander the chance to admire a man who competed on the fields of the first World Cup and who, sixty-four years later, observed the last one, USA 1994, with lucidity.

F.V.: I went to Montevideo as a backup. To win myself a spot in the starting eleven, I had to win an election against other great inside-rights, which was my position. It was me, Arrillaga, Zito, Marassi, and another guy who I don't remember.

A.C.: And who voted?

F.V.:The officials of the federation . . . and a representative of Independiente was asked by another representative, from Gimnasia, which was my club: "Vote for the kid for me." Because of that vote, I won the spot.

A.C.: How long before the tournament did this take place?

F.V.: I think it was about a month before.

A.C.: And the coach's opinion didn't carry any weight?

F.V.: The coach was Olazar, but he didn't form the team. The team was decided on between Cherro, Nolo Ferreira, Zumelzu, the most experienced players, and the executives . . . . In those days you couldn't make any substitutions or anything like that. . . . They injured our goalkeeper, and we couldn't replace him: Our opponent, "el Manco" Castro, hit him, leaving him on one leg. That's how the Uruguayans were: They won by bullying us. That's why when I look back on that World Cup it still angers me . . . I can't believe that we lost it.

A.C.: Of all the stories that surround that game, which ones are true? The fear of some of the Argentines, the intimidation of some of the Uruguayans . . .

F.V.: Some of the things are true. . . . I always say the truth is reflected by the final score, so it's not worth bringing up old controversies; but there were players who felt daunted, and that's why we lost. It's the truth. No one can certify it, but if someone from the old guard who was at the stadium that day still lives, he'd confirm what I've said.

A.C.: Why did that happen?

F.V.: It's that, in those times, the Argentine player was much softer. Today, they are more macho . . . they used to shoot from outside the penalty area, because they were afraid to enter.

A.C.: And before the final? How did it feel to be competing in the World Cup?

F.V.: Everything was very nice, an unforgettable experience. Our delegation was staying two hours away from Montevideo, in Barra San Lucia. That's where our training camp was. . . . Carlos Gardel would come [he is referring to the legendary Argentine tango singer] to play bingo with us, we were all such good friends!

A.C.: Were you the youngest one in the group?

F.V.: Yes, I was the youngest one. Monti and Paternoster, the oldest ones, would come up to me and say: "Hey, 'Panchito' say something, so we can learn to recognize your voice."

A.C.: Is it true that Nolo Ferreira did not leave his law studies behind during the competition and actually went back and forth between Uruguay and Argentina to attend his classes?

F.V.: Yes, but it isn't true that he missed any games because of it as it was once said. . . . The one who missed the semifinal was me, because I had injured my knee. The team's leaders wanted me to save myself for the final and, before the decisive game against the Uruguayans, they tested me out. I remember that they took me to a chicken coop behind the hotel where we were staying, and they made me kick the wall hard; it was a terrible thing. . . . It's that I had received a blow to my left knee in a strange situation: Playing against Chile, I sent a cross to Stabile, who scored the goal. I celebrated it a little to much, which didn't please the Chilean half who came from behind me and kicked me in the knee. I carried that pain with me for the rest of my career. But in those days, I had a tremendous desire to play, so I felt great. . . . The real problem was that the environment, the atmosphere, was hellish.

A.C.: People always talk about the Argentine players, being intimidated. Like the story of Luis Monti, the team leader—how was it?

F.V.: Poor guy, they threatened him so much.

A.C.: Why did they single him out?

F.V.: Because he had played against the Uruguayans many times and had gotten into many tangles, many fights. So the people took it out on him. During a game played in Peru, he had hit, I don't know who . . . Lorenzo Fernandez, I think, who himself was the most malicious of them all. I wasn't afraid: I did whatever I wanted to against him. But he had this face and huge legs that made him look like a lion, and he tried to scare our players . . . with some, he was successful. Seeing as I was so young, I didn't feel any danger at all, even though, whenever he passed by me, he would say: "Next time I see you, I'll drown you in grass, you snot-nosed kid. I'll kill you. . . ." But, since the only good thing about me on a soccer field was the guts I put into the game, all my fears left me as soon as I stepped on the field.

A.C.: Nowadays, there is a lot of talk about violent play on the soccer field. Back in your day, was there a lot of intimidation, or scare tactics?

F.V.: I don't think that things were *that* bad. There was more bark than bite. . . . That's why I say—and I know because I played with them—that yesterday's players were more easily intimidated. The Argentine soccer player chickened out, I saw it in my time. I mean, look at the 1930 final. We were calmly ahead 2–1, one of my shots hit the crossbar, we could have assured ourselves the win, but . . .

A.C.: Was the game even?

F.V.: It was until they scored their third goal. After that, it wasn't: Had we gone on, they would have ended up with eight goals. We were playing with a goalkeeper who had one of his legs injured, thanks to that incident with "el Manco" Castro. I asked one of the veterans—Carlos Peucelle—to see if one of the men on the field could defend the goal, because they didn't allow substitutions yet. He answered: "No, 'Pancho,' I'm not getting involved." Of course, there had already been controversy in choosing the team's lineup . . .

A.C.: How did that come about?

F.V.: There was a meeting, with all the players and all of the executives. That's where it was decided that, among other things, Monti would play, even with all the threats flying around . . . and let me tell you, Monti didn't cry over just anything. They were about to put Chividini—who really wanted to play—in his place. He hadn't played in any of the games—he was a kid with extraordinary strength. But in the end they decided on Monti. When a Uruguayan player fell down, Monti went to help him up. It was the kind of attitude that doesn't help in a final. . . . But why bring all of that up again?

A.C.: Well then, tell me about that Uruguayan team, which went on to make history as the first World Champion.

F.V.: They were older, almost all of them retired the very next year. They couldn't beat us. They played with Scarone, Castro, Iriarte, Andrade, Lorenzo Fernandez, Gestido . . . Gestido, who was in the military, was a true gentleman. When Lorenzo Fernandez sought me out to talk trash and hit me, Gestido would tell me, "Play cool, kid, he's crazy. . . ." I always tell that story. In any case, I was never afraid to go out and play. I'll go even further and say that because of my style, I would have been able to play in today's soccer. Understand, I'm not saying that out of vanity, only so you understand how it was back then.

A.C.: And of course one can't talk about that first World Cup without mentioning the problems.

F.V.: No, no, of course not. In the first game we played in the World Cup—which was not in the Centenario, but rather in Parque Central—the trouble started. But the Uruguayans had started it. . . . There was already a lot of anger targeted against the Argentines in those days. They thought we were all a bunch of showoffs, and looking back now, maybe there was a bit of truth to it.

A.C.: When you couldn't play in World Cup 1934 because you were playing in the amateur league, did you think you were really missing out on something?

F.V.: Well, yes . . . for me, having played in the first World Cup had been the ultimate. I still feel that way about it today, when I see the shirt I wore, which my daughter still keeps. . . . I had given it away, and she almost killed me when she found out: She went and got it back. I gave everything away. It never occurred to me that it would all be worth a lot of money later . . . I don't even have any pictures.

What he does have—and this is indeed priceless—is the love and company of his family: "I have a daughter (Maria Teresa) and two stepsons. I married a second time, and Maria Teresa married the son of my second wife. So everything stayed in the family. . . . It's thanks to them that I still get by. I've had this sports betting and lottery agency for twenty-five years. I was the coach of my first club, Gimnasia y Esgrima de La Plata, for two years: In the first year, I saved the team from relegation, and everyone called me 'the Wizard'; in the second year, I was sacked . . . that's soccer. I didn't have the character for the job: Had I continued as coach, I would have surely been six feet under a long time ago. I screamed a lot, so the referee would approach the bench and tell me, 'Mr. Varallo, I'm very fond of you, but I'm going to have to eject you.'"

A.C.: You were a special guest at World Cup 1994, a Cup filled with technology, filled with advances. What did you think, compared with the World Cup you had participated in?

F.V.: *Uuuhhh!* I was with Platini, who told me he had heard of me by way of *El Gráfico* magazine. With Di Stefano, with Puskas, who are in good shape because Real Madrid always offers them some job, to keep them close by . . .

A.C.: What most surprised you?

F.V.: I'll tell you the truth: That tournament was so cold! I loved how Argentina started out, with Maradona. But later, the disappointment with all that had happened to Diego was terrible . . . how sad! Everyone was crushed. The executives who had accompanied me to the United States wanted to take me to Boston and stay until the final, but I wanted nothing to do with it anymore . . . I was so disappointed. For me, everything was over. How could it not be? I mean, I am Argentine and I am still their biggest fan, even today.

Italy 1934

"I don't know how it can be done, General, but Italy must win the World Cup . . ." As would happen on more than one occasion, soccer was getting mixed up with politics. Or, at least, it was getting taken advantage of by it. General Giorgio Vaccaro, president of the Italian Olympic Committee, listened to the words of *Il Duce,* Benito Mussolini, and as he left the Venice Palace, he set himself to the task with the single-mindedness and discipline of a soldier. The fascists who governed Italy would spare no expense: It was no longer only about building stadiums, which would sprout like mushrooms in all the cities of the country; it was now necessary to win. And luckily a few things began to go their way.

To begin with, an avalanche of registrants fell on the organizers before the February 28, 1933 deadline. Of FIFA's fifty affiliated federations, thirty-two sought to participate in the second World Cup. The problem was that there were only enough spaces for half of them. The "avalanche" of that time may seem trifling today: World Cup France 1998 will have thirty-two teams participating in the final round. Spain 1982 had already increased the number of final participants to twenty-four from the original sixteen.

The overwhelming response forced FIFA to implement the first qualification rounds. Small groups of two and three teams were formed, some according to geographic proximity. Oddly enough, Italy, the home team, was required to participate in a qualifying round. Their opponent in this round, not surprisingly, was Greece, the most inexperienced team in Europe. Playing against the Greeks, who had organized their national team just four years earlier, was tantamount to a free ride.

Some very important absences also smoothed Italy's path. Uruguay, offended by the lackluster European turnout at their World Cup four years before, gave the Europeans a taste of their own medicine. Also, the move toward professionalism in the Uruguayan league was generating a lot of controversy, which needed more immediate attention. Therefore, the *charrúas* became the only World Champion in World Cup history not to defend their title. Argentina presented an amateur team because of the refusal of the newly professional clubs to release their players. Formed by players of the second and third division, the team came to Italy without a prayer. Argentina's fabulous 1934 league championship showed that their best talent had indeed stayed home. By that time, South American players were already in demand by the economically powerful Italian clubs, and Argentine clubs were unwilling to lose their stars at the start of what was to be a golden age in Argentine soccer.

Soccer of the highest caliber was being played near the River Plate of Argentina and Uruguay, but, unfortunately, it would never debut on an international level. Something similar occurred with the British, who again stayed home, depriving the world of Stanley Matthew's superb dribbling and Dixie Dean's goals. On the other side of Europe, the regional representatives of what would later be known as the Soviet Union grew in strength, but it would be a few more years until they would appear at a World Cup.

And so, the stage was set for conquest by Italy.

Two executives, Giovanni Mauro and Ottorino Marassi, saw the excellent opportunity that presented itself and, taking advantage of the government's desperate need to project a positive image internationally, organized everything in such a way that, when it was all said and done, they had netted more than three million dollars. It was a preview of things to come: the use of the World Cup to enhance the image of the host country, while earning it a pretty penny. This formula would repeat itself over and over again, with other characters and even bigger numbers.

The show began on May 27, with play distributed to eight cities (Florence, Turin, Naples, Genoa, Milan, Bologna, Rome, and Trieste), but also with an obvious organizational blunder: Half the teams that went to Italy—including the United States and Argentina, who had crossed the Atlantic—had to go back home after playing only one game, because it was a single elimination tournament.

That said, things went pretty much as expected. In Giovanni

Berta stadium in Florence, Germany rolled over Belgium 5–2. The Germans took full advantage of their two great stars (playmaker Fritz Szepan and goal-scorer Edmund Conen) and rigorously followed coach Otto Nerz's game plan: the English-style W–M system—which, as will be seen, marked another milestone in the evolution of tactics. The Belgians' physical endurance was not enough against the physical play and one-on-one defense of the Germans. The result was inevitable. In Benito Mussolini Stadium in Turin, the famous Austrian *Wunderteam* of Hugo Meisl limped through its match with the French, finally beating them in overtime. The final score read 3–2 after the first ninety minutes had left a 1–1 score. Thepot and his French teammates played their characteristic creative game, putting a wrench in the gears of Sindelar and his Austrian cohorts, who were unaccustomed to facing such bold opponents. The only difference between the teams, in this first game in history to go beyond ninety minutes, was a goal made by Schall while he was offside—a detail that went unnoticed by Dutch referee Van Moorsel. In Ascareli stadium in Naples, Hungary enjoyed a belated revenge against Egypt by beating them 4–2. The Africans, who had disgraced the Hungarians ten years before when they eliminated them from the Paris Olympics, now fell without resistance.

Luigi Ferraris stadium in Genoa was the setting of the best game of the first round: Spain—at the peak of its glory—beat Brazil, 3–1. Still without important achievements at the international level, the Brazilians had come to Italy intent on making a good showing, but serious internal disputes had once again prevented them from fielding their stars from the Rio and Sao Paulo leagues. The coach, Carlo Rocha, ended up playing an almost secret role, since he didn't have the backing of the front office. In spite of that, Brazil participated in a spirited match. Irarragorri, on a penalty kick, and Langara put the Europeans ahead, causing Brazilian goalkeeper Roberto Gomes Pedrosa to have a nervous breakdown. But Leonidas—the first appearance by the man who would be the first great star of Brazilian soccer—narrowed the lead. Minutes later, another man, who would later play an indirect role in soccer history, took a direct role in a unique situation. Many years later, Waldemar do Brito would discover Pele, but that afternoon, he had more urgent business to attend to. In an attack he launched, he was fouled in the penalty area by a tackle so vicious that he was left unconscious. When he came to, his teammates were still arguing over who should be in charge of kicking the penalty. "Me," he commanded, without hesitating, reminding them that he was a specialist. But apparently he was still not fully recovered: His straight, powerful shot was met by the fists of Zamora, the great Spanish goalkeeper. Afterward, Langara increased Spain's lead, and Brazil repeated its sad history: returning home after only the first round.

In Bologna's Littorale stadium, an inexperienced Argentine team delighted the fans but ended up losing against Sweden (3–2), who showed off the awesome attacking power of their forwards, Jonasson and Kroon. It was there that the Argentines inaugurated (not surprisingly) a discussion that would eventually divide their soccer world: whether to play well or play to win? Whatever the case, the first round losses left South America without representatives.

In Milan's San Siro, a Netherlands team that thought itself invincible tumbled before the individual talent (Trello, Abegglen III, Minelli, Kielholz) and the relatively modern tactics of Switzerland, who surprised them with a 3–2 win.

In Trieste's Littorio stadium, Czechoslovakia was a machine of skilled play, bulldozing Romania by a score of 2–1. The game premiered the goal-scoring power of the man who would be the tournament's leading scorer, Oldrich Nejedly.

Lastly, in the P.N.F. of Rome, the home team, Italy, debuted by flattening the United States 7–1. But that deserves its own paragraph.

Benito Mussolini was not a big soccer fan. But the opportunity this tournament offered to obscure his totalitarian image seduced him. So he started to show up wherever a ball was being kicked. He also made an appearance, of course, in the hotel where the Nazionale was staying. His talk with the players was very frank and to the point. . . .

"Boys, win. If not, *crash* . . ." *Crash* meant, plain and simple, that heads would roll. The coach Vittorio Pozzo and his men understood it more clearly than anyone. On that team, there were four naturalized Italians from Argentina defending the *azzurra*—Orsi, Monti, Guaita, and Demaria. One of the four, Raimundo "Mumo" Orsi, remembered it like this:

During February and March of 1934 we trained two or three times per week. The Cup started in May, which is why we had already set up camp in Rome in April. We worked day and night. During the day, we worked out in the gym, and at night, soccer. A lot of work with the ball. Pozzo insisted that our more skillful South American group, including the Brazilian Guarisi, try to teach some secrets to our Italian teammates. We formed a sensational roster. . . . Pozzo was very studious and I remember his visits to our rooms as if they had happened yesterday. He would come quietly and say: "How are you? What do you need? What can I help you with?" Yet, five minutes later—and without most of us realizing it—he was telling us the strengths and weaknesses of the opponents we were about to face, but never building them up in our heads. The night before our first game, he told me: "Mumo, tomorrow Czerkiewicz will guard you. I wouldn't worry too much about it, he's terrible. The key is to fake outside and go inside. Then, cross the ball behind you and Schiavio will kill them with his headers. . . ." It was truly prophetic. Schiavio made three goals on three of my assists. I made two off rebounds and Meazza and Ferrari completed the seven goals that we made against the United States.

Those results led to an all-European quarterfinals (the saving grace for the South Americans was that the teams they sent weren't their real teams), which included four matches of the highest quality and two that were truly outstanding.

In the less important games, Germany eliminated Sweden and Czechoslovakia defeated Switzerland without too much difficulty: 2–1 and 3–2 respectively. The other two matchups had their own stories to tell. . . .

In Bologna, in what was, at that moment, the biggest rivalry in Continental soccer, Austria beat Hungary 2–1. Head to head: two powers that had been competing since 1902; the two best center-forwards on the planet: Sindelar and Sarosi; an identical way of playing soccer, with a religious devotion to ball possession. The teams went into the game with a mutual respect for one another, but that afternoon, on May 31, everything changed.

The playing field was turned into a battlefield, with fouls of every shape and size. The Italian referee Mattea totally lost control. It was Sindelar's *Wunderteam* that took the lead and Sarosi—the only Hungarian to keep his composure—narrowed it. But it was not enough, and Austria waited to face the winner of the other great clash.

In Florence, more than one game was necessary to decide Italy's triumph over Spain, which finally ended 1–0. Just as in the Amsterdam Olympics six years before, two hours of play were not enough to break the tie. Like the other semifinal duel, it was more of a war than a soccer game. Statistics prove that this is no mere exaggeration: Only eleven of the twenty-two players were fit to play the tie-breaker the next day—that's right, only twenty-four hours after the first game and its corresponding overtime. Moreover, Italy caused injuries to both Spanish goalkeepers. One of them, Ricardo Zamora Martinez, one of the greatest goalkeepers in the history of world soccer, was crucial in the first match, which ended 1–1, stopping at least five prime scoring chances.

Unfortunately for Spain, one of the men unable to play the decisive game the next day was Zamora. His replacement—Nogues, a good player although nowhere near Zamora's level—figured in the key play of the game. It came eleven minutes into a game that had already claimed its first casualty, the Spanish wing Bosch. Curiously, the play happened two different ways, depending on which news report you read. The Italians reported: "Everything is resolved eleven minutes into the game, when, after a corner by Orsi, coming from Nogues's right, Atilio Demaria jumps to find the ball. Behind him the imperious Meazza surges and, with a supreme jump toward the sky, gets to the ball before both his teammate and the Spanish goalkeeper, who had desperately dived off his goal-line. The Spaniards protest the play, considering it illegal because of a foul by Meazza. In their view, the *azzurro* center-forward had leaned on the back of an opponent. In fact, a photo proves that the forward came in contact with no one, friend or foe." The international media said the following: "Italy won 1–0 on a Giuseppe Meazza header, taking advantage of Argentine Demaria's obstruction of Spanish goalkeeper Nogues. The goal was protested but the motion was denied. So too were the two goals converted for Spain by Regueiro and Quincoces, which the Swiss referee Macet annulled. In this game, Italy was a bit more gentle than in the last, injuring only four Spanish players: Bosch, Chaco, Regueiro, and Quincoces. The officiating was so biased that the Swiss Federation immediately suspended Macet for life."

John Langenus—who had been the referee of the 1930 final and who was now a journalist—boldly titled his article: "Spain, the Real Champion of the World."

Television wasn't around then, so today our opinion of that final depends on our point of view. The testimonials of those who were present and can still remember are surely tinged with the passing of time and their inevitable bias. It is all so different from the unimpeachable proof we have today. Sixty years later, Italy and Spain met again for the quarterfinals of a World Cup, but this time in Boston in the United States. As happened sixty years before, a controversial play went unpunished by the referee, but this time no one bothered to complain. More than one television camera showed how Mauro Tassotti elbowed Luis Enrique in the face while they battled in the penalty area. Hungarian referee Sandor Puhl completely ignored it, but this time around no one disqualified him. On the contrary, he was rewarded, but I'll get to that later.

In Italy, the celebration continued. The VIP boxes were quite a sight, with the noble presence of the prince of Piedmont and the princesses Giovanna and Mafalda, as well as Benito Mussolini, accompanied by his youngest daughter.

One can be sure Mussolini's daughter did not accompany him to the training camp of "his" team, after it had beaten Austria in a great semifinal match (1–0). The opponent for the final would be Czechoslovakia, who had beaten Germany 3–1 in the other semifinal. The night before the decisive match, *Il Duce* gathered them together for a little pep talk: "Gentlemen, if the Czechs play fair, we'll play fair. That's the most important thing. But if they want to play dirty, then we Italians must play dirtier. . . . Good luck tomorrow and don't forget my promise: *crash.*" As if they needed reminding . . .

With that pressure on them, Italy faced the final. Moreover, they had to confront a real, solid, and prestigious rival, Czechoslovakia. By the way, what were they like? How did they play?

During the 1930s, in response to the change in the offside rule in 1925, Herbert Chapman, coach of London's Arsenal, produced the strategic innovation known as the "System," also known as the "W–M," after the shape this formation traced on the field. It consisted of three backs, a "roving" center-half, two halves, two insiders to make the plays and, farther up, the wingers and the center-forward. In the World Cup, the "System" was attempted only by Germany, which finished with a consolation prize offered for the first time: the third place game, played between the two losers of the semifinals. By a score of 3–2, Germany beat an Austria handicapped by the absence of its biggest star, Mathias Sindelar.

Italy and the other countries remained true to the style that had worked so well for Uruguay and Argentina, but distinguished the different lines of the team even more than the South Americans had four years earlier. Behind were the backs, in the middle were the halves, then came the insiders, and well advanced, the two wingers and the center-forward. The Italians called it the "Method."

The Czechs had their own system: a great goalkeeper, Planicka; a formidable midfielder, Cambal; a great little striker, Puc; and a scorer who did more than score, Nejedly. He would end up being the tournament's top scorer, with five goals, even without scoring any in that unforgettable final. On that day, June 10, the team that literally couldn't afford to lose got off to a bad start.

Seventy minutes into the game, Puc put the Czech team in front. Here's how Orsi, one of those who had the "crash" very much on his mind, remembered it: "It was another hard-fought game. They went ahead, but thanks to a rebound, I was able to tie the game with only ten minutes left in the match. Guaita accelerated from behind, and as he saw Schiavio beating his defender with a sprint, he gave him a long, high pass. In the air, Schiavio crashed against two defenders, the three fell, and the ball came to me. I was covered, but Planicka hesitated, and he gave me just enough time. When he came to block my angle, I tapped the ball from right to left. We went to overtime and, because we were in better shape physically, we won the title (ninety-five minutes into the game, Schiavio, assisted by Meazza, scored the winning goal, 2–1). I still remember the delirium of the crowd, Mussolini's upturned chin . . . I think we won it all because Vittorio Pozzo was ahead of his time and like a good father, without pressuring us, he showed us the way. In that time, he already knew the defects of all our rivals; he knew how to get through to us and make good on his advice. . . ."

Italy exploded. Like blood running through veins, the celebration pulsed through every street in the country, in a fervor of passion and patriotism, as would happen every four years thereafter. Mussolini authorized a payout of $17,000 for each of the players, with which, according to them, "we could buy a nice home." Add that to the tournament's million-dollar profit, and a simple equation begins to take shape: The World Cup = economic success.

VITTORIO POZZO
(Italy)
Italy 1934

"Italy won the World Cup yesterday. The final, like the quarter-final and the semifinal, was of epic proportions. So tough and disputed was the game that it exhausted half of the players, and an overtime was necessary to decide the winner."

That's what Vittorio Pozzo, coach of the winning team, wrote with his own hand for the Italian newspaper *La Stampa* on June 11, 1934. Today, there is no possibility of getting a more precise or valuable statement than that one, since all the protagonists of that heroic struggle are no longer with us. . . . Therefore, we are left with the valuable words of the man about whom Raimundo "Mumo" Orsi—one of the men he coached—once said: "I think we won it all because Vittorio Pozzo was ahead of his time and like a good father, without pressuring us, he showed us the way. In that time, he already knew the defects of all our rivals; he knew how to get through to us and make good on his advice. . . ."

In that article written the day after winning the title, Vittorio Pozzo went on like this:

There has not been a single easy opponent in this World Cup; Italy, without a doubt, has had the best teams put in its path. Spain, Austria, and Czechoslovakia, true soccer bastions, have been the three obstacles that have given rise to the toughest, most dramatic, and most passionate games of the tournament. It is clear that Italy did not walk a rose-covered path to the championship. Neither the caliber of their opposition, nor luck favored it. The projected total time of play for a team in the finals was 360 minutes; but, between the first round, the quarter-finals (including an overtime, and a tie-breaking replay), the semifinals, and the final (which included another overtime), the Italian team played 510 minutes of soccer. This shows that the *azzurri* played almost two championships while the opponents played only one. . . . The Italian squad has gone through a minor hell to win the title. Even the Czech national team, which throughout the tournament had impressed no one, yesterday dug in and showed a style of play and a fighting spirit that shocked the skeptics. . . .

And, as for the team's reaction to being down 0–1:

But from that moment on, our national team grew in stature. Puc's goal acted like a jockey whipping a good horse. It spurred on our men, whose pride had been wounded by the goal, causing them to put everything on the line and use the moral and physical strength they had accumulated over the course of the tournament. The *azzurri*'s comeback was an example of will and fortitude. The goal defended by Planicka had to withstand waves and waves of attacks brought about by the Italian front line, which had been given a boost by Guaita and Schiavio's swapping of positions. When Orsi equalized the score after a great individual play, crowned by a shot that was superb in both power and aim, all the fear disappeared immediately. It seemed clear that only an accident could keep them from winning the game. . . .

What a performance by the *azzurri!* Their triumph constitutes the greatest prize that can be aspired to, the highest peak that can be climbed by a soccer player. This title rewards the seriousness, moral purity, sacrificing spirit, and will of a handful of men who, in order to defend Italy's colors, have not hesitated to isolate themselves from the rest of the world for forty days, depriving themselves of every comfort, and adjusting to a harsh discipline. Never had a national team done what ours did to prepare for a World Cup. It's only fair that this victory belongs to us.

France 1938

Europe was on the brink of destruction, and so was soccer. Spain was stuck in the middle of a terrible civil war, making it all but impossible to get some great players—like the "Divine" Zamora—on the soccer field. Germany had already invaded Austria, annexing the country and its soccer players, too. Austria's biggest soccer star, Mathias Sindelar, could not handle it. With the added burden of his wife's disappearance, he fell into a deep depression that first ended his sports career and then, just after the end of the World Cup, his life. On January 23, 1939, he turned on the gas in his kitchen and asphyxiated himself.

Amidst all this turmoil, the third World Cup was organized. This time it would be played in France, a country that loved—and still loves—other sports, such as cycling and rugby, more than soccer. South American teams again gave the competition the cold shoulder. After having its candidacy for organizing the tournament rejected, Argentina felt particularly betrayed that FIFA had broken the official pact of alternating the site between Europe and the Americas. But Monsieur Jules Rimet, the "father" of the World Cup, held his ground. Putting diplomacy aside, he said: "It will take place in my country." At the Berlin Congress, held on August 15, 1936, forty of FIFA's fifty-four affiliated countries voted in favor of Rimet's decision.

Rimet's grandson, Ives, was chosen to draw the lots that would determine the makeup of the first-round groups. It was a gesture that would be imitated years later by another official anxious to make history: Brazilian Joao Havelange. It was not the only thing

Havelange would imitate. Faithful to Rimet's original vision, the Brazilian would continue to make the World Cup a successful enterprise, both athletically and financially.

Even with the reverberation of bombs nearby, FIFA was unflappable and the tournament was already showing signs of maturity. For example, some important changes had been made: Now the defending champion and host country automatically qualified for the competition; every team had to present an official roster of twenty-two players; and FIFA paid for the transportation of seventeen people per delegation in second-class berths and covered the price of lodging, with a per diem of three dollars per person per day. Moreover, from five days before their first game until two days after their last game, the players were each given fifty cents per day to cover incidental expenditures. Also, if the final game ended in a tie, the two teams would be declared cochampions.

The format of the competition, however, would remain the same as in 1934, with direct elimination: Lose just once and you pack your bags. Cruel, but effective.

The qualifying rounds had left no surprises, but they had left some interesting side-notes. Thirty-six of FIFA's fifty-four affiliated countries had entered the competition for the sixteen final berths. Austria won a spot after beating Latvia and Lithuania on the playing field, but lost on the battlefield at the hands of Germany. Norway and Poland eliminated the always dangerous Yugoslavia. Brazil and Cuba qualified without having to play a game, since they were the only American representatives. Asia made its debut in the World Cup with the presence of the Dutch East Indies team, which also qualified without having played, thanks to the Japanese, who forfeited their place because they were waging a war against China.

The British countries continued to watch the World Cup from the sidelines. The English politely turned down the invitation to replace the Austrians, citing "not having enough time to adequately prepare the team" as their excuse.

On paper, it looked like an easy win for Italy. The Italians did not have the physical proximity of *Il Duce* this time around, but did get his message, which was, as always, very clear: "Win or Die," said the telegram that the men of the *azzurra* received the night before their debut. Only two World Champion players, Ferraris and Giuseppe Meazza (now the captain), remained from the team that won it all in 1934. Shining alongside the two were several members of the gold medal–winning 1936 Olympic team, almost all of whom were suspected of playing in that competition illegally, because of their alleged professional status.

In any case, Italy's first game was not an easy one. In Marseilles, after their fascist salute drew boos and jeers from the public (which otherwise displayed excellent behavior, considering the battles that surrounded them), they struggled to defeat Norway 2–1. In the center of the Italian attack, the man who would become the team's leading scorer began to distinguish himself: Silvio Piola.

The luck of the draw had left Germany and Switzerland the responsibility of opening the tournament. Germany's newly "annexed" Austrian players could not adapt themselves to the "system" and a big upset resulted: Switzerland—the true inventor of *catenaccio,* as the Italians contended—won 4–2 in a tie-breaking match. This after having tied 1–1 in the first game and its corresponding overtime, in which the Austrian Galucher scored for his new team. The Swiss, with a no-holds-barred defense and blazing counterattacks, overcame the firepower of the Germans.

The great match of that first round was, without a doubt, between Brazil and Poland on July 5 in Strasbourg. The South Americans had finally ended the regional disputes that had been so detrimental to their international soccer commitments. The conflicts over, they could now proudly show off the jewel of the "land of the samba": the "Black Diamond," Leonidas Da Silva. The words of Diego Lucero, an eyewitness, give a portrait of Da Silva's character and breakthrough performance that is more precise than any:

Leonidas was a small, black kid. He had perfect features, astonishingly beautiful eyes, and curly hair. As a player, he was simply phenomenal. A classy yet effective dribbler, he cut through the enemy defenses like lightning, and he shot at the enemy goal with the precision and power of a born goal-scorer. The things Leonidas did in the first half of that historic game against Poland on July 5 in Strasbourg can be ranked among the most beautiful and brilliant plays in soccer history—artistic, rhythmic plays that carry the secret of soccer magic, and a grace that can make the ball speak. Leonidas was a flash of joy and glory that easily danced through the entrenched Polish defense. It was all done with the ease of someone who knows instinctively how to do something and then does it. In that first half, he made three goals, but then a deluge of rain set in, and the Polish managed to transform Brazil's 3–0 lead into their 4–3 favor. Then, Leonidas, living up to his name, became a lion in battle, wreaking havoc in the mud on the players from that sunless land. At one point in the game, his shoe got stuck in the mud. "The Black Diamond" took his foot out of the shoe and kicked the ball with all his might to tie the game. That goal went into the record books as the "stocking goal." In the end, Brazil won 6–5.

The surprising Cubans, not a great team, eliminated Romania, although they also needed two games. Its big stars, curiously, were two goalkeepers: Carvajales and Ayra. The former played in the first game, but could not play in the second game because he had to honor the primary commitment for which he had gone to Europe: to commentate the game for a Cuban radio station.

France, with the decisive presence of forward Nicolas, easily turned back Belgium 3–1, at Princes' Park in Paris. Similarly, Hungary finished off first-time participant Dutch East Indies with a convincing 6–0 in Reims.

The quarterfinals were now set, with the addition of Sweden, which got by thanks to the absence of Austria.

On June 12 in Bordeaux, the inevitable "ugly game" present in every World Cup took place. This time around it was Brazil and Czechoslovakia's turn to hit one another instead of playing soccer. By the end of the first half, the field of play showed only nine players against ten while the scoreboard showed a 1–0 advantage for Brazil, with a goal by Leonidas. One of the few players who escaped the mayhem, Nejedly, scored the equalizer, deadlocking the game and making it necessary to play a tie-breaking match two days later. The first match left a balance of nine Brazilians and eight Czechs injured. In the second game, the Brazilians emerged victorious after the referee called back a valid Czech goal, in which the ball had already crossed the line and a Brazilian defender cleared it from inside the goal.

The Swedes debuted in Antibes against Cuba and produced the largest margin of victory in a World Cup game up to that point: 8–0. It could have been even worse but for Cuban goalkeeper Carvajales, who left the microphone aside to go back in goal. The loss, which eliminated the Cubans, didn't leave them totally disappointed. On their way back home, they made a stopover in New York, where they saw Joe Louis knock out the German Max Schmeling, just as the Swedes had knocked them out. For the Swedes, some tough matches would follow.

In Lille, before the game against Switzerland, the Hungarian coach, Karoly Dietz, spoke with a confidence bordering on arrogance: "If we lose, I'll walk back to Budapest." Both Sarosi and Zsengeller responded to his call by sealing the easy 2–0 win.

With Germany out, the only team left that symbolized the prevailing political unrest was Italy. As luck would have it the Italians were to play the home team next, and to make things worse, the French people had just elected a democratic government. In that legendary Parisian stadium of Colombes, the French made their feelings clear with emphatic jeers and a barrage of hostility toward the *azzurri,* who saluted with their right arms extended forward. At the same time, these men—fascist gestures aside—displayed a level of soccer on the field with which anyone would want to be associated. The Uruguayan Andreolo had become a worthy replacement for the great Luis Monti; Meazza remained the leader that he had always been, with a perfect partner in Colaussi; and Silvio Piola was the goal-scorer chosen by Vittorio Pozzo's clinical eye. At exactly five o'clock on June 12, the Belgian referee Baert had ordered the start of play. Ninety minutes later, after a 3–1 win sealed with one goal by Colaussi and two by Piola, few doubts were left that Italy would win the title.

In reality, the only other team that could even hope to stand in their way was Brazil. But they were doomed from the start. First, they paid dearly for having had the quarterfinal against Czechoslovakia go to two games. What made it even worse was that the two games were played in a forty-eight-hour period, and they had to face Italy only forty-eight hours after that while Italy got to their semifinal match against Brazil with a full four-days rest. Adding to Brazil's misfortune, they could not count on their big star—and the great star of the World Cup—Leonidas, due to an, at best, confusing set of circumstances. In fact, there are two versions of the story surrounding the "Black Diamond's" absence. The first, told by journalist Lucero, claims that the forward was injured. The other, with no attributable source, but repeated through the years, says that the coach, Pimenta, had decided to rest Leonidas and Elba de Padua Lima (Tim), another key player, for the final!

The story seems absurd, but it makes sense when confirmed by another anecdote, which also serves to give a feeling for the times and personalities. The semifinal match was to be played in Marseilles, and there was only one direct flight to Paris, scheduled to leave one hour after the game. Obviously, it was ideal for the winner, who would play the final in the capital three days later. But who would the winner be? Brazil reserved all the seats, using the names of its respective players. The Italian coach Vittorio Pozzo humbly and respectfully confronted his rivals at their training camp to try to correct the situation. "I think it is a good idea to reserve the seats," he said. "But what do you say if we don't reserve them under any particular names? That way, either team can use them, depending on who wins." The resounding "no!" was heard all the way to Rio de Janeiro and Rome, with a Portuguese accent and a tacked on. "It won't be necessary." Pozzo excused himself and left.

Italy won easily 2–1, with one goal by Colaussi and the other by Meazza on a penalty kick for a foul that the Brazilians have disputed ever since. In any case, no one at that time doubted Italy's superiority or Brazil's immaturity.

In the other group, Hungary advanced with even more ease, after their 5–1 victory, which showed that the Swedish had no business being in the semifinals. Afterward, in the third place game, Brazil also refused to take mercy on the Swedes: Leonidas reappeared, scored two goals, and no one could deny him the title of top scorer of France 1938.

At that point, the World Cup was barely eight years old, but many things had changed in the style of its participants. They were more experienced, more professional, and they now took more safety precautions.

Italy got to the final with the enviable record of 22–0. There had technically been a loss a few months after winning the 1934 title, but it was not taken as such. The Nazionale had decided to go after impenetrable England at Wembley and lost 3–2, but the tight game was more of a disgrace for England than a loss for Italy. Coach Pozzo was continually refining his ideas and trying out more skillful defenders who would allow the team a better exit from its own defensive zone. As the players caught on, Pozzo realized it was possible to beat anyone. In this particular game—their second consecutive final—Pozzo changed their routine. He took advantage of that same plane that left for Paris from Marseilles the day of the semifinal, and from Paris they journeyed to the solitude of St. Germain where he isolated his players in absolute calm.

When June 19 came, they appeared in Colombes stadium with serenity reflected in their countenance and in their gestures, saluting the fans with smiles and answering the journalists amiably.

On the other side, the Hungarians—who could count on players like Gyorgy Sarosi, a clerk who was also a forward or midfielder of absolute clarity—had the "problem" of having too many important players to fit on one starting team. They arrived tense and nervous. The changes in their lineup this time around had been forced by injuries.

On needed only to compare the faces of the two teams to realize how the game would go. Italy stayed with the lineup that had gotten them to that stage, with players who knew each other's moves blindfolded. The team formed by Olivieri, Foni, Rava, Serantoni, Andreolo, Locatelli, Biavati, Meazza, Piola, Ferrari, and Colaussi went ahead at six minutes, with a goal by Colaussi. Hungary responded almost immediately, equalizing with a goal by Titkos. Piola and, before the end of the first half, Colaussi extended the Italian lead. Two stars of that French World Cup ended it in their own inimitable style. First, Sarosi provided a last gasp of hope to the long-shot Hungarian dream. Then Piola, in his own unique way, put the ball in the net to close the score, 4–2.

Once again Italy was the champion. This time, Giuseppe Meazza could lift the Cup free from suspicion of favoritism from referees or the crowd. They would get to keep the Cup for longer than was originally planned. Fourteen months after that June day in 1938, Hitler would order the invasion of Poland in what was the beginning of the end. World War II had begun, a war which would claim many lives, redraw the map of Europe and—much less importantly—would not permit a World Cup until 1950.

France continued the tradition of generating positive cash flow: 374,937 spectators with an average of 21,000 fans per game. Soccer was once again a worldwide success.

SILVIO PIOLA
(Italy)
France 1938

He's eighty-two years old, his health is only so-so, and he carries a sad smile. Silvio Piola, an institution in Italian soccer, still gets excited when he talks about the ball, about the goals, about . . . soccer. Perhaps because of that, he dedicates so few words to it. "Goals were my life. I'm still the record holder in Italy: I made 290 in first division defending the colors of Pro Vercelli, Lazio, Juventus, and Novara. Only Zoff played more games than I did in first division, and only Meazza has scored more goals than I did in the Nazionale: thirty-three of his against thirty of mine. How great he was . . . poor Peppino . . ."

Meazza–Piola was the great clash of the titans: the Pele–Di Stefano, the Maradona–Van Basten, of 1930s Europe.

One of them, Meazza, Inter's glorious idol, symbolized the Nazionale Azzurra who had won the World Cup 1934. His name lives on today, memorialized by Milan's eponymous soccer temple in the San Siro district.

The other, Piola, signed and sealed the second title four years later in France. He scored five goals in four games and was the perfect complement to Meazza.

"What pleasant memories the French World Cup brings up. Winning was beautiful, but I remember it as being difficult, complicated. At that time, Italy was ruled by fascism, Mussolini was the head of state, and many exiled Italians who had escaped the dictatorship lived in France. Before the games would begin, all of us players used to extend our right arms toward the stands: It was the fascist salute, which was almost always met by boos. . . . The truth is that we didn't understand very well; for us it was the most nat-

ural thing in the world to salute like that. I don't think we understood that our extended arms were a slap in the face to our compatriots. Something that we only learned with time . . ."

Goals, salutes, fascism, and hate. That 1938 World Cup had not
been an easy one for Italy, nor is it easy for Piola to sum it up . . .

"In the second game, we played against France; we won 3–1."

He repeats it with statistical accuracy, but without even a hint of
emotion. Intentionally, he ignores his own importance to that game:
Two goals of his had broken the 1–1 deadlock in the tense
atmosphere at Colombes stadium, whose crowd had showered a
totalitarian Italy with boos.

Afterward, it was necessary to get past Leonidas's Brazil—a task
made easier by Leonidas's absence due to injury—and another
doppietta[1] by Piola decided the final against Sarosi and Zsengeller's
great Hungarian team. "Colaussi–Piola, Colaussi–Piola, and the Cup
for Italy," wrote the journalists of that time about Italy's conquest.
In the prestigious magazine *Guerin Sportivo,* today's journalists remember him like this:

> Before the appearance of Gigi Riva in the sixties, he was the synonym
> for the word "center-forward" as far as Italian soccer is concerned.
> These were his characteristics: an imposing physique (at least for the
> time; he was 1 meter, 78 centimeters tall) made him very fearsome in
> the air-game. His build—he seemed made of stone—allowed him to
> go into the penalty area with the spirit of a conquistador: Before he
> could be stopped, Silvio Piola gave rival defenders a piece of his mind.
> When Angelo Schiavio retired from soccer, Pozzo saw that it was nec-
> essary to solve his center-forward problem. The choice of Piola left
> him satisfied, seeing that Piola scored two goals against Austria in his
> first game in the Nazionale. His caliber was acknowledged by the
> English masters themselves (whom he scored against with a handball
> in 1939), who saw in him the ideal center-forward for their style of
> soccer.

That's how they saw a man who refuses to talk about the soccer
of today. "The thing is that I was always a bit difficult on the field.
Off the field, I try to seek out some peace. I don't like to talk about
subjects that don't concern me. Maradona? Baggio? Each of them
does their own thing, like I did in my day. . . . Do I watch soccer on

---

[1]*Doppietta:* literally meaning "double-barreled gun," it refers to a player scoring
twice in a single game.

TV? Very little, only every once in awhile . . . sometimes I'll watch a World Cup game—it's the only thing that ever catches my eye. It doesn't excite me that much anymore . . ."

He was more excited when, until a few years ago, he would take out his rifle and go hunting in the forests surrounding his Pied-montese residence in Novara, half an hour from Turin and half an hour from Milan. There, he became as good a shot as they say he used to be in the enemy penalty area. Nowadays, he chooses not to disturb his own memories.

"Today's soccer? I liked mine more," he says. And that's it.

Brazil 1950

The war was over. Since that ominous September 1, 1939, sixty million innocent people had lost their lives in a massacre that will never be justified. Nothing would ever be the same. Still, on July 1, 1946, FIFA officially reconvened in Luxembourg and decided to resume the World Cup, starting with one in the Americas. At the same congress, they also agreed on a new name for the cup. The trophy, in the shape of *Winged Victory,* would now be called the Jules Rimet Cup, after the official who had done the most to bring it about. A few days later, everything was confirmed: Brazil was selected as the organizer of the 1949 edition—Europe, with their war wounds still fresh, had no way of confronting such a huge task— and Switzerland was chosen as the organizer of the following one, scheduled for 1953.

The years stated above are not errors. By the time the Paris Congress convened on January 18, 1947, the organizing committee realized that there would not be enough time for everything to be put in place and, therefore, decided to postpone. Thus, the resumption of the World Cup would have to wait until 1950.

Three hundred sixty-seven days later, on January 20, 1948, in Rio de Janeiro, the Brazilians started work on an awe-inspiring edifice that they later christened in their own inimitable style: "The eighth wonder of the world, the Maracana!" For two years, work continued day and night to level the ground, from which more than 50,000 cubic meters of earth were removed. By the time they were done with the monstrous stadium, they had used 464,500 tons of cement; 1,275 cubic meters of sand; 3,933 cubic meters of stone; 10,597,661 kilograms of steel; and 55,259 cubic meters of wood. It was clear that Brazil wanted to organize an *o mais grande* (grander) World Cup.

Of course, for that they had to do some number crunching and, when they analyzed the finances, they came to several conclusions. With the bottom line in mind, the organizers proposed a modification to FIFA: Cast aside the system of direct elimination, which allowed only sixteen games and, therefore, only sixteen contributions to the box office; replace it with four groups of four teams, with the four winners of the respective groups playing a final round, for a total of thirty games.

The international organization was unconvinced by this proposal, and the Brazilians' response was to adopt a pressure strategy: If FIFA did not accept the idea, Brazil would not organize the Cup. Finally, FIFA gave in, but not without a price: FIFA vice president Henri Delaunay, a pioneer of the World Cup, resigned in protest of the change.

Analyzing it in hindsight, the idea had interesting implications. The problem was that, when the time to play came, only thirteen of the sixteen classified teams showed up. France decided not to participate after requesting that the organizers change an insurmountable schedule: They had to play against Bolivia and Uruguay in Porto Alegre and Recife, an almost impossible trip at that time; Austria and India excused themselves, citing the economic hardship of the long voyage to South America. Given the circumstances, the groups had to reshuffle and the format that would later be used in most of the tournaments was only partially implemented.

There were, as in all World Cups, significant absentees.

One was Argentina, which again got hit from all sides: first, when the South American Soccer Confederation endorsed Brazil's bid to organize the tournament and later, because of Argentina's strained relations with the Brazilian federation. The previous year, the AFA (Argentine Football Association) had decided not to send a team to the South American championship in Brazil, because of the exodus of their best players to Colombia. The reaction of the neighboring officials was to prohibit any soccer relations between the two countries, a measure that did not please the Argentines, who considered it excessive and unfriendly. Only when the new president of Brazil, Getulio Vargas, assumed office after the end of the World Cup and after his personal intercession through his ambassador to Argentina, was it possible to reopen ties between Brazil and Argentina.

Another absence—an obvious one—was Germany. Its national team had been outlawed as punishment for the crimes committed by its leaders during the war. Only after the FIFA Congress of 1950 would Germany be allowed to participate in the next tournament.

Italy, although technically present, was clearly handicapped. The recent plane crash that had killed the entire Torino team—the cornerstone of the Nazionale, where eight of the eleven starters played, among them Valentino Mazzola (father of Sandro Mazzola, who would later star in Mexico 1970)—was a hard blow. So much so that when the Italians decided to make the trek to South America, they chose to go by sea, even at the risk of placing themselves at a severe disadvantage. The ship, a luxury cruise liner, was not built for athletes and, like in the old days, they went through fifteen days of ludicrous training sessions, including balls going overboard. Moreover, upon arrival in Rio, they found themselves in a luxury hotel filled with beautiful and seductive Argentine dancers. . . . Legendary tales tell how the Italians had guarded the World Cup during the war—such as the one that recounts how Italian federation official Ottorino Barassi hid it under his bed and even inside a block of cheese to protect it—but the Italians had already resigned themselves to the fact that the Cup would not be theirs for much longer.

Nevertheless, there were also new or returning participants. At long last, the British teams came out of isolation, deciding to participate in the World Cup for the first time. After eliminating one another in the qualifying rounds, the expected finalist remained standing: England. Of course, the end result of the Cup would not be so predictable.

Municipal stadium, popularly called Maracaná stadium, after the extraordinarily poor neighborhood surrounding it, was built in record time: twenty-two months. General Angelo Mendes de Morais, prefect of Rio de Janeiro, expressed his expectations clearly: "I did my job," he told the Brazilian players, "now it's your turn." Everyone was dreaming of immortality. And on that note, filled with national pride and confidence, they heard the starting whistle of the fourth World Cup, the first to identify the players with numbers on the back of their jerseys.

On June 26, Brazil inaugurated the new stadium, and no detail was overlooked: Celebration and music covered up the organizational mistakes, and the rival (if one can call it that)—Mexico—was the perfect foil, poised to receive the four slaps Brazil gave it and allow the Brazilians to continue the party on the field. As Group 1 played, Brazil tied Switzerland (2–2) and barely beat Yugoslavia (2–0), proving that victory in the tournament was not going to be easy. The Brazilians, however, did not seem to notice, preferring to put their faith in the idea that everything would be taken care of by Ademir's goal-scoring prowess (which came true) as well as by the fervor of their fans (also true, but inconsequential).

Group 2 quickly showed that, in this game, fame and precedent are not enough to win. The great England debuted with a triumph against Chile (2–0) and soon after found itself facing the United States, the tournament's biggest surprise.

The English team was made up of the best players from a country whose soccer was considered a model for everyone, and at right back was a brilliant player who would later coach England to the World Championship in 1966: Alf Ramsey.

The American team was formed by a very select group: an Italian goalkeeper, Borghi; two Portuguese forwards, the Sousa brothers; a Belgian back, Maca; and a Haitian forward, Gaetjens. Moreover, among them was a carpenter, a teacher, a gravedigger, two postmen, a machinist, an interior decorator, and a day laborer. It was almost the same as fifty-four years later when, as the home team, the Americans counted a German, a South African, two of Argentine descent, and two Uruguayans in their ranks.

From all this, an indisputable conclusion can be reached: Then, as now, the contribution of immigrants to soccer in the United States has been undeniably valuable, even though it may not be acknowledged today.

Perhaps at that time, when the heroic feat was achieved, many expected it would turn out differently. Here's the way it went: The game started just as expected, with an intense siege on the United States goal, defended by Italian-American goalkeeper Borghi. But lack of luck—as well as precision—impeded the English from opening the scoring. Then, thirty-nine minutes into the first half, Haitian Larry Gaetjens beat everyone to the ball, and English goalkeeper Williams was unable to contain his shot. From that moment on, the British dominated the action even more intensely than they had before the goal, but they were still unable to alter the scoreboard. At the end of ninety minutes of play, the American triumph was as much a reality as the general disbelief surrounding it. . . . So much so that much of the English media decided not to report news of the loss, and one newspaper even went to the extreme of reporting that the score was incorrect. The real score, according to the paper, was England 10, United States 0. The real one, as we know, was different.

Looking back, two stories from two other World Cup competitions bring to mind the American upset over England: The first, which happened on the field, when North Korea ended Italy's dreams of a World Cup win in 1966; the other when, during World Cup 1994, a Danish journalist pressed the wrong key on a sophisticated computer and sent out an article—prepared before the game—recounting Romania's victory over Sweden—when in fact it ended up the other way around.

Group 3 was one of the groups that had been left incomplete by the no-shows. Only three teams fought for the top spot and Sweden provided the surprise. Even with an incomplete team, they easily beat a crestfallen Italy and an outmatched Paraguay. The Calcio club of Milan already attracted the world's greatest stars—as it does today—and three of the greatest Swedish players in history—Gren, Nordahl, and Liedholm, the famous "Gre-No-Li" trio—played for Calcio and stayed in Milan. The Swedes had other players to make up for their absence—Jeppsson, Skoglund, Andersson, K. Nordhal, Gard, and Sundqvist. The Italians had their eyes on these players too, but not until after their defeat, which proved that winning a World Cup for the third straight time was just a fantasy.

Group 4 was the most thinned out by the absences. Uruguay, in an unexpected gift received from the Brazilians, only had to play one game, against Bolivia. The final score of 8–0 speaks for itself, yet it does not even begin to measure the Uruguayan team's amazing will to win. But, as happened before, the story seemed to have already been written: the Brazilians saw themselves lifting the Cup toward the heavens, and each game was nothing more than a perfunctory exercise.

That is how the final series started.

Showing their power on the field, the Brazilians effortlessly flattened the, until then, tight Swedish team (7–1) before laughing in the face of the Spanish "fury" (6–1), confirming Ademir (nine goals) as the undisputed goal-scoring king, and Jair as his faithful squire. Uruguay sweated against Spain (2–2) and also had to work to beat Sweden (3–2), making it clear that it could count on a great player like Jose "Pepe" Schiaffino, as well as the unbreakable will of the whole team. Coincidentally, the match between the two European teams (Sweden and Spain) became the third place game (Sweden won), and the match between the two South American teams (Brazil and Uruguay) became the grand finale. . . .

The statistics provided a profile of each team. Brazil reached that historic day with four points—thirteen goals for and two against while Uruguay got there with three points—five goals for and four against. Tactically, each team had its own strengths. The Brazilians had already adopted the idea that was all the rage in Argentine soccer: three backs (one in the middle and one on each side) and a center-half to guide the team from the midfield. Up front, the players were arranged diagonally, with Ademir and Jair constantly moving and switching to try to avoid being caged by the W–M formation.

Of course, Uruguay wanted nothing to do with this "system" and remained faithful to its old "method." Instead of the solitary back of the English system, there were two central defenders who mutually covered one another, depending on how their adversaries advanced ("I go out, you cover. You go out, I cover."); two halves on the wings who closely guarded other team's forwards; and a classic center-half, helped by the two insiders who took turns retreating back toward him. That defensive zone was called "the little cage." Before the final game, coach Juan Lopez, hoping to trap Zizinho, Ademír, and Jair, formed the cage with center-half Obdulio Varela and backs Tejera and Matias Gonzalez. He told Gonzalez: "Don't leave the penalty arc of the zone. Don't let yourself creep out of it." He had all the cool that was lacking outside in the streets, where Brazil was one huge party confident that they would lift the Cup in victory after the game.

So widespread was the belief that the game was a lock, so intense was the certainty that theirs was an unbeatable team, that any of the 203,567 spectators present—even though the stadium was built for a capacity of only 183,354—would have bet the house on Brazil without a second thought. Even Uruguay's own management told their players that it would be a victory just to lose by a reasonably close margin. One of them, Dr. Jacobo, approached Omar Miguez and whispered to him as though he wanted him to pass the message along: "What's important is that these people don't score six goals. If they score only four goals, our mission will be accomplished . . ."

When Obdulio Varela, the captain, found out, he asked his teammate: "How come you didn't throw him out of the hotel?" Then Schubert Gambetta rose in support of his captain: "The management are cowards." From that moment, Obdulio and coach Juan Lopez began a psychological exercise that could be summarized in the captain's own words: "Only when we are champions will our mission be accomplished."

Their work continued unhindered. They got to the stadium and went into the stuffy, noisy locker rooms before going out to a small park for fresh air. Everyone was so relaxed that Gambetta was still sleeping in his chair less than one hour before the start of the most important game in his life. As the team went out onto the field, Varela approached Miguez and said: "Doesn't their goalkeeper look like an idiot? Don't tell me that you can't make two goals against him." He then went up to Gonzalez, who had the tough job of guarding the dangerous Chico: "If you let him touch the ball even once, you'll have to deal with me later." Finally, the captain announced to his team, "Boys, today I really feel like running!"

That's what they did from the start, although the game seemed to unfold just as everyone had predicted. Brazil had control of the ball, their attack always close to goalkeeper Roque Maspoli. Nevertheless, from where he stood, things didn't look quite so bad: "When the game started, they began to play very rough, but they made a mistake. They went after Ghiggia and Julio Perez, two cool, imperturbable players who weren't disturbed by the rough play. The fouls were called and they just got right back up again, without the slightest sign of discomfort. That's when I think the Brazilians began to lose. But after they got ahead 1–0, the atmosphere became hellish. . . ."

Friaca scored the first goal, two minutes into the second half. That's when the key scene, which was to become part of soccer mythology, took place. . . . While all Brazil—literally *all*—celebrated, Obdulio Varela calmly took the ball out of the depths of his net, put the ball under his arm, and stepped proudly toward the center circle. As soon as he got there, he pompously began to protest to the British referee Reader, unleashing an argument he did not understand . . . but the Uruguayan captain achieved his objective: slowly, like a giant, loud radio that gradually lowers in volume, the screaming of the crowd became a murmur, then a whisper, and, finally, silence. Frozen silence. More than two hundred thousand pairs of eyes were hooked on that strange scene and, for an indeterminable length of time, the Brazilian heat turned into cold sweat. . . . When play finally resumed, it crossed more than one

Brazilian's mind that maybe this story wouldn't have such a happy ending.

Twenty minutes later, Varela opened play to the right, Ghiggia got to the ball, and crossed it to Pepe Schiaffino, who didn't miss: "Crossing the field diagonally, Ghiggia appeared near the line of the goal area in the position of an inside right. He gave me a perfect pass from the wing, and I volleyed the ball hard, with the inner part of my right foot. When Barbosa dove, the ball had already entered the goal inside the near post. I saw the ball hit the upper part of the net. It was the tying goal. In spite of this, the Brazilians went on celebrating because, even with the tie, they were champions anyway. . . ." But in the midst of hundreds of thousands of fans sitting comfortably under the Brazilian sun knowing that the tie gave them the Cup anyway, Omar Miguez's eyewitness report gives the impression that something had definitely changed: "It was in the stars that, against all odds, we would win. We feared no one. Had Maspoli played center-forward, he would have scored two goals and had I played goalkeeper, I would have saved two penalty kicks."

Alcides Ghiggia, seven minutes from the end, proved him right. "Julio Perez approached the line and we did our classic play, the 'yours and mine' [presently known as a 'give and go']. I passed him the ball, he gave it back to me on the wing, I faked Bigode out, kicked the ball ahead of me, and then went after it. Schiaffino joined up again, waiting for a backward pass as he had in the first goal. Barbosa, the Brazilian goalkeeper, also thought that the ball was going to Schiaffino and stepped forward to intercept. When I lifted my head to make the pass, I saw the gap that Barbosa had left between his body and the near post, so I shot the ball with some spin. Barbosa flew, but it was too late. Because of the spin, the ball curved and continued toward the net, even though it hit Barbosa's hands. It was strange—our shouting was the only thing you could hear. . . ."

It seems easy to imagine it. A deadly silence. The "Maracaná shocker" was complete. Just before a corner kick, Gambetta heard the three whistles of the English referee, took the ball with his two hands and kissed it. . . . Right away, the few Uruguayans present in the stadium invaded the field, although very few others in the stadium were still watching. In the midst of the confusion, the trophy disappeared for a short time and, by the time it fell into the hands of Jules Rimet, Obdulio Varela had already shouted: "With or without the Cup, we are the champions. . . ." Finally, FIFA's president handed the Cup to Varela: "I found myself alone with the trophy in my hands, not knowing what to do. Then I found the Uruguayan captain Varela and, as if we were in hiding, I turned the Cup over to him, extending my hand without being able to utter a single word. . . ."

Outside, the samba was no longer being heard: The happy Brazilian music had been replaced by wailing sirens. Ambulances sped to save those who were felled by heart attacks or who sought to escape their unbearable pain through suicide. Police tried to detain—somewhat reluctantly—those who attempted to go after the people they held responsible for the fiasco, such as Brazilian coach Costa, trying to kill them with their own hands.

Forty-five years later, Costa would tell the Brazilian magazine *Placar*: "When the game ended and the crowd left the stadium crying, we went into our locker room. We were crushed, ashamed, full of guilt. While I was there with the players, I could not wait to just get home. I would have liked to escape without speaking with anyone, but it was impossible. We had to wait a good while before we could leave the Maracaná. I remember that people were worried about me and tried to distract me. So they started to talk about other things, but inevitably, it went back to the game; it was impossible to talk about anything else. Years later, I found myself in Europe with Sweden's coach, who showed me the gold medals that they got for being World Cup runners-up. We didn't even get a telegram from the Brazilian Football Confederation. I know that the loss in the final was a major disappointment, but I also think that we deserved something for our dedication and for the campaign that we waged."

Many years later, the venerable, noble, and great Obdulio would admit: "We won because we won, nothing more. Brazil was a machine: they assaulted our goal with shots and played soccer in the truest sense of the word. Get it through your head: if we had played one hundred times, we would have won only that one. . . ."

Many years later, the great Chico would come to a similar conclusion, one that would sum up many other upsets throughout the history of the World Cup: "The best don't always win." Adding to his testimonial of that fateful game in *Placar*: "When the referee ended the game, I ran off the field. The feeling was total devastation. I don't remember speaking with any journalist or any

Uruguayan player. They may have spoken to me, but I really don't remember. I went to the locker room, and there everyone was silent, it was truly as if someone had died. Then I went to my house on Barao of Carai street in the Flamengo district . . . I remember talking to people, but I was totally disoriented, I couldn't concentrate at all. I remember that that night I couldn't sleep. Then, for the next week, I had the same dream: that the game had not been played yet and Brazil still had a chance to be World Champion."

Exactly forty-four years and one day later, Brazil would be crowned the first four-time champion in World Cup history. The title would come after a poor performance; amidst arguments that Brazil wasn't really the best, almost losing to a team—Italy—that definitely was not the best; and with a conservative style of play that was somehow influenced by that old—but still haunting—pain of the "Maracaná shocker."

OBDULIO VARELA
(Uruguay)
Brazil 1950

In 1990, on the fortieth anniversary of the "Maracaná shocker," a Brazilian journalist traveled to Montevideo to interview Obdulio Varela. He rang the bell at his house at 3030 20 de febrero Street, in the Villa Española district. Even with the passage of time, the un-mistakable outline of the star appeared behind that brown door and heard the journalist's pleadings in the best possible *portuñol*.[1] But there was no response. He wanted nothing to do with an in-terview. So the journalist sat down and waited. For five straight days he sat on the curb in front of the house, waiting to be let in. But still nothing.

Finally Jacinto Obdulio Varela—the leader of 1950, the man with the ball under his arm, the myth—took pity on him and let him in. That journalist must have been the last . . . because Obdulio doesn't want to talk anymore. And he wants to remember even less. "I can't even play *truco*[2] anymore," he laments, excusing himself.

He still maintains the image of a man who is frank, dignified, and proud in his simplicity. He has long nails—very long—and on every September 20, he wakes up to the sound of a military band playing in front of his house, where he has lived since 1964. There, he lives out his days meekly, accompanied by his wife, and every now and then he enters that corner of his mind, which he himself calls "the corner of memories," filled with images and pictures turned yellow

[1]*Portuñol:* a mix of Portuguese and Spanish. The word is formed by "portu" (Por-tuguese) and "ñol" (Spanish).
[2]*Truco:* literally meaning "trick," a popular card game played in Argentina and Uruguay.

by time. It is also filled with ghosts. . . . He doesn't want to talk about them either—it upsets him too much. The last thing he let the world hear was a severe, sharp, and precise criticism: "Maracaná was an accident. It's a mistake to think that it lasts forever. . . . It caused Uruguayan soccer to take a nap."

In 1966, sixteen years after the "Maracaná shocker," the prestigious Uruguayan journalist Franklin Morales interviewed the "Dark Chief." It was the first article in which he spoke about the Maracaná and the last issuing statements so severe, he never wanted to repeat them. Surely, he considers them his final statements, his unalterable experiences. . . . Here's what he said, and what he would say today, that is, if he would say anything at all.

When Brazil was playing their qualifiers, I went to see them in person at the Maracaná. How beautifully they played! They looked like chess pieces: small, moved by who knows who. They were perfect, they weren't mere mortals. I left the stadium satisfied by what I had seen. That was soccer! Those were players! In my opinion, the best players in the world are Brazilian, because of their showmanship and agility. Some of the players looked like dancers. Now, years later, I remember Didi. When he brought up the ball, the defender didn't know what to do. He controlled the ball with both feet while weaving his way through the rival defense. Well, in 1950, there were a lot of Didis.

The Maracaná shocker? It was like winning the lottery. We bought a ticket and won the big one. The Brazilians had a great team. We did too, but a game like that is always won with the help of luck. The ball under my arm after we went down 1–0? A lot has been made of that . . . Rossi or Perucca would have done the same thing. The second half had just started, Friaca's goal had come, the stands were on fire, sparks were flying everywhere, and I had to do what I did. I had to delay putting the ball back into play as much as possible because, if we had started up again immediately, they would have scored five [goals]. I achieved my goal: They went from being happy to booing; they got nervous. We calmed down, and that's when I gave up the ball. I was close to being kicked out of the game, so I was lucky even there. Afterward came Schiaffino and Ghiggia's goals. That was it.

The situation was very tough. Brazil was a machine. Get it in your head: We won because we won, no more. They put our goal under siege . . . it was crazy. If we had played one hundred times, we would have only won that one. Up front, everyone played badly, except for Ghiggia and Julio Perez. Schiaffino was lucky enough to score. Omar [Miguez] was always very eccentric, an exciting player to watch. Our defense was strong. We had the luck to have a player like Matias Gonzalez in back. Incredible player. So was "el Mono" (the monkey) Gambetta. They felt the pressure of the Brazilian attack. It looked as though their faces were even changing color.

There is so much ingratitude. People think everything was perfect in the Maracaná, that we worked hard to win, because afterward there were enough medals to go around. Of course, let's not forget that we got silver ones while the executives got the gold. About three days before the final, Dr. Jacobo called Omar [Miguez] and told him: "What's important is that these people don't make six goals. If they score only four goals, our mission will be successful." The guys told me everything that was going on, so when he came and told me what had been said, I asked him why he hadn't kicked Jacobo out of the hotel. It's what he deserved. In the locker room, there were similar messages: Play with kid gloves, they said, our aim was accomplished by just reaching the final. When we were alone on the field, we all got together and agreed, "The management are cowards. Only when we are champions will our mission be accomplished." And that's how things went; luck was on our side.

After the game, in the hotel, there was a huge party, so they told everyone not to leave. I wasn't about to let them take away my freedom. I'm my own boss. I asked Americo Gil (head of the delegation) what could be done, and he told me to do whatever I wanted. The executives went to a cabaret, and they wanted to keep us locked up! Please! Matucho (Figoli, the team masseur) and I took over, and we started to drink wine. We gulped down one bottle. Then another. Then another. I was totally out of it. Later, we went for a walk, and we got to a friend's brewery. There I ran into all the journalists, who were eating. They introduced me to journalists from France, from Italy, from God knows where. They invited us to join them, but instead we went to the counter and started to chug down some beer. A bit later, I ordered a couple of hot dogs. Just as we were about to leave, I told Matucho: "You pay, because I didn't bring any cash." "I didn't either," he told me. We didn't have a penny . . . the things that happen! How embarrassing! Luckily, they were friends, so I told them, "I'll come back and pay you tomorrow." Right then, a group of Brazilians, who had come from the country's heartland to see the game, came in carrying flags and banners. They started to talk about the game with the owner. "What a player that Obdulio is," and this and that, they went on. "You know who that is?" the owner asked them, "Obdulio himself." Then the Brazilians started crying, "What a player you are," and this and that. Then, they invited me to go drink some whiskey with them. I told Matucho, "Look, I'll go to show them that I'm not afraid, but I'm not so sure they don't want to throw me into the river." I got back to the hotel at seven in the morning, thinking everyone would be asleep. Jesus, Mary, and Joseph! Sleeping, my ass! They were so over-emotional they didn't sleep. I sent from one room to the next, making everyone sign the little flags, and I got to *Juancito* (little Juan) Lopez's room, where Maspoli was, too. When the big guy sees me, he asks me, "Did we really win yesterday, Obdulio?" "Leave me alone, Roque." I hit up Americo for some cash and went to cover my tab for the beer. On the way back, I drank another bottle of whiskey. Had there been any left by the time I got back, with the scavengers there, God help me!

Almost eighty years old, the thoughts of Jacinto Obdulio Varela— the "Dark Chief," the "Great Captain," the "Great Chief," the "Eternal Captain"—have not changed a bit. He neither wants to hear about, nor talk about soccer. And he wants to see it even less. His image has already been cast in bronze, along with the image of Jose Nasazzi, in the *Historical Monument of World Soccer,* in front of Centenario stadium. His feats have inspired books (Roberto Mancuso's *Obdulio, el último capitán*[3] and Antonio Pippo's *Obdulio, desde el alma*[4]), stories (Osvaldo Soriano's "Obdulio Varela, el Reposo del Centro Medio"[5] and "Obdulio" by Eduardo Galeano), and even plays *(Tango del Penal,*[6] directed by Italian Giorgio Galleone).

He pretends not to notice. Sometimes he falls back into the "corner of memories" and, still contemplating all the greatness stored there, prefers to be left alone with the tranquility offered by his wife, and the incomparably peaceful Montevideo. If anyone still thinks it's all a myth, that's their problem.

[3]*Obdulio, el último capitán (Obdulio, the Last Champion).*
[4]*Obdulio, desde el alma (Obdulio, from the Soul).*
[5]"Obdulio Varela, el reposo del centro medio" ("Obdulio Varela, the Last Centerhalf").
[6]*Tango del Penal (Penalty Kick Tango).*

Switzerland 1954

The world was not at peace, and international soccer had its own share of conflicts. With the cold war between the United States and the Soviet Union at its height, FIFA became riddled with internal disputes that convinced the legendary Jules Rimet that his job was just too draining. As the United States tested the H-bomb in the Pacific—a bomb hundreds of times more powerful than the one dropped on Hiroshima—FIFA left behind its offices on Rue Saint-Honoré in Paris, which had survived the war under security against Hitler's threats, and moved to Zurich, where it remains to this day. As a result, the fifth World Cup was played . . . at home.

After Spain failed to beat Turkey in a three-game series ending with a tie and a victory for each, a drawing was held. A kid by the name of Franco Gemma picked a ball out of a hat, and luck favored the Turks. Spain was out. The South Koreans made the tournament for the first time, at the expense of the Japanese, who were to become their eternal rivals, both on and off the field. The rivalry continues today, with both countries vying for the right to organize the 2002 World Cup.

From the other half of the world, the two finalists of the unforgettable 1950 World Cup arrived in different states of mind. Uruguay came basking in the glow of their legendary victory, having kept most of the players from their 1950 team, including Maspoli, Rodriguez, Andrade, Miguez, Schiaffino, and, of course, Obdulio Varela, in spite of the fact that he had recently turned thirty-seven. Brazil came still bearing the painful memory of the loss four years before—a memory that had kept them from play-ing any games outside their country for two years. The team they fielded in Switzerland included only two survivors of that tragic encounter—Bauer and Baltazar. Among the new faces were Didi, with his excellent playmaking talents, as well as Djalma San-tos and Nilton Santos. The Brazilians and Uruguayans would be the only South Americans present. Once again, Argentina decided to watch from the sidelines. Instead of playing, they sent a giant from another era—the famous "Infiltrator" Guillermo Stabile, now Argentina's national team coach—to observe and evaluate the participants. Argentine soccer had been without Alfredo Di Ste-fano, who had been sold to Europe in an interesting transaction. When River Plate, Di Stefano's original club, sold his rights to Barcelona, Millonarios of Bogota, the last team in which "the Di" had played, also transferred him to Real Madrid. In Spain, the local Federation resolved the problem with a Solomon-like solu-tion. Di Stefano, it was decided, would play one year for each club. In the end, however, Barcelona was compensated, and the great Al-fredo helped build Madrid's now legendary club more than any other figure. Barcelona had better luck in securing the talents of an-other great player: Hungarian Ladislao Kubala. Unfortunately, Kubala was kept out of the 1954 World Cup after the Hungarian federation asked that he be disqualified because he had played for Spain's national team. He would eventually get his chance, but followers of Switzerland 1954 never had the pleasure of seeing him play.

It was a situation that, years later, would cause FIFA to alter its rules. After the rule change, any player who had ever defended the colors of his national team could never do so for another, even if he changed citizenship. As a result, the Colombian-born Carlos Fer-nando Navarro Montoya would not be allowed to defend the goal of his adopted country, Argentina, in USA 1994. In any case, back to 1954. . . .

There was one serious, confident, and clear favorite: Hungary. In 1952 they had won the Olympic games in Helsinki. On the very day of that victory, Sir Stanley Rous, president of the English federation, approached Hungarian coach Gustav Sebes and challenged him to a game in London, just as they had done with the Italians after they had been awarded the gold. The Englishman obviously didn't know what he was getting into.

The date for the match, November 25, 1953, was not chosen at random. Rather, it was planned by the home team to take advantage of the weather in the English capital at that time of year, which the English were accustomed to. But it didn't make much difference on the day of the game. Awestricken fans witnessed what turned out to be a Hungarian-hosted soccer clinic. In the humid and uncomfortable fog that the English thought would favor them, that fabulous Hungarian team filled the hosts' net with goals. In the end, without any regard for tradition, the Hungarians had given England a 6–3 beating. That night, the fog-shrouded Wembley stadium was illuminated only by the light of the Hungarian stars: Grocsis, Bozsik, Lorant, Budai, Kocsis, Hidegkuti and, of course, Ferenc Puskas. In addition to being a distinguished soccer star, the short, stocky Puskas, who was already twenty-seven years old, was also a major in the army. He was known as "the Colonel."

The rematch in Budapest produced an undisputed 7–1 win, proving beyond a shadow of a doubt that Wembley had not been an accident. The game allowed the Hungarians to add to an already impressive record, which got them to the World Cup undefeated in their last thirty-one games, a winning streak that spanned four years. It is no wonder that the world already knew them as "Aranycsapat," the golden team.

Perhaps because of an overall dedication to the aggressive soccer that everyone likes to see, a shower of goals rained on Switzerland, making that Cup the most prolific of all as far as scoring. Meanwhile, the tournament's new format drew more than one protest: In each group of four teams, each team would play only two games before the quarterfinals. So in Group 2, for example, Hungary would not play Turkey. Consequently, a confrontation between the favorites and Germany was of key importance, as we shall see.

In Group 1, which took place in Lausanne and Geneva, Didi's Brazil started out by clobbering Mexico (5–0) before suffering against Yugoslavia (1–1), achieving their qualification for the next round without having to cross paths with France. According to prestigious Italian journalist Gianni Brera, the Brazilians—who wore their now traditional yellow and green jerseys for the first time—had a problem. It was recorded like this in *Guerin Sportivo*: "The Brazilians play the W–M and they frequently and willingly abandon their stopper Brandaozinho. The right and left backs Santos (referring to Nilton and Djalma) merrily advance to kick crosses from the wing. If the cross is cleared, Brazil finds itself with only one defender, Brandaozinho. The stupidity of this practice is amazing." The French, for their part, were unceremoniously eliminated from the tournament. At least they were spared Mexico's shame: They participated in their third World Cup, unable to tie—let alone win—a single game.

In Group 3, which took place in Zurich and Bern, Uruguay calmly advanced while filling the nets of both Czechoslovakia (2–0) and Scotland (7–0). A tight Austrian team advanced with Uruguay's Celeste to the next round, defeating the same rivals by the scores of 5–0 and 1–0.

Up until 1954, on the international stage at least, the stories of the mastery of English soccer players had been left unverified. In Group 4 (played in Basel, Lausanne, Bern, and Lugano), however, England advanced to the next round for the first time, after tying Belgium (4–4 after overtime) and beating Switzerland (2–0). The Swiss also qualified, introducing a style that Swiss coach Rappan named the *catenazz*. Later, the Italians would make that style famous throughout the world as *catenaccio* (defensive tactics). In Switzerland 1954, however, the Italians refused to use it and wound up giving one of their worst performances in history.

Group 2 (played in Zurich, Bern, Basel, and Geneva) produced a bigger crop of goals than any of the others. The group was formed by Hungary, Germany, Turkey, and South Korea, which was the punching bag of the first three. The four teams scored forty-one goals in five games, an average of 8.2 per game. Some of the games were predictable while others were surprising. One of the latter included the much awaited game between Hungary and Germany, which ended 8–3 in favor of the Magyars. Sepp Herberger, the German coach (who had annexed the Austrian players to his national team, after Hitler had done the same with the country), decided to rest five of his starters (Turek, Laband, Morlock, Ottmar Walter, and Schaefer). For Herberger, the loss to Hungary was as calculated as their win in the tie-breaker against Turkey—which advanced the Germans to the next round. The coach used the game against Hungary, he later confessed, to discover their strategy without risking his players' prestige or health.

In the quarterfinals, Uruguay halted the English advance by a score of 4–2. The *charrúas* were helped with inspired performances by Ambrois, Schiaffino, and Obdulio Varela, who scored a goal in one of his last games wearing *Celeste* on his chest. Austria unlocked the Swiss defense in a game that ended with an un-precedented—and to this day unmatched—final score of 7–5. Germany had no trouble defeating Yugoslavia, and Hungary prepared to face Brazil. In retrospect, they must have been more like war preparations, because the game, expected to be one of the most passionate soccer duels of the time, turned into a battle of another sort. The Battle of Bern . . .

A historic match was expected, but it made history for all the wrong reasons. It was the biggest soccer scandal to date. It all started after the Hungarians got ahead 3–1. The Brazilians soon lost control and started to kick things other than the ball. Their actions attracted the attention of the referee, who responded by expelling both Nilton Santos and Bozsik at 60 minutes. As a side-note, the expulsion of Bozsik was unique: The Hungarian was a Congressman in his country at the time, undoubtedly making him the first dignitary expelled from a field of play. But the aggressions didn't end there.

Aside from an attack that hit the goal post, Brazil's aggression was channeled in a whole other direction. Humberto Tozzi joined Nilton Santos in the locker room before the final whistle, and immediately the Brazilian players started chasing Kocsis, even though he didn't have the ball. His speed, which was crucial when dribbling through his opponents, this time helped him escape and save his famous "Golden Head."

After the game ended, Maurinho attacked Buzansky and the hostilities began anew. . . . Puskas, who had not played, got into an argument with Pinheiro and broke a water bottle over his head. Brazilian coach Zeze Moreira threw a shoe at the vice president of the Hungarian Sports Committee, injuring his face. In the meantime, police fought with photographers, in a battle that consumed the entire field. In the midst of what looked like a riot, an alarmed crowd, who had expected another kind of show, looked on as the fight continued into the locker rooms. Calm was not restored until long after the game had ended.

According to FIFA, it was all Brazil's fault. Bozsick and Puskas were pardoned and Hungary had the chance to show—as if they needed to—that they were capable of actually playing soccer. They took advantage of that chance in their next game, which marked another milestone in Switzerland 1954. It was to be a true party: the party of Lausanne.

For the Magyars, the upcoming semifinal game against Uruguay was supposed to be the ticket to another matchup—this time decisive—against the Germans (who surprised almost everyone by easily turning Austria away, 6–1). It was also a chance at redemption after the embarrassment against the Brazilians. This time, they lived up to expectations in what was truly an amazing game.

Once again, rain was an element that added to the emotion of the game, but neither side needed to use the bad condition of the field as an excuse. After moving ahead 2–0 (Czibor and Hidegkuti), the Hungarians dedicated themselves to having some fun, playfully passing the ball back and forth. Facing them, however, were eleven men not accustomed to giving up. With the class of "Pepe" Schiaffino, the fervor of the naturalized Argentine Hohberg, and the will of the entire team—a will that would always be the trademark of *la Celeste*—they managed to tie the match, with only four minutes to go. Then one of the most dramatic scenes in the history of the World Cup was played out: Hohberg, physically exhausted and overcome by emotion like almost everyone in the stadium, almost fainted and had to be revived with smelling salts on one side of the field.

When he reentered the game to play the overtime, he was already fully recovered and had the strength to lead the first and best attacks of the overtime, all of which were beaten back by Hungarian goalkeeper Grosics. But an injury suffered by Rodriguez Andrade—"One of the best defenders I saw in my life," according to Puskas—forced him to be treated outside the field. His absence was fully taken advantage of by the Hungarians. Kocsis first tipped the scales in favor of Hungary and later extended the lead in what was, for many, the real final of the World Cup.

The official final, which was coming, didn't seem like an even match. . . .

For the first time, television would beam images of the game around the world. It was still a minor presence, but it set the stage for the inevitable. Sixteen years later, the final of Mexico 1970 would be seen by 800 million people. For now, at least, it served to support an idea that had already been affirmed: the World Cup was the best reflection of the evolution of the game. As for the evolution of Switzerland 1954, the picture was crystal clear.

The main strength of Gustav Sebes' team was the quality of its individual players; nonetheless, the Hungarians were bringing about the first tactical revolution in soccer history. All the players complemented one another in countering the aforementioned W–M system. In the back, they positioned themselves similarly to the Uruguayans of 1950, with two central defenders. The difference was in the Hungarians' brilliant and overpowering offense. Sebes gave his center-forward, Hidegkuti, more freedom to roam by retreating him a little, allowing him to create plays with Boszic. At the same time, he advanced his insiders, Kocsis and Puskas, creating a double-edged sword that took on the rival central defender with a two-on-one advantage. As if that weren't enough, they were helped by two wings, Toth and Czibor, who were positioned slightly behind the insiders. The wings and insiders formed a "magic square" from midfield forward that was lethal in placing maximum pressure on the rival defense. The revolution was under way, with the path being paved for the future 4–2–4. The only thing left for the Hungarians was . . . to win. To block the Hungarians' path to the Cup, Sepp Herberger offered the tremendous physical capabilities of his men, their unshakable discipline on the field, and a characteristically German iron will. The Germans also relied upon the classiness of Fritz Walter, the goal-making abilities of Rahn, and the strategic genius of Herberger who, in the first round of the tournament risked a blowout to uncover the tactical secrets of his opponents.

More and more coaches were beginning to realize the importance of tactics. The report written by the Argentine coach Guillermo Stabile for his federation shows that a critical dialogue had already begun:

> The Hungarian team was the best. They are excellent players, and they practice high-quality soccer, but they aren't amazing. They have a defense that is, at best, uneven, but a magnificent attack [. . .] Had Argentina participated, it would have given an outstanding performance [. . .] Europe, in general, has purged from soccer anything that is not effective, practical, and direct [. . .] I do not believe that we will make the mistake of disciplining our game to such extremes with tactics and systems. The best of what Argentine players have to offer is their natural skill. They have incredible skill, but it is important to insist that it be focused on making goals and not become an end in itself. I am convinced that a balance can be achieved between the practical and the beautiful.

Argentine soccer started a debate that would continue through our time, with the respective sides led by César Luis Menotti (World Champion in 1978) and Carlos Salvador Bilardo (World Champion in 1986 and runner-up in 1990).

Ferenc Puskas awoke on the morning of July 4 with his right knee injured, after the battles against Brazil and Uruguay. It was Puskas himself who begged the coach to let him play. Finally, Sebes gave in. He surely didn't want to deprive his team's leader—an important presence even when not in top form—of the almost certain opportunity of a victory lap. . . .

> We quickly went ahead 2–0, as everyone expected, with a goal that I scored and another by Czibor. But suddenly, as had happened to us before, the half ended 2–2. How did Germany play? They were a very well-organized team defensively with two great stars: Fritz Walter, the brain, and Rahn, a great winger. In addition, they were tactically extraordinary. Eckel, the stopper, was in charge of guarding me and Mai defended against Czibor or Kocsis. They took away our ability to create openings and beat us with the only thing they had over us: strength. Rahn scored the winning goal that shocked the world. The truth is that I still haven't found an adequate explanation for what went wrong. It's as inexplicable as having lost out on the family vacations promised by the government in Budapest as a reward for winning the championship, a result that everyone took for granted, especially the international soccer press. They had labeled us the best team in the world, without taking two fundamental facts into account: Soccer is always full of surprises, and we had completed our most brilliant cycle between 1950 and 1953. Actually, the team was born around 1946, after the ravages of war, built around Honved. Like all teams, it evolved, reached its peak, and declined. In 1954 we were on the downslide from glory, something we noticed only when it was too late. . . .

Once again, the best team was not the champion. Germany was the spoiler. They would be tagged with that label again in 1974, playing at home, when they would snatch the title away from Holland. Thus, the curtain fell on Switzerland 1954, which left these statistics to tell the story: a combined attendance of 943,000 with an average of 37,720 spectators per game, a number less than the one expected by the organizers, who were already starting to discern the economic and commercial side of a World Cup; an incredible average of 5.38 goals per game, the highest in history; and, not to be overlooked, this was the World Cup in which television made its first appearance. All in all, it was quite an achievement. Many years later, the World Cup would not be able to live without television. And, although few seem to notice, without goals either.

FERENC PUSKAS
(Hungary)
Switzerland 1954

They called him "The Colonel." The nickname could have referred to his rank, Major in the Hungarian army, or to his appearance: short, but proud, with his flat combed-back hair, wide-open eyes, and skill to lead. That image doesn't only exist in pictures; Today, with the added authority the years have given him, memories of his days as conductor of the "Hungarian Ballet"—the nickname given to the team—come out of him with little effort.

Ferenc Puskas lives in Budapest with his wife, and proudly carries the title of Manager of the Hungarian Soccer Federation. "I'm not coach or anything. My job involves a little bit of everything. For now I live here, but I leave whenever I want. I travel the world, I see soccer, I visit my daughters. . . ."

A.C.: Do you remember those images from Switzerland 1954?

F.P.: Of course. In spite of it all, it's a great memory.

A.C.: Why is it that the "Hungarian Ballet" evokes such great memories, even in defeat?

F.P.: We were, without a doubt, the best of our time. Even the Germans, who beat us, recognize that. We played with a goalkeeper, three defenders, two midfielders, and five forwards. We shuffled our positions during the game, we moved throughout the entire field, and we kept control of the ball for most of the game.

A.C.: So how was it that you lost against Germany after having beaten them 8–3 in the first round and after having gone up 2–0 in the final?

F.P.: Well, because we got overconfident. In only fifteen minutes, they tied us, then we got nervous, and luck wasn't on our side. . . . All of that together worked against us.

A.C.: Was Germany much worse than you guys?

F.P.: No way. They had less skill, but they were also tougher. Tough, but within the rules, so I can't complain. They played their game.

A.C.: Is any present team comparable to that of Hungary?

F.P.: No, and I don't think there ever will be.

A.C.: Why?

F.P.: Because today, 99 percent of the teams play to defend themselves. . . . Today's soccer is truly very strange, different. I like soccer, not fighting.

A.C.: It's obvious that, for you, everything about yesterday's soccer was better. Could any of today's players have been stars in yesterday's game?

F.P.: Well, unfortunately we have "el nene," who did that stupid thing.

A.C.: Are you referring to Maradona?

F.P.: Who else? He was the only player capable of changing the face of the last World Cup.

A.C.: Didn't you like USA 1994?

F.P.: No. I didn't get it. Most of the teams played with a goalkeeper, nine defenders, and a lone striker. I don't know what this is called, but I don't like it, nor will I ever like it.

A.C.: What do you attribute this to?

F.P.: I don't know if it's because of a lack of skill or if it's a tactical problem, but the objective is clear: Don't lose. Everyone is satisfied with a tie. I've seen the last seven World Cup competitions, and it gets worse every time. . . . The public is being bored.

It is difficult to be bored by his tone, filled with a Spanish accent and charged with a conviction that can only be admired, whether you agree with him or not.

Sweden 1958

FIFA's promise to have Europe and South America take turns organizing the World Cup was broken almost as soon as it was announced: Switzerland 1954 was followed by Sweden 1958. It was no coincidence that both countries were neutral during the war. No bombs were being heard in the world, but the chill of the cold war was being felt. While the United States and the Soviet Union looked at each other suspiciously, Sputnik orbited through space; to the alarm of England, Egypt permanently nationalized the Suez canal; and the Algerian Liberation Front waged a war of independence against France.

Somewhere in the midst of all that, as always, was soccer. It was now without Jules Rimet, who passed away on October 16, 1956, at the age of eighty-three, but with the addition of the UEFA (Union of European Football Associations), which modeled itself after the South American Confederation, formed several years before. UEFA's first act, the introduction of the Champion's Cup, is another example of the evolution of the game. Every four years soccer became more of a show; every four years it grew.

One thousand five hundred journalists applied for credentials; fifty-six radio stations, including eight from Brazil, prepared to broadcast; and 40 million spectators watched it on TV. They saw everything, including the opening ceremonies, where King Gustav, watching from his box, again showed that the tournament is an event in which both athletic and national pride are mixed. For better or worse, it is an aspect that will never be lost.

Fifty-two countries registered to qualify for sixteen finalist positions, with the qualification rounds showing some surprises.

Uruguay was out, with a 5–0 loss against Paraguay in Asunción adding to the embarrassment. Also absent would be Italy, eliminated by Northern Ireland, protagonist of the first story of this World Cup. Because of religious reasons, the players from Ulster asked not to play on Sundays. FIFA said no and, in consequence, Northern Ireland sent a roster of only seventeen players to Sweden, since five decided not to sin and stayed home. With the Uruguayans and Italians out, the winners of four of the last five World Cup competitions were absent.

There were other side-notes, both good and bad.

On one hand, the Soviet Union competed with the Western world, eliminating Finland and Poland in the qualification rounds. In the Cup, they showed off one of their great sources of pride: Lev Yashin, known as "The Black Spider," considered Europe's greatest goalkeeper.

On the other hand, England showed up severely handicapped as a result of the terrible plane crash suffered by English champion, Manchester United. The plane crashed as the team returned from Belgrade, claiming the lives of four national team starters (Byrne, Taylor, Coleman, and Edwards) and wounding one of their young stars (Bobby Charlton).

The new format of this first Nordic World Cup would have a long life: four groups of four teams each, with the top two of each classifying for the next round, and, from that point forward, knockout rounds until there were only two left to play the final.

The final was precisely where Brazil wanted to go. From the days of the "Black Diamond" Leonidas, twenty years before, and through the *mais grande* disappointment in 1950, they had always had a great talent, but also great disorganization. This time around, they vowed to get it together. The "scratch" got to Sweden with a plan thought up by Joao Havelange (then president of the Brazilian Sports Confederation) and headed by Paulo Machado de Carvalho. The team staff also included Dr. Hilton Golsing (the man responsible for saving Pele's knee, although legend states that the team's big, bald masseur Mario Americo deserves credit); dentist Mario Trigo, who extracted a total of sixty-two teeth from the players, solving one of the team's worst health problems; trainer Paulo Amaral; and coach Vicente Feola, who had the team training for the entire four months leading up to the World Cup. What stood out more than anything else was that a psychologist, João Carvahales, appeared on the staff for the first time. He quickly gave his diagnosis: "When there are exaggerated feelings of responsibility, expectations are always weighing heavily on the mind, causing an anxiety-ridden team. That's what happens to Brazilian players in the World Cup. This time, things will be different, we will treat the problem in depth. . . ."

It may never be known whether it was his work or the amazing talent of the Brazilian players that put this incomparable soccer machine in place. Another anecdote, however, gives at least a partial answer. After Brazil tied England (0–0) in the second game of the first round (after having beaten Austria at the start), with their qualification for the next round still at risk, the players themselves, after severe self-criticism, forced a meeting with the coaching staff to demand changes. In response, Coach Vicente Feola stated: "I will form the team that you guys want, because you are the ones who will win or lose." In that meeting, the team's three leaders, the captain Bellini, Didi, and Nilton Santos, demanded the replacement of Dino Sani and Altafini by Zito and Vava. They also demanded the immediate addition of both Garrincha and Pele, who, for different reasons, had not played up to that point. Their addition played a major role in destroying the Soviet Union, forcing Soviet coach Gabriel Katchalin to exclaim: "I can't believe that what we saw this afternoon was soccer. I have never seen anything so beautiful in my life. . . ." More importantly, they had provided an overwhelming response to the rumors surrounding their initial absence from the field. Garrincha's psychological profile said that he was "irresponsible and incapable of following the simplest order." With respect to Pele, doubts were based more on his right knee which refused to heal, badly injured in the last friendly match before the Cup. Long afterward, "number ten" would recount, "Mario Americo and the props manager Chico de Assis dos Santos boiled water, wet a towel in the pan, and immediately wrapped it around my knee. Tears fell from my eyes but not a peep came out of my mouth. While he pressed the towel against my knee, Americo would say to me, 'Daddy will make you alright.' He didn't leave me alone for a single moment and, in the end, he cured me. . . ."

Edson Arantes do Nascimento—Pele—was only seventeen years old. But already, anyone could see that a king was being born. . . . However, Mr. Saporta, a scout for Real Madrid, did not seem to notice. His employers in Madrid sent him a message, which said, "We want you to bring us the best soccer player in the world." "I've already found him," he answered. "His name is . . . Raymond Kopa."

With so much hindsight it is easy to judge. But it is still hard to accept the mistake of the scout who perhaps allowed himself to be blinded by the heat of a tournament with so many big names.

Group 1, which looked like one of the most even, was played in Halmstad, Malmö, and Helsingborg. Germany retained both the core of the team that had given them the title four years before and their characteristic physical strength. The latter would help them expose the weaknesses of a team that would become one of the big disappointments of this World Cup: Argentina.

The *albicelestes* came to the tournament as the South American Champion, but without the players who achieved that glory. Those fabulous "dirty faces" (Sivori, Maschio, Angelillo) lit up their continent and also the Italian club teams, which continued to attract the best South American players thanks to the economic power of their contracts. Without the "dirty faces" and with the blindness that comes with overconfidence—epitomized in Guillermo Stabile's report on Switzerland 1954, claiming that no team was better than Argentina—the national team was run off the road. Stabile's men lost 3–1 against Germany, beat Ireland 3–1, and then fell with a loud thump against Czechoslovakia. Only thirty-five years later would Argentine soccer face a setback comparable to that slap: the 5–0 massacre at the hands of Colombia, before the astonished crowd in Buenos Aires' own Monumental stadium, during the USA 1994 qualification rounds. The failure of a generation of brilliant players—Lombardo, Pipo Rossi, Labruna, Corbatta, Carrizo—proved that games are won and lost on the field, that words are not enough, and that players' physical conditioning and preparation are becoming more important on the international stage. After the loss, the coach said: "We learned a hard lesson. Now, upon our return to Argentina, we will have to change all of our plans if we want to once again beat the Europeans. . . ." Labruna then added: "We went in blind, completely blind, because we were neither physically nor technically prepared to play three games in one week." The statement is not surprising coming from a man who had gone to Sweden with the extra weight of thirty-nine years. According to Federico Vairo, however, it was not only the weight of years that Labruna brought to the field: "In River [Plate] it wasn't noticeable because we used a buttoned shirt, but with the tighter shirt used by the National team, it was easy to see his paunch. . . ." And, less noticeably, "Pipo" Rossi played with a copper wire around his waist, due to rheumatism.

Group 2 was played in Västerås, Norrköping, and Örebro. That is where Wisnieski, Piantoni, and Vincent, not to mention Raymond Kopa and Just Fontaine, reigned. With what would become their perennial style, the French dazzled the crowd with an attack so powerful they sometimes forgot to defend. With Fontaine among their ranks, it was a luxury they could afford, and his goals led the French march to the quarterfinals: He netted three in the victory against Paraguay (7–3); two in the shocking, but not critical, loss to Yugoslavia (2–3); and one for the qualification-clinching win over Scotland (2–1). Fontaine, called the "Chinaman" because of his sloping eyes, had been born in Morocco, the son of a Frenchman employed in a cigarette factory. He was on his way to a record that, even in World Cup 1994, has never been matched: he would convert thirteen goals, at an average of over two per game.

Yugoslavia qualified along with France. In those days, the Yugoslavs enjoyed the same strengths and suffered the same weaknesses as players today from the different republics that were formerly Yugoslavia: the talent to win it all, but the character to let it slip away.

In Group 3, set in Stockholm and Sandviken, Sweden's older team looked experienced while Hungary's older team looked slow. The home team took advantage of Liedholm and Gren—whose combined age was almost eighty—who in turn fed Hamrin Somonson with precise passes. Without being remarkable, they won a spot in the next round: 3–0 against Mexico, 2–1 against Hungary, and 0–0 against Wales. In contrast, the defending World Cup runner-up saw that their old stars (Grosics, Bozsik, Hidegkuti) just did not contribute in the way they once did. They wound up losing a tiebreaker with Wales, which proudly boasted John Charles, although without much effectiveness. The Juventus player was the subject of a dispute—won in this case by the Welsh federation—that would continue through the years: the fight between soccer federations over the refusal of clubs to release their foreign players to their national teams. Years later, FIFA would resolve the problem with a decree: The clubs had to hand them over.

Göteborg, Uddevalla, and Borås had the opportunity to see the fabulous attractions of Group 4: Yashin's saves for the Soviet Union that wound up eliminating England, again abandoning the hunt early; as well as the magic of the Brazilians. The South Americans had chosen the small and placid city of Hindaas, five hundred meters above sea level and an hour from Göteborg, as the site of their training camp. There, in a hotel as serene as a postcard, where rich Swedes went for their honeymoons, they trained as they dreamed, often by running around a pool where modern Swedish women, many of them topless, took in their country's scarce sunshine and the gaze of the Brazilian players. But of course, the players had something else to think about: soccer.

It was in Göteborg that Pele scored his first World Cup goal, in the quarterfinal match against Wales. "I always remember it with love, because it was the first," he would say years later about the goal that gave his team the win and a place in the semifinals. The Brazilians, with a totally neutralized Garrincha and faced with the rough tactics of the Welsh (who played without their injured star, Charles), played their worst game of the tournament. But Pele saved them. . . .

At the same time, with the unwinding of the other matches, a terribly difficult semifinal was taking shape: Perennial goal-scorer Rahn gave Germany the win over Yugoslavia (1–0); Sweden showed it was the master of its own home-field against the Soviet Union (2–0); and France and Fontaine went on scoring against Northern Ireland (4–0). The results produced a matchup between the host and defending champion: Sweden versus Germany. It was a game with four crucial scenes, all of them goals. . . .

One–zero in favor of the visitors. Uwe Seeler, appears both in the play and on the international soccer stage, a man who would be at the center of so much throughout the years. He crosses the ball to Schaffer for the first score.

One–one. Liedholm, in a controversial play, controls the ball with his hand before passing to Skoglund and ties the game.

Two–one. From twenty-five meters out, Gren nails the ball into a corner of the goal. The ball bounces off the goal's support and reenters the playing field, but no one doubts the legitimacy of the score: It was one of the best goals of the World Cup.

Three–one. Two minutes from the end, a dribbling clinic by Hamrin ends in a goal and unleashes a cool Swedish-style celebration.

The time for Brazil–France came too. If Wales can be remembered as Brazil's worst match of the Cup, the game against the

French would be the most difficult. For the Brazilians, the beginning of the game was a party. In the second minute, Vava pierced the net, ending a typical Brazilian play with short passes among Didi, Garrincha, and Pele. But the Brazilian party soon turned into a duel when the always dangerous Fontaine got serious and equalized the score. The deadlock would be broken by a misfortune that, in those days, could not be remedied: The leader of the French defense, Jonquet, suffered an injury, but substitutions were not yet allowed. Considering the Brazilian magic, the game was as good as over, as Didi would prove just two minutes later. After that came a beautiful little dance by Pele, who was already trying on his crown. The final score read 5–2 and Brazil danced to the final to the rhythm of the samba.

At the time, many felt that Sweden 1958 was contributing nothing with respect to tactics. In hindsight, however, many interesting developments can be seen. With players as talented as the Brazilians, it was possible to try new things; what they did was to take one step further what the Uruguayans did defensively in 1950 and what the Hungarians did offensively in 1954. Vicente Feola, the same man who had transferred responsibility to his players (or, to be more exact, confirmed it), gave his players a tip: "Do what you're supposed to do tactically. More than anything else, cover each other." He constructed a zone defense with four backs, in which Nilton Santos excelled. Further up, two midfielders with great vision and precision (Zito and Didi) launched the attacks. Up front, he put the power, skill, talent, and scoring combination of Garrincha, Vava, and Pele, supported by a man whose versatility made him a player before his time (or a man of all seasons, if you wish): Zagallo. Old Lobo, as he was known, would later become unique in history for having won four World Championships (as a player, trainer, coach, and assistant coach), and for converting the famous 4–2–4 of the Brazilians into a 4–3–3 when he retreated to midfield. In light of all this, talk of a tactical regression seems disrespectful. Perhaps the explanation is that the pundits were so overwhelmed by the magic of the Brazilians' individual talents that everything else, including tactics, became secondary.

The experts weren't the only ones overwhelmed. There were also, of course, the poor Swedes, who found themselves facing a team capable of eclipsing everyone, even their formidable stars:

Liedholm and Gren, two respected heroes of European soccer in general and their own club Calcio; Gustavsson (who played in Bergamo for Atalanta); the forwards Hamrin (who shone at Fiorentina and who later played for Milan and Napoli); Skoglund (Inter); and legendary goalkeeper Karl Svensson, who never accepted the flood of offers to play in the English League, always preferring to continue playing as an amateur.

Whoever assumes, after looking through pictures, watching videos, or hearing stories, that the Swedes got to the final only because they were the home team, is mistaken. The problem was simply that they were facing Brazil. The issue is also that, compared to the present, defenders in those days gave their rivals' forwards . . . more time and space. Somehow, therefore, everything was easier.

Surprise invaded the beautiful Stockholm stadium quickly. Three minutes into the game, thirty-six-year-old veteran Liedholm showed his class, making the score 1–0. Legend states that Didi walked to the center circle with the ball in his hands, like Obdulio Varela had in 1950. The only difference was that, unlike the Uruguayan captain, he didn't start to protest. "I was only thinking about one thing: giving the ball to Garrincha," Didi would later say. The goal, and the situation it put the "scratch" in, forced the Brazilians to respond to the doubts about their poise. Could the team come back? Could Garrincha's crazy skill make a practical contribution?

The answer on both counts was a resounding "yes." Right away a run by Garrincha ended just inches off target; at nine minutes, the great right winger again burst through the mark of Axbom and Parling and then perfectly crossed the ball behind him for Vava to put into the net. Everything was now back to normal, and everyone knew how the game would end. The only thing that remained to be seen was how many goals the Brazilians would score and who would score them. The second question had an obvious answer: Pele. By the end, he had two, but the first fifty-five minutes of the game best sums up his genius: In the heart of the penalty area, he stopped the ball with his chest, confusing a Swedish defender; as it came down, he tapped it delicately over the head of a second defender; he then met up with the ball again, before it ever touched the ground, nailing it into the net with his right foot, barely missing the goalpost. It was a jewel. At that point, the Swedish crowd, who gracefully accepted the 5–2 Brazilian win, gave Pele a standing ovation. By the end, 868,000 fans had filled the stadiums, an average of

24,800 fans per game, all of them convinced that Brazil was home to the masters of soccer.

Perhaps not even the Brazilians themselves realized they had just forged the first golden link in a chain called *tetracampeonato* (four-time championship), a chain that would take them thirty-six years to complete.

PELE
(Brazil)
Sweden 1958

"There are too many memories that come to mind when people ask me about the 1958 World Cup. And to think that at that time I was only seventeen years old makes me treasure it even more . . . seventeen years old, imagine that! It's a dream, that's what it is: my debut against Wales, the goal that qualified the team for the next round. What comes to mind—and it's almost as if I could hear it now, at this very moment—is the national anthem of my country playing, and me surrounded by foreigners. I don't know, but it occurs to me that someone must have asked himself: 'What's that kid doing there in the midst of so many giants?'"

That kid cried and all the giants stretched their arms to hold him. The image was immortalized in a picture, and that picture shook the world. Everyone understood, then, that a new king of soccer had been born: Edson Arantes do Nascimento, known to everybody as Pele. Today, after so much time and so many goals, and the passing of his crown, it is difficult to understand why it was so surprising. Ater all, what's so strange about a genius like him occupying that place, no matter what his age?

P.: It's that we're talking about a roster of cracks, chosen after a period of tryouts attended by the best soccer players in the country. In truth, we had almost everything, we lacked nothing: an excellent roster, magnificently prepared; a trainer; a full-time physician; a dentist; masseurs; assistants; and even a psychologist. . . . All of this, at that time, was a novelty, especially when you consider that we are talking about Brazilians.

A.C.: And you? When did you start attracting attention?

P.: After that match with Wales, the press started to cast their eyes on me. Before, they asked me only about that bothersome inflamation of my knee that would not heal. But after my goal, they were interested in a lot more. Even people that I, obviously, did not know began gathering around me. Among them, the Swedish girls, with their straight, blonde hair such as I had only seen in pictures of dolls.

A.C.: Compared to the present, how was the soccer of that time?

P.: It was different. More offensive, less commercial, with a different meaning. Now, the only important thing is winning, and the beauty of the game tends to be lost in the quest for victory. It is a bit worrisome, because the beauty of soccer is disappearing and with that comes the alienation of the fans, from both the stadiums and the television sets. The economic and security problems also contribute to this, and the trend can only be reversed by the appearance of a great number of quality soccer players. We used to play in front of two hundred thousand spectators in the Maracaná. Today it would be unimaginable.

A.C.: And how does one reverse this negative trend?

P.: Without a doubt, one must protect the player responsible for the show. It is ludicrous to see a player go out to the field to entertain the fans only to become the punching bag . . . he must be protected at all costs.

Chile 1962

"Because we have nothing, we will do everything." It is impossible to deny the power of this statement, and the event that it inspired. That was Chile as it prepared to host the seventh World Cup, and that's what Carlos Dittborn, its principal driving force, said, putting it into words better than anyone else. Both as feat and as phenomenon, the World Cup had become a palpable reality in every soccer-loving country in the world, and everything from love of the sport to national pride was projected onto it. The patriotism of the Chilean people was challenged when, four years after being named host of the tournament and two years before the opening of the event, an earthquake threatened to destroy their dream. Any analogy to what Mexico would experience twenty-four years later is no mere coincidence.

It was then, with the earth still shaking, that Dittborn, born in Rio de Janeiro, but whose parents were Chilean, stood before FIFA and the whole world and spoke those now famous words. He had been working for a long time, and he would keep on doing so until . . . death. A month before the opening ceremony, when he was only thirty-eight years old, his heart failed him, surely overcome by emotion as well as by stress. What is certain is that he never saw the outcome of his labor nor the realization of his dream, so poignantly expressed in that historic statement. A few days later, his widow gave birth to a son. Raimundo Saporta, Dittborn's rival at the time of the choosing of the site and a bigwig at powerful Real Madrid, the undisputed European soccer king of the period, went to the hospital to pay tribute to the child and the child's late father, in the way he thought most appropriate: He made the child a lifetime member of Real Madrid. In the street, people were crying before a gigantic poster of the man "who had done everything" posted on the building of the *El Mercurio* newspaper.

Springtime weather welcomed the sixteen national teams that had qualified from the original field of fifty-six, a new record of registrants. Among those qualified were all the champions of the previous competitions (Uruguay, Italy, Germany, and Brazil), but the qualifying rounds had eliminated both Sweden and France, respectively second and third in the previous tournaments.

The relationship between television and the World Cup was just beginning, and the Cup allowed Chile to inaugurate their new communications capabilities. Moreover, an idea was beginning to take shape: For the host country, these tournaments represented an open window to the rest of the world. Surely for that reason, the Chileans wanted to show the world their entire territory, from one end to the other. The geographical distribution of the four groups was in as many sites, scheduled to play between May 30 and June 17.

In the capital, Santiago, the locals hosted Switzerland, Italy, and Germany. Feeling the pressure of playing at home, Fernando Riera prepared an impressive and solid roster, with men like Leonel Sanchez, Jorge Toro, and Tito Fouillioux. On June 2, against Italy, Chile played a game that would set the tone for the rest of the tournament with two stories that would heat up the atmosphere until it became unbearable.

The Italians had come to South America with their own stars, a young Gianni Rivera among them, as well as with the added power of the famous *oriundi,* South American natives who could defend the colors of the *azzurri* because of their Italian heritage, such as the Argentines Maschio and Sivori and the Brazilian Altafini. These players were seen as traitors to their heritage and were treated as such. Moreover, two articles written by Italian journalists fanned the flames even more. Corrado Pizzinelli, a journalist for Florence's *La Nazione,* sent to Chile before the World Cup to cover political issues, and Antonio Ghirelli, a specialist for the *Corriere della Sera,* wrote articles that offended the Chileans, increasing the already anti-Italian climate. In fact, it wasn't a game: It was a battle; the inevitable battle of every World Cup. The result was a broken nose, for Maschio; two Italians ejected (David and Ferrin); many blatant fouls; and several scuffles—one, in particular, in which Maschio received his broken nose, was not penalized. Today, you can see on video how Leonel Sanchez hit him but, on that day, neither the horrible British referee nor his linesmen saw anything.

Many years later, one of the Italian journalists involved in this episode would write in *Guerin Sportivo:*

> The radio stations would spew out an avalanche of invective day and night directed not only against the Italian journalists but against all Italians . . . Italian people, Italian players, and the Italian national team. It was a hot issue. Their intention was to create an atmosphere of hate and intolerance when the *azzurri* came on the field in the second game of the group against the hosts (the first had been an uneventful, scoreless tie against Germany). Everyone knows how it ended. Not satisfied with having created a hellish atmosphere to intimidate our players, which included a couple of *oriundi* marked as traitors to South America, the Chilean officials took the liberty of designating a referee, the Englishman Aston, who was sensitive to the power of the home-field advantage and, above all, to FIFA's advice to favor the home team in order to increase box office receipts. Not only are Aston's terrible deeds inscribed on the pages of history, they are among the most bitter pages in the history of international soccer: He changed the pace of the game, favored the Chileans at every turn, looked the other way during their defenders' fouls, and took advantage of a ridiculous situation to expel two Italians. Even though we ended the game with nine players, we were so much better than they were that we missed out on a draw by a hair. It was a total outrage.

"An outrage." That, at least, was the Italians' feeling. What is certain, in any case, is that the negative atmosphere of that one game contaminated the rest of the tournament as a whole.

In that same group, Germany took the lead almost without trying, thanks to a chubby and dangerous forward, Uwe Seeler, and the sweeper Karl Heinz Schnellinger, guide of the German *catenaccio*. Chile, still trying at all costs to put on the best performance of their history, came in second.

Viña del Mar, 145 kilometers away, was the most beautiful of all the sites. That's where the Brazilians set up camp, trying to maintain the organization that had taken them to their peak. Vicente Feola was no longer coach because of illness, and his place was taken by Aymore Ferreira. They had a trouble-free debut against Mexico and then tied against Czechoslovakia. That tie set them back in more than the usual sense, since Pele, the kid who had gained renown four years before and was now a man in search of a definitive crown, was sidelined by an injury. Twenty-five minutes in, an inspired shot hit the post and went out of bounds, taking with it his dreams of playing in the World Cup.

The Brazilians would begin to breathe a little easier in their next game, against Spain, when the young Amarildo scored a goal and showed that, at the very least, he could stand in for the great "number ten."

For the Spaniards, on the other hand, their start was an absolute disappointment. Like the Italians, they had appealed to the great stars who had graced their country's championship. But they lost Alfredo Di Stefano to injury before the start of the tournament, and the constellation formed by the Hungarian Puskas and the Uruguayan Santamaria, led by the Argentine coach Helenio Herrera and accompanied by native stars such as Gento, was noticeably suffering his absence. They lost against Czechoslovakia as it began its stealthy advance; they narrowly defeated Mexico who, featuring Carbajal in his fourth consecutive World Cup, would later surprisingly defeat the Czechs; and they fell against Brazil. They left for future analysis a subject that is still talked about today . . .

How should national teams be formed? Should they consist only of native players? Or should they be based on players from a country's club teams, regardless of their nationality? A while ago, Italian television magnate Silvio Berlusconi suggested the latter idea. FIFA has always supported representation based on country of origin, to such an extreme that even a change of citizenship is no longer sufficient: If a player has ever played an international game for his national team, he can never play for any other.

In Rancagua, Chile, a small mining town of fifty thousand inhabitants situated very close to the capital, England won their first World Cup game since the 1954 qualifiers. Argentina was disappointed once again. Hungary gave a virtual clinic, showing the world exactly how the game should be played, and Bulgaria came and left in sorrow. Since they had arrived, everyone had christened the Hungarians "the ballet." Just as in 1954, but with other names, it was simply a pleasure to watch them play. The dancers included Sarosi, Sandor, Rakosi, and Tichy under the tactical guidance of coach Lajos Baroti. They advanced with such overwhelming force (2–1 against England, 6–1 against Bulgaria) that they rested their best players during the third game (against Argentina). They tied 0–0, enough to qualify them for the quarterfinals.

Once again, the Argentineans suffered a predictable disappoint-

ment. In those times, the national team was not a top priority—
which became a slogan after the team lost again in 1974—and
self-destruction caused by lack of organization or short-sightedness
was a common occurrence. That is how the prestigious journalist
Juvenal remembered it in *El Gráfico* magazine, writing about the
team: "They came out playing like a hurricane, with a goal by Facundo three minutes into their debut against Bulgaria, and, little by
little, lost their luster until they were all washed out, without color
or life." Afterward, via commentaries by Argentina's own experts
(Rattin, Roma, Pando), the mistakes made by coach Juan Carlos
Lorenzo gradually came to light. Those errors involved changes in
the lineup and positioning of the players that were not very well
thought out. One case in particular serves to illustrate: that third
game against Hungary (it ended 0–0), after the victory against Bulgaria and the defeat against England (3–1). Juvenal tells the story
like this:

> For that third match, Lorenzo also changed the goal-keeper. Julio
> Dominguez replaced Antonio Roma who, according to Lorenzo, had
> "lost the game against England." Why? Because against the direct or-
> ders of the coach, put on paper, Roma had cleared two balls to his
> right (the English players' left) and two of the runs originated by
> Bobby Charlton, culminating in the first two English goals as a conse-
> quence of two passes to the wrong side. "He was ordered to always
> punt to the left and throw the ball out of bounds if he did not see
> open teammates," was Lorenzo's obsessive post-defeat explanation.
> Did he actually think that if Roma put the ball out of bounds the ball
> would then never come under the control of the attacking duo of En-
> glish soccer?

In the end, the only positive aspect of Argentina's participation was
the emergence of left back Silvio Marzolini, who would soon show
himself to be the best in the world in his position.

For the British, that victory against Argentina represented their
first celebration in a World Cup in eight years, since the qualifying
rounds of 1954. It was also their pass to the quarterfinals, breaking
a long history of suffering in the first round. In any case, their performance in Chile was a small preamble to their fine perormance
four years later, still led by Charlton.

Arica turned out to be a remarkable site. Located two thousand
kilometers north of Santiago, in the middle of the desert bordering
on Peru, it received two South American teams (Uruguay and

Colombia) and two European teams with little power in soccer politics (Yugoslavia and the Soviet Union). The Russians, who had just won the first European Cup, counted on Lev Yashin in goal, and that was their biggest attraction. They started off by defeating Yugoslavia (2–0) and right afterward participated in one of the most spectacular games in World Cup history against Colombia. It went like this . . .

Fourteen minutes into the game played on June 3, the Europeans were ahead 3–0! Valentin Ivanov and Cislenko had made it possible. Even with Aceros narrowing the score and the first half ending 3–1, the game seemed already sealed. But the men coached by the legendary Argentine Adolfo Pedernera didn't give in. Playing an attractive style of soccer, which many years later, under the leadership of Pacho Maturana, would again place them on the world's stage, they turned the game around. Between sixty-seven and seventy-seven minutes, they tied the game 4–4!

The European press crucified Yashin, and a few rash journalists went so far as to say the best goalkeeper in the world was now finished. At the same time, they glorified the South Americans who, although they would later fall, put themselves on the map with their gutsy play.

Silently, the Yugoslavian team of Sekularac, Scoblar, and Jerkovic, who was collecting enough goals to place himself amongst the top scorers of the competition, advanced at the expense of Uruguay, which had been favored to accompany the Russians to the next round. Velibor Milutinovic's compatriots played with their usual style and, since they specialize like nobody else in training coaches, they showed up with a team that had four of them: Cilic, Lovric, Rusevljan, and Mihajlovic! Of course, to keep in step with the atmosphere of the tournament, they did their share of butchering. In their first game, Mujic fractured Dubinski's leg and had to go back home. In the decisive match with Uruguay—which still had Pepe Sasia around to remind it of its glory days, even though it didn't advance—Sekularic had encounters with almost everyone.

Upon reviewing the initial group play and comparing it with previous years, what one is left with is a sense of mediocrity. It should have been the World Cup to end all World Cups because of players like Pele; Alfredo Di Stefano; the Hungarians Ferenc Puskas and Florian Albert; the Spaniard Luis Suarez; Enrique Omar Sivori; the Brazilian Jose Altafini; the "Bambino de Oro" Gianni Rivera; the Yugoslavians Sekularac and Skoblar; the Soviets Yashin and Voronin; the Czech Masopust (awarded the Golden Ball that year by the French magazine *France Football);* the Englishmen Greaves, Moore, and Charlton; and the Uruguayans Rocha and Cubilla. Instead, it went down in history as the World Cup of violence and tainted referee calls. Pele was almost immediately injured. Di Stefano did not even get to play (and lost out on his chance to play in a World Cup), and great teams, such as Spain and Italy, fell early.

In the quarterfinals, the most interesting game was Brazil–England. The powerful attacking duo formed by Hitchens and Greaves stood a good chance of ending the Brazilian hegemony, which was less dazzling than four years before. But it didn't go that way, above all because of the appearance of a magician: Garrincha. The man who guarded him, Wilson, left the field humiliated; the avalanche of fakes and breakthroughs left Wilson stumbling to pick up the pieces. That night, Garrincha made two goals, assisted Vava on another, and qualified the "scratch" for the semifinals.

For Hungary, the Chilean World Cup was like being reborn only to die again seconds later. Once again, as in Switzerland 1954, they displayed a style that was rich in skill, and they reached the quarterfinal match with confidence against the surprising Czechs. It was, in fact, the Czechs who suffered an unexpected defeat against Mexico, but qualified for the quarterfinals anyway. That afternoon in Rancagua, the cause of Hungary's misfortune had a name: Willy Schrojf. This Czech goalkeeper snuffed out every play generated by Tichy and Albert, among others. Then Scherer, on a counterattack, made Hungary relive the unbearable experience of being better than the opposition, but not being able to show it. Instead of playing their game, the Hungarians yielded to the sinister wind in the air and tried to beat Czechoslovakia at their own rough and tumble game.

Against Germany, Yugoslavia showed it could do more than just hit; it could also play soccer. Three minutes before the end, with a goal by Radakovic, the Yugoslavians became semifinalists. In the closing minutes, there was a final opportunity for Uwe Seeler to confirm reports of his prowess, but Soskic, the Yugoslavian goalkeeper, denied him, securing his team safe passage to the next round.

In far away Arica, Chile continued on its way. A tackle by Landa left the great Lev Yashin of the USSR badly injured and with diminished perspectives. Cislenko's score-narrower was not enough. The European champions were left out, and Chile tasted their best result in World Cup history.

The semifinals separated South America from Europe, guaranteeing an intercontinental final.

In Santiago, Chile versus Brazil. That June 14, 76,594 fans packed Santiago's Nacional stadium, the greatest attendance of the tournament.

Only 150 kilometers away, in Viña del Mar, only five thousand spectators showed up to see Yugoslavia–Czechoslovakia.

It is worth revisiting the better attended of the two games first. Up to that point, Brazil had played as if it were a local team. From the very first, the Brazilians had shown themselves to be the principal catalyst behind Chile's organization of the World Cup. Moreover, their usual ease in getting along with people as well as their essentially charming game had made them a crowd favorite. But now national honor was at stake for both teams. To defend their honor, the Chileans would go to any length and the least they could do was to boo their opponents. It was Garrincha's day all over again. At nine and thirty-one minutes into the game, he put Brazil in front and silenced the crowd. Before the end of the first half, Toro had narrowed the gap. That gave a glimmer of hope to the home team, but what it really needed was a miracle and it was not coming any time soon. With Zagallo's decisive strategic sense; Vava's assertiveness, scoring the two remaining Brazilian goals for the 4–2 result; and Garrincha's magic touch, they straightened things up. As if to further emphasize the defining characteristic of this World Cup, its best player, Garrincha, ended up in a fight. Landa had already been expelled (it was about time, since he had already provoked more than one incident during the tournament), but the great winger was tired of receiving blows and decided to respond with one. He punched Rojas and was ejected by the frail-looking Peruvian referee, Yamasaki. When he was exiting the field, a rock hit him and wounded his head. End of story, sad and final . . . and that's where they were headed—to the final.

Seeking the same objective, although not with the same amount of drama and with a smaller audience, Czechoslovakia—no longer a surprise—finished off Yugoslavia. It was a duel that would be repeated in time: the refined skill of the Yugoslavs against the physical and tactical strength of the Czechs. Underscoring the general mediocrity of the tournament, the victory went to the team with the best goalkeeper up to that point, Schrojf, and a relentless forward, Scherer, who stayed focused up to the last seconds of the game, scoring at eighty-one and eighty-nine minutes. The final would read 3–1 for Czechoslovakia.

And so there they were, the two finalists face to face, without any big surprises and without any major spins, except for one strategic change that Brazil put forward, which is summarized below.

Influenced by the passing of time and its team's innate ability, Brazil went from the 4–2–4 formation, which they had used with success in Sweden 1958, to the modern 4–3–3, which would be used universally for many years. The new formation proved perfect for their aging but seasoned players, nine of whom had been champions in 1958.

In the defense, they replaced their two central defenders, with Mauro and Zozimo replacing Bellini and Orlando, but they kept as their right and left backs the Santos duo, Djalma and the thirty-six-year-old Nilton, whose nickname "The Encyclopedia" spoke volumes about his knowledge of his position. In the middle were the usual suspects: Zito, who was brilliant in the World Cup, and Didi, who at thirty-four was declining. They received support from Mario Lobo Zagallo, a man before his time as far as tactics, with amazing mobility and quickness, who would later be a record four-time World Champion. Zagallo gave the team the new, distinctive, and decisive touch it needed, retreating from his position as striker to become a player of the entire field, capable of recovering balls and then making the direct link to the strikers. Many years later in 1994, with the same Zagallo on the coaching staff (under Carlos Alberto Parreira) of World Champion Brazil, his role would be discussed and studied in depth, in an attempt to fashion a team full of versatile, well-rounded players.

Up front, the appearance of the twenty-two-year-old Amarildo assuaged the fears caused by Pele's absence. Although it would be impossible to say that Brazil didn't lose a little in the exchange, it would also be fair to say that the difference wasn't overwhelming. Next to Amarildo in the attack, the forceful Vava and the magical Garrincha were poised to rewrite all the rules.

The key to Brazil's power in the field was that experience replaced speed, and the possession of the ball became its highest expression. As long as they had the ball, they reasoned, the opponent couldn't score.

And as if that were not enough, they were also superstitious.

Here are two examples. On one hand, they made the entire delegation from the 1958 championship travel to Chile. The only ones missing were Feola, who was sick, and Orlando, who had professional obligations in Argentina. On the other hand, they arranged to fly with the same airplane and the same crew with which the team had arrived in Sweden four years before. The problem was that the pilot of the plane had shaved his beard. At the insistence of the team, he had no choice but to grow it back.

There was only one shadow that could darken their horizon: the specter of Switzerland 1954. That year, teams that began with less quality but improved as the tournament advanced, and playing a physical game—as had been the case with Germany—had demolished favored opponents like Hungary. The Czechoslovakia/Brazil comparison during Chile 1962 was inevitable.

The three basic pillars on which the Czechs relied seemed to be unshakable: the goalkeeper Willy Schrojf, an iron curtain, up to that point; midfielder Masopust, the team's true architect; the forward Scherer, the team's authentic finisher and a believer in the still-existent principle that games last ninety minutes and that a goal can be scored up until the very moment the referee blows his whistle three times.

The only thing left to do was to go out onto the field. Before that, however, two stories were unveiled that made this World Cup one of the most peculiar in history. The first regarded Pele's desperate desire to play in the final, frustrated by a group of physicians who put their nationalistic passion aside and acted in an objective manner, confirming that his physical condition would not allow it. The other involved the authorization for Garrincha, who had been expelled in the semifinal against Chile, to play, as a result of pressure from the Brazilian government and an express and unusual request from Czechoslovakia that he be included in the rival team! Perhaps the Czechs were looking to win the affection of the fans or for a strategic advantage, given that the wonderful wing would have to play with four stitches in his head.

These two situations would be unimaginable today: losing one's best player to a minor injury and allowing a player on the field who had been ejected from the previous game. But it was not so long ago . . . we are talking about 1962.

Again all the predictions, Czech coach Vytlacil sent his players to the attack from the start. This surprising strategy paid some quick dividends: Masopust put his team ahead 1–0 after fifteen minutes. It was only the first link in a chain of surprises summarized in the bitter reflection of the Czech coach after it was all over: "Had they told me I would lose the final because of two errors by my best player, I would never have believed it. . . ." But that's the way it went. Two minutes after Vytlacil's score, Brazil's Amarildo shot and scored when everyone expected a cross, confirming that it would be a dark day for Willy Schrojf, the Czech goalkeeper . . . the best player on his team. Schrojf ruined everything: the offensive game plan, by which they had managed to take the ball away from the opponent and keep them far away from the goal—the dominance that made utopia look possible.

Later, Schrojf made a mistake on a cross (his specialty had been cutting off balls in the air) and permitted a header by Amarildo, making the final score 3–1. With gifts like these, Brazil didn't even need Garrincha, who played with a fever and who was well controlled by the layered guarding of Novak and Jelinek. Thus, Brazil celebrated their second straight World Cup. It lacked the suspense of the Maracaná, the quality of 1954, and the brilliance of Sweden . . . but it had a just outcome.

The yellow of the Brazilians' shirts was flying high, but at the same time the yellow warning light announced violent play, ill-intentioned officiating, all surrounding a competition that was growing by leaps and bounds.

MARIO ZAGALLO
(Brazil)
Chile 1962

Sitting down to talk with Mario Lobo Zagallo ("please, Lobo is my name, not my nickname, and my last name is spelled with two ls") is like speaking with soccer itself. . . . It's that, beyond the fact that the main topic of conversation was a World Cup, the man's accomplishments are simply mind-boggling. Perhaps it would suffice to say that he is the only man on Earth to have won four World Cup competitions: as a player in Sweden 1958 and Chile 1962, as coach in Mexico 1970, and as an assistant coach in USA 1994. But I think a meticulous, objective list of his accomplishments would be more respectful, to drive my point home more forcefully. He's married to Alcina de Zagallo. He has four children—Maria Emilia (thirty-eight), Paulo Jorge (thirty-seven), Maria Cristina (thirty-four), and Mario Cesar (thirty); four grandchildren—Renata, Paula, Daniel, and Paulo. His career as a player started in America, before playing for Flamengo between 1950 and 1958, winning three straight championships from 1953 to 1955. After World Cup Sweden 1958, he was transferred to Botafogo, where he played until 1964. Botafogo gave him his start as coach in 1966, and he led it to the championship in 1967 and 1968. Afterward, his coaching career took him to the following places: the Brazilian national team (World Champion, 1970), Fluminese (Champion, 1970), Flamengo (Champion, 1972), Kuwait's national team (Persian Gulf Champion, 1977), Botafogo, El Helal (a Saudi Arabian club), the Saudi Arabian national team (which qualified for the 1980 Olympic Games in Montreal), Flamengo (winner of the Guanabara Cup), and the national team of the United Arab Emirates (who qualified for World Cup Italy 1990). In 1991, he returned to the Brazilian national team . . .

Given this amazing résumé, limiting the interview to only one World Cup—in this case Chile 1962—is almost disrespectful. But Zagallo himself would volunteer to relate that great feat to everything else in history and everything that the future holds for soccer . . . the main objective of this book.

A.C.: Lobo, to help introduce the subject, give us another detail. . . . When did you start to watch soccer?

M.Z.: I started out in the youth leagues in 1947, and I watched World Cup 1950 while I was in the Flamengo farm system. I was about nineteen years old, serving in the army, and the day of the final I was in uniform, guarding the stands at the Maracaná . . . from that moment on, I have only soccer memories.

A.C.: What do you remember about Chile 1962, a World Cup that you participated in?

M.Z.: In general, the game was very different compared to today, both the atmosphere behind it and the game itself.

A.C.: Was it better or worse than today?

M.Z.: Different . . . for example, at that time, we had been dealt a hard blow with Pele's injury in the second game against Czechoslovakia, and the team felt it greatly. The loss of a player of his caliber at the start of the tournament caused me to think that things would go badly for us. . . . Yet, many years later I confirmed the fact that a team cannot rely on only one player. That's what comes to mind, for example, when I think of the Argentine national team in USA 1994, which went over the edge after Diego Armando Maradona's disqualification.

A.C.: In any case, according to what you've said publicly, Pele was the greatest soccer player that you had ever seen.

M.Z.: Ah, yes, yes. He was complete: he kicked the ball with both feet, headed the ball very well and was calm in front of the enemy goal when he finished. . . . At that moment, he was replaced by Amarildo, who had a heavy responsibility weighing on his shoulders, and he handled it very well. We also had Garrincha, another great . . . so unpredictable, even to us, his teammates, but also an undeniable key to victory. Of course, there was a great team surrounding him, nothing was achieved by individuals alone.

A.C.: For example?

M.Z.: For example, in 1958 I had disobeyed the coach: Instead of playing forward, I played a dual role on the left side. I knew when I had to attack and when I had to go back to recover the ball. At that time, the Brazilian press destroyed me. Today, I remember it and laugh, since time has shown that any team without a player to fill that role is lost. In any case, it wasn't the only thing.

A.C.: What else?

M.Z.: Well, it's a little anecdote. Before the Cup, during a practice session in Viña Del Mar, which was where we played our first-round games, I lost a San Antonio pendant that I always wore around my neck. . . . I started to look for it, and I told my teammates, "If I find it, we'll be champions." I found it, and I still wear it to this day . . . and I haven't done too badly in World Cup competitions.

A.C.: That's for sure. But I still have some questions. Did you like the soccer that you played and also coached in the past or today's—which seems more physical?

M.Z.: As I told you, everything is different. In 1962 we had more freedom to move on the field, although not everything was left to chance. . . . But you can't really compare. In 1962, like in 1958 and 1970, there was more space, more freedom to create, more time to play the ball, and more opportunities to show off one's skill. Soccer in general has changed very much since World Cup England 1966. That's where "fighting soccer" started, the soccer we see today.

A.C.: What does the future hold, Lobo?

M.Z.: Well, by 1962 we had already evolved from the 4–2–4 to the 4–3–3. In USA 1994, in order to win the title, our team adopted a clear 4–4–2. Under my current game plan, Brazil tries to play a 4–3–1–2 . . . don't be surprised if the future World Cup games—the true reflections of the strategic changes in our beloved soccer—give us the possibility of seeing a team unfold in a 4–6–0 formation, with all of the players, both attacking and defending, without fixed positions . . . that's where we're headed, no doubt.

Why not? Maybe he'll get to celebrate another title, with that strategy or with some other one, but always with Brazil and always in the Cup. Those two words are synonymous with Mario Lobo Zagallo.

England 1966

Europe versus South America. By this point, there was already a declared war between these two contenders on two different fronts. The first was the fight to be named the organizer and the second, the lifting of the Cup. It would be a long time until other continents, like Africa or North America, for example, entered the fight that seemed to be in its apogee in 1966.

Englishman Sir Stanley Rous was heading FIFA, and it surprised no one that the site chosen to host the eighth World Cup was, in fact, England. West Germany, hoping to be helped by their 1954 title, and having fought for the honor of hosting the event since 1958, attempted to challenge their candidacy, but it was no use. In 1960, during the FIFA Congress in Rome, England won the nomination by a vote of thirty-four to twenty-seven.

It was no longer surprising that seventy-five teams signed up for the classification rounds, once again a record-breaking number of countries entering the competition for a place among the final sixteen positions. What was surprising, however, was the first theft of the World Cup trophy.

On January 5, 1966, Sir Stanley Rous received the Jules Rimet trophy, the dreamed-of *Winged Victory*. On March 20, that object of desire disappeared from Central Hall in Westminster, the site chosen for it to be exhibited before the world.

Quickly, Scotland Yard mobilized their men throughout the British Isles, in search of the stolen cup. Seven days later, a new name had to be added to the list of stars that are part of the World Cup. Pickles, a trained dog, found the gold statuette wrapped in newspaper and thrown in a garden in Bealah Hill, a suburb of London.

From that moment on, everything was ready for soccer to be played in the same land in which the game was invented.

"Gentlemen, I don't have much to tell you. I only have to let you know that England will win the next World Cup." The forceful words of Alf Ramsey, right after taking the reins of the national team in place of the legendary Walter Winterbottom, served to summarize his team's attitude: England was ready to go to any lengths to be victorious and would not accept any other result.

Until then, the English had been satisfied with a soccer reputation that had gone unproven in the international sphere. Their reputation as masters placed them above others in expectation, although actual results placed them below many in reality. Although the same is true today, in those days—especially before their 1966 Cup—it was even more true.

With Winterbottom in charge, the English national team had reaped only frustration: in Brazil 1950 when they were eliminated by the amateur players of the United States; and in 1953, when the marvelous Hungarians humiliated them in their own Wembley Stadium with a historic 6–3 whipping.

With those precedents in mind and the added frustration of having lived them on the playing field itself, Ramsey proposed to change it all. He used the same tools as coach that had made him succeed on the field. As a left back, his ferocity, discipline, and determination had made him a standout and, with those same attributes, he began to take new measures as coach. As if he needed any more reminding, the English were whipped again. This time, they lost to France (5–2) in the European Cup (England had participated to end their chronic isolation once and for all), marking the end of their backward W–M formation.

In truth, Ramsey proposed a change of mentality and, with that, of men. First, he caused a scandal when he excluded Jimmy Greaves, one of the country's most talented players, from the national team. To understand, imagine leaving 1995 *Pichichi*[1] Ivan Zamorano off the Chilean national team or leaving 1995 *Capocannoniere*[2] Gabriel Batistuta off Argentina's.

Afterward, of course, his decision generated a controversy that went beyond soccer into the social realm. The press, up to that time

---

[1]*Pichichi:* the title given to the Spanish league's leading goal-scorer.
[2]*Capocannoniere:* Literally meaning "top gunner," it is the title given to the Italian league's top goal-scorer.

conservative, became extremely vocal. Ahead of his time, Ramsey answered its attacks with an almost irrefutable response: results. Before the start of the tournament, they played seventeen games, coming away with twelve wins, four draws, and only one loss. Even with that, it was rare to see Ramsey with a smile on his face.

Czechoslovakia and Yugoslavia, respectively second and fourth in the previous World Cup, had been eliminated in the qualifying rounds. Among the Europeans, Sweden and Scotland also had to watch the action from home. On the South American side, all the big teams made it. The Africans stayed away deliberately. The continent's fourteen candidates decided to boycott the competition, believing they deserved their own spot, rather than having to share one with the Asians and the Australians. For the next World Cup, they would get it.

So the sixteen finalists—a number that was beginning to look small considering the growth of the competition—were decided upon. It is worth mentioning that thirty-two national teams—exactly twice as many as in 1966—will participate in World Cup France 1998. But back in the British Isles circa 1966, seven cities stood ready to receive sixteen guests.

London hosted Group 1: England, Uruguay, Mexico, and France.

Birmingham and Sheffield hosted Group 2: West Germany, Argentina, Spain, and Switzerland.

Liverpool and Manchester hosted Group 3: Portugal, Hungary, Brazil, and Bulgaria.

Middlesbrough and Sunderland hosted Group 4: Soviet Union, North Korea, Italy, and Chile.

Because each city already had a stadium, the English did not have to spend too much on infrastructure, and the majority of the stadiums were just remodeled for the occasion. Such was the case of legendary Wembley, the soccer cathedral, which saw its capacity increase from 126,000 to 150,000. In fact, it was at Wembley on July 11, 1966, that, with the Queen of England and her husband, the Duke of Edinburgh, in attendance, the World Cup was kicked off.

The first game of Group 1 started the competition. In this opening match, Uruguay dealt England an eye-opening blow. With strict discipline, protection offered by Mazurkiewicz's goalkeeping, and Rocha's talent, Uruguay closed off all paths for England, leaving the score unopened, to the disappointment of those who filled the stadium. England did not set themselves apart from the Uruguayans in that game or within the group since they both advanced to the quarterfinals easily by defeating France and Mexico. For Mexico, the game against Uruguay catapulted their goalkeeper, Antonio "la Tota" Carbajal, into the record books. Carbajal had lost the starting spot before the World Cup, after having played the four previous Cups. He won it back, however, for the game against the Uruguayans, setting a record that still stands today: He is the only player to have played in five World Cup competitions.

The scores in the first round reveal the key to the English system: only four goals for, but none against—the best evidence of Ramsey's new strategy.

In Group 2 there were few surprises, with two teams advancing with two victories each and a draw between themselves. Argentina, which had lost 3–0 to Spain on tour before the official competition, now took revenge on the "Red Fury," beating them 2–1, and showing what distinguished Juan Carlos Lorenzo's team, which played with a distinct European style: left back Silvio Marzolini's performance, Ermindo Onega's uneven but always unique talent, and Artime's goals. Germany, in addition to the famous goal-scoring Helmut Haller, introduced a new twenty-year-old kid with great presence and skill: Franz Beckenbauer.

In these first two groups, things were going relatively smoothly. The drama was reserved for the other two groups, with Brazil and Italy as the protagonists of two stories that will be remembered forever.

In Group 3, Brazil, once again coached by Feola, looked ready to add to their two consecutive championships. With that in mind, they again combined experience and youth, in the same dose that had given Aymore Moreira positive results. As expected, everything revolved around Pele, who was the game's focus in the successful debut against Bulgaria and also the focus of his rival's aggression. Trying to make up for their technical inferiority, the Bulgarians resorted to violence. They provoked foul play. Zecev sought out Pele's right knee, and Brazil's key to victory went bye-bye. In Brazil's next game, Hungary unmercifully took advantage of "the King's" absence. Portugal also wanted to take advantage of this . . . but Pele returned to the field for that game, and the bandage on his knee became the preferred target. The Portuguese player Morais, acting with the complicity of referee McCabe, had perfect aim. Once again, for the second consecutive time, Pele was left out of a World Cup; but this time, his teammates would be left out with him.

In Group 4, Italy waited to taste the glory it had not savored since the 1930s. To that end, the Italians took drastic measures, including the exclusion of *oriundi*[3] (the case of Maschio, Sivori, and Altafini four years before) and the decision to designate a permanent coach (it would be the late Edmondo Fabbri), in the style of the legendary Vittorio Pozzo. Like today, the club competition in Italy was very fierce, and teams like the 1963 European Champion AC Milan and Helenio Herrera's revolutionary Internazionale were at the top of international soccer. But their style of play was not applied to the national team for lack of appropriate players (Suarez, a Spaniard, and Jair, a Brazilian, were key factors in Internazionale's victories, for example), and fights began to undermine a team that was, at first, thought to be made of steel. They had started off well, especially in avenging themselves against the Chileans. Afterward, they lost against the Soviets, but their advance to the next round seemed safe, since their defining game was against North Korea. And that's where the story begins.

In hindsight, one wonders whether the confidence felt by the Italians before confronting the North Koreans was the same as that felt by the Argentineans (before losing to Cameroon in 1990) or Colombians (before losing to the United States in 1994). In any case, the moral is clear: It doesn't pay to be overconfident, ever.

Substitutions were still not allowed, so coach Fabbri's decision to start an injured player, Bulgarelli, was even stranger than it would be today. To no one's surprise, he had to leave the field after only a few minutes after crashing into an opponent who would soon enter the history books. His name was Pak Doo Ik, a dentist, and he hustled non-stop, as did the rest of his teammates. Forty-one minutes into that unforgettable game against the Italians he shocked the world. Not backing down before such legendary names as Faccetti, Mazzola, or Rivera, he aimed at Albertosi's goal and hit the bull's-eye. North Korea had beaten Italy, eliminating them from the World Cup and providing one of the hugest upsets in World Cup history.

Even after that, as history shows, the big teams would still never learn.

On that day in 1966, even the Italian officials were so overconfi-

---

[3]*Oriundi:* Literally meaning "native" in Italian, in this case the term refers to players born in South America who, because of their Italian roots, were allowed to play for the Italian national team.

dent that they opted not to attend the game. The president of the Italian Federation, Pasquale, returned to his country to attend to personal matters, and the rest of the delegation decided to go to Birmingham to see Brazil play Portugal. So they got the bad news second hand, rather than seeing it with their own eyes. Afterward, the Italians attempted to outwit their fans. They delayed their arrival in Italy by eight hours and announced that the plane was to land in Milan, even though they arrived in Genoa. But the fans weren't fooled. They were waiting for them at the airport with handfuls of coins and rotten fruit.

The battle between the continents was about to reach its decisive stage. Europe had placed five teams in the quarterfinals, with South America adding two, and Asia one, thanks to the surprising North Koreans. Once again, attention was placed on two games with, at the very least, strange characteristics.

Looking back, the idea seems so ludicrous it's hard to believe it happened. For the England–Argentina matchup, a German referee, Kreitlein, was designated while an English one, Finney, was chosen for the West Germany–Uruguay clash.

Both referees gave a regrettable performance, and in both games the European teams won a place in the semifinals. Can an objective reading be made of all this?

Yes. For the Argentine affair, a transcript of journalist Juvenal's article sent while he was *El Gráfico* magazine's special correspondent said:

World Cup 1966 is over for us. Until Saturday at 1:38 P.M. (Greenwich time), it was a realistic dream. From that moment on, it was out of our hands because we were left a man short against a team that had to beat us. When England scored their goal only thirteen minutes from the final whistle, they sealed a memory that could have been better, but is not in any way disagreeable or bitter [. . . .] We had serious warnings about the officiating. Information supplied by Spanish and South American friends warned us about German referee Kreitlein. And those warnings were confirmed as soon as the game started [. . . .] With that we entered the last ten minutes of the first half. A foul was called on Perfumo for tackling an English forward from behind. Rattin got between the referee and Perfumo's attempted protest [. . . .] Rattin's gestures were neither angry nor offensive. We saw his gestures: His index finger leaning downwards on the palm of his other hand as if he were calling "time out" in basketball and indicating the sign of captain with his fingers [. . .] Roma kicked the goal kick to Marzolini, and Rattin kept on talking to Herr Kreitlein in Morse Code. From a distance, it appeared he was trying to say, "Please give me a moment, I am the captain." All of a sudden the German's index finger signaled "out." The expulsion had no justification [. . . .] Neither physical violence, nor aggression, nor disrespect for the referee were ever apparent. Leaving a team one man short in a World Cup quarter-final match, without a good reason, appeared to be an enormous error [. . . .] Argentina's mistake was never using the air game and, while they kept the ball from being controlled by the English, they were never able to get their attack past stage one. Argentina would have been better served trying to break past the English defense with two or three passes to the open field [. . . .] The strategy they employed would have worked to keep an honorable score, without goals against, but it could never work to win the game [. . . .] The loss of time after Rattin's expulsion, and the ending with Pastoriza's assault on the referee and Onega's spitting at the game's commissioner, cannot be justified. Even if it was a reaction to the injustices of the referee, we cannot, under any circumstances, defend these actions, which undermine our case and make us look bad.

In all honesty, a very valid testimony. Those final images would remain forever in World Cup legend: Rattin, the recently expelled captain, took the English flag off the corner pole and sat on the red carpet, at the other end of which sat the Queen. Finally, as if the bias of the referee had not been enough, English coach Ramsey later blurted out the epithet, "Animals," to describe the Argentineans, ruining Argentina's image for several years after.

For Uruguay, things went even worse, if one can compare unjust defeats. When things were still 0–0, the English referee Finney ignored a clear penalty committed by German defender Schellinger, who pretended to be a goalkeeper, blocking a shot with his hands. That wasn't all. After eleven minutes, Haller scored a goal and, in reaction to the first Uruguayan protests, the referee expelled two of them, Troche and Silva. With nine players on the field, the South Americans could not stop the European storm. The Germans overwhelmed them with a flurry of goals (4–0). A new Continental injustice had been committed.

In Sunderland, Hungary once again shrunk from its role as favorite, losing this time against the Soviet Union, again because of a disgraceful performance by its goalkeeper, Gelei.

In Liverpool, North Korea showed it was ready to give more than one surprise (as Italy already knew) while Portugal showed that, thanks to one player, it had the potential to be a world power. In an unmatched game, the Asian team got ahead 3–0 at twenty-four minutes, taking advantage of the Portuguese goalkeeper, Costa Pereira. But of course soccer is played with eleven players, and within the ranks of the Portuguese eleven was Eusebio.

He was a black forward, born in Mozambique. A true gazelle with superior power, speed, and precision in his shot. He was the ultimate forward, one would could command millions and millions of dollars today. Three minutes after the last Korean goal came Eusebio's first, and he didn't stop until the tide was turned at 4–3. He left the last goal for his teammate Jose Augusto but the victory was all Eusebio's. Today, a monument immortalizes him in Da Luz stadium in Lisbon, home of his club, Benfica. In England, he took Portugal to a semifinal of a World Cup. He left his mark and earned his eternal nickname: "The Black Panther of Mozambique."

It was the World Cup of controversy and duels. Also of styles. In the semifinals, for example, Portugal opposed the new English tactical order with the best weapon it had: the inspiration of its men. It was not enough, and Eusebio left the field in tears. On the other hand, it was the home team's most convincing performance.

The other semifinal matched two teams with the same view of the game. Germany and the Soviet Union played their hands to the limit, with deeds that were as risky as they were terrible, all before the passive eye of Italian referee Lo Bello. One play shows what that match was all about: At forty-three minutes, the German Schellinger took the ball away from Cislenko with a tackle that endangered both players. That play launched Haller's score-opening goal, causing a protest from Cislenko, who was then ejected. It is, at the very least, interesting to note that Germany was benefited by the expulsions of the Argentinean Albrecht, the Uruguayans Troche and Silva, and the Soviet Cislenko. Would they ever pay for so many favors? The only thing left was the final . . . against the English.

The home team revolved around a wise and generous playmaker who was willing to use the entire field: Bobby Charlton.

In the back, they had a great goalkeeper, already considered the best of the tournament: Gordon Banks. In front of him, a line of four backs, one of whom stood out, both in appearance and in importance: Bobby Moore.

In the midfield roamed a unique player who always made himself right at home. He played like a sweeper in front of the back four, and he was destined to fill many important roles, such as recovering the ball, pressuring the most important rival player, and roughing things up when things weren't going their way: His name was Nobby Stiles. With him ran the above-mentioned Charlton, Martin Peters, and Alan Ball, the midfielder who joined the attack most often.

Up front were Roger Hunt and Jimmy Greaves, but as stated earlier, he was replaced by Geoffrey Hurst, who was less skillful but more powerful. .

On the other side was a team of the highest caliber. Germany counted on a goalkeeper who would only be outdone by the classy Sepp Maier: Hans Tilkowski. In front of him was the most outstanding part of the team, the defense, where Schellinger and Beckenbauer stood out. From the midfield forward, the clarity and scoring of Helmut Haller joined forces with Wolfgang Overath and, way up front, a forward who was already tested: Uwe Seeler. The man in charge of coordinating them was Helmut Schoen, successor to the legendary Sepp Herberger as coach of Germany.

On July 30, 1966, Queen Elizabeth II was already in her honorary box at Wembley Stadium when the two teams went onto the field. England, in red, allowed Germany to wear their traditional white jersey. It was their only courteous gesture.

The game had one key duel: Bobby Charlton versus Franz Beckenbauer. The home player would wind up winning it, but without humiliating his rival, who would one day also become a legend. The game was dominated by England from the get-go. It launched its men forward with the understanding that defeat was not an option, especially considering all the bitter moments it had endured in World Cup competitions past. The game was highlighted by a lot of goals.

Twelve minutes into the game, with the English mostly on the attack, Haller took advantage of a faulty header by Wilson and beat Banks for the first time.

At eighteen minutes, the previous goal already a distant memory, Geoffrey Hurst took advantage of Hottges' loose defense and equalized the game.

Up to that point, the goals reflected the nerves, defensive errors, and great offensive concentration of both sides. From that moment on, two unexpected episodes would come to define the game, along with its scandalous aftermath.

At seventy-eight minutes, with everyone expecting the game to go into the tiring thirty-minute overtime, a ball was launched into the German end by . . . a German defender. Martin Peters accepted the gift and beat Tilkowski making it 2–1.

After eighty-nine minutes, with the English already celebrating, Jack Charlton, Bobby's brother, committed an unnecessary foul on Haller, just meters away from the English area. Haller himself kicked the cross, which Schnellinger and Seeler let pass. Banks also saw the ball pass by before Weber finally decided to put it in the net for the suspenseful 2–2 tie.

That's how regulation time ended. The overtime would be thirty minutes of pure emotion; but even more than that, thirty minutes of controversy.

Controversy because the goal that tipped the scales in favor of England is disputed to this day, with its image repeated over and over again. Granted television was not as advanced then as it is today, but soccer is so unpredictable that nothing guarantees that that play could be made sense of even by today's cameras. Only a deep, detailed study done in 1995 by Oxford University scientists showed, with the assistance of a new slow-motion technique, that the ball never completely crossed the line. On the field, the play went like this: Eleven minutes into overtime, Hurst received a cross from Ball and shot violently at the German goal; the ball bounced off the lower part of the crossbar and then onto the grass. Was it in front of or behind the line? That is the question.

The rules state that the ball, in its entirety, must cross the line for the score to count, but it simply could not be verified. In that fatal second, the Swiss referee Gottifried Dienst was left frozen, as was Soviet linesman Bakhramov. In the case of the latter, his one gesture had a clear meaning: no goal. Had he thought differently, he would have run toward midfield. However, the referee moved closer to speak to him. First, he shook his head, clearly meaning no; then, he nodded, meaning yes. Right at that moment, Wembley exploded . . . the 3–2 was fact, as was Hurst's glory as the only player in history to score a hat trick in the final. Later, a fourth goal would come but, by that point, it only mattered for the record books.

The third goal would inevitably become the symbol of a World Cup filled with doubts and controversy. It ended with a result that might be more than the product of chance: For the first time in thirty-two years, the home team won the championship.

BOBBY CHARLTON
(England)
England 1966

Even when he was young, he already had those "Englishman" qualities that distinguished him in the soccer world. Bobby Charlton was famous for his bald head, but even more so for his intelligence and maturity on the soccer field. Perhaps all at once after the accident that changed his life, he grew up on and off the field. Miraculously, he survived the February 1958 airplane crash in Riem Airport, Munich, in which most of his Manchester United teammates lost their lives. A player who covered the entire field, he inspired his whole team while also defining it. But when he remembers the keys to victory in 1966, he doesn't begin by mentioning his own name.

B.C.: Alf Ramsey, our coach, was quite a revolutionary. Adapting to his system was not very difficult because, for the two years preceding the Cup, we played a lot, and we won all of the games. . . . The system was understandable and easy to explain, especially for the midfielders: Their role was like that of a springboard, jumping backward or forward, to attack or defend.

A.C.: But the relationship between you guys was not so simple . . . it began with some problems.

B.C.: We didn't question him and, because of that, absolutely no conflicts developed. The ones with the problems were our rivals, who found themselves before an undecipherable team. In truth, Ramsey adapted his system to his team, which did not have forwards good enough to implement the most commonly used game plan. So we surprised everyone by coming up with a new one . . . then it was our opponents who had to adapt their system to ours.

A.C.: And no one questioned his decisions?

B.C.: Alf Ramsey was the boss and was given respect worthy of his position. No one questioned his decisions because we understood what was best for the team. . . . We didn't even question his leaving Jimmy Greaves off the starting lineup. It was a decision that upset Greaves greatly, but we all accepted Ramsey's decisions.

The image of Bobby Moore in his teammates' arms, the one of Charlton with the ball at his feet and his arm extended, directing his teammates . . . flashes of the best moments.

B.C.: The most pleasant memory is, of course, having won that World Cup. It would have been a big disappointment had we not won it . . . we had good players, a good system, a good team, and a great deal of confidence. But, more than anything, we were convinced that we were the best.

A.C.: And today? Would you still be the best?

B.C.: I don't like to make comparisons, but I will say something that makes me feel torn between the two periods. First, I'll say that I'd like to play in today's soccer. Second, I can confirm that the soccer of that time was more fun. How do I justify both things? Simple. I would love to be a soccer player now because everything is much more professional, more . . . organized. But, as always, there is a "but." Before, fans had a better time at the stadium, and the stress to win at any cost did not exist.

A.C.: But not everything about those days was golden. The England–Argentina game had all the ingredients of a game charged with stress.

B.C.: I've never understood what Rattin did in that game. Having himself thrown out of a game was a criminal act against his team. It was like throwing the game away before it was over. In those days, and even more so today, one could not impose upon referees and, in truth, that's what he did. . . . Being the captain of his team, he should have respected authority. . . . I never forgot that incident, and I've always considered it unprofessional.

A.C.: It wasn't the only controversy in that World Cup. There is a picture of you celebrating Hurst's controversial goal as soon as the ball hits the grass. Did you see the ball cross the goal line, or was it just an act, to pressure the referee?

B.C.: In no way was it acted out. I always thought, and I still maintain—that it was a legitimate goal. On the contrary, I immediately thought the referee wouldn't call it. . . . But, either way, we knew we were the best, with that goal or without it. . . . Even Franz Beckenbauer himself has recognized that it's a minor point.

A.C.: Speaking of which, tell me about that opponent.

B.C.: It was very difficult to play against that young Beckenbauer. He was very resourceful, fast, and elegant at the same time and very difficult to defend. I'll tell you something strange: It was my job to guard him and his job to guard me. We canceled each other out and didn't contribute much to the game . . . but I was ready to run that risk knowing I was surrounded by better teammates than Franz.

A.C.: Does the best player in history come from that list, or have they been surpassed by those of other eras?

B.C.: Throughout the history of the World Cup, I've seen many great players. I think it's impossible to compare a goalkeeper with a midfielder or a defender with a forward. . . . For that reason, I'll list players in no particular order: Pele was magnificent in every way; Di Stefano—who we were never able to see in a World Cup—was incredibly intelligent; Puskas was a man before his time; Cruyff was a great architect of the game.

A.C.: Would you be so bold as to list who you think is the best?

B.C.: Well, I'd have to go with the man who has the least to do with this work, because as I said, he never played in a World Cup: Alfredo Di Stefano. He was so complete. But more names are coming to mind, and I know that I'm being unfair . . . the history of soccer is too great.

A.C.: And the best of your World Cup, England 1966?

B.C.: My teammate Bobby Moore, an incredible defender and leader. Overath and Beckenbauer among the Germans, and Rattin, when he was on the field.

So often have the English been called soccer masters that anyone would be perplexed by the large gap between accolades and actual results. England has only one World Cup victory, won in their own home. Then, never again . . .

A.C.: Why, Bobby?

B.C.: In our time, Ramsey knew how to pick a team that could win each game. That was his philosophy: one game at a time. That's something that England has lacked ever since. The right mix of men may not have appeared for a winning team, but it's also true that there hasn't been a man like Alf Ramsey, with the clinical eye necessary to pick the best eleven and go out and win.

Mexico 1970

At this point, it was already a custom: The fantastic universal re-
union, the Olympics, was used to announce the host of the World
Cup six years hence. Moreover, the site constructed for the multi-
sport event was taken into consideration for later use by soccer. It
was the first intermingling of these two organizations, which were
called upon to compete and fight together, although not always loy-
ally. And so—during the Tokyo 1964 games—FIFA opted for Mexico, certainly keeping in mind that in 1968, two years before play
was scheduled to begin, Mexico City would be in charge of organizing the International Olympic Committee's big event. It was an
extra guarantee that work would be finished when the time came
to play ball.

With those arguments in hand, FIFA, which was becoming powerful enough to do whatever it wanted, didn't listen to any of the
protests, and Mexico's bid was sealed, with fifty-nine votes against
the thirty-two received for Argentina's candidacy. It would therefore be the first World Cup above sea level—the main reservation
the Europeans, especially England, had about Mexico—as well as the
first Cup in which many rule changes took effect.

For example, yellow and red cards began to be used in order to
avoid doubts with respect to the disciplinary actions of referees
(the case of the Argentine Rattin and the German referee Kreitlein
was fresh in everyone's memory). It was also established that an indirect free kick would be distinguished from a direct one by a referee's raised arm. Finally, but probably most important, teams
would be allowed to make two substitutions per game, with no re-
striction as to the position of the players coming in or going out. It

took forty years to make that decision, and it would take another twenty-eight—in time for France 1998—to allow a third substitution.

As a side-note, another debut was made. Until now, the country's delegations had included doctors, trainers, masseurs, and even psychiatrists. Now, Sweden included a cook: Peter Olander, private chef of King Gustav Adolphus himself.

The World Cup was getting more and more eccentric while the world just kept on spinning. In Chile, leftist Salvador Allende took power; in Paris, Greek statesman Mikis Theodorakis went into exile after being a prisoner of the military state; and in Sweden, Russian Alexander Solzhenitsyn received the Nobel Prize. And the ball kept on rolling. . . .

The qualifying rounds, which once again broke a record with seventy-one participants, left behind some illustrious names (Hungary, Yugoslavia, Spain, Argentina) as well as the bitterness of a war. That's right, Honduras and El Salvador took their passion for the game off the playing field and onto the battlefield, in what is known as the Soccer War, which left a bloody aftermath.

On May 31, 1970, in the amazing setting of Azteca stadium, the majestic "Colossus of Santa Ursula," the championship started. The home team and the Soviet Union were the participants in the opening game, and they ended in a 0–0 tie, a result that has become common in opening games. But this one went down in history: Puzach replaced Serebrianikov at halftime in the first substitution in soccer history.

Beforehand, a colorful opening ceremony had confirmed, as if it were necessary, that the World Cup was turning into a demonstration of national pride. And the likes and dislikes of the fans were very thinly veiled. The Mexicans obviously received the biggest applause, but in second place came those renowned diplomats of soccer, the Brazilians. In Guadalajara, they passed out flags, opened their training camp to the public, and signed autographs to the point of exhaustion. The boos and jeers went to the English. They had decided, because of the altitude, to come a month before the competition, but during a stopover in Bogota, where they played preparatory games and acclimated themselves to the altitude, their captain, Bobby Moore, was arrested, accused of stealing jewelry in an airport shop. The war—Europe versus South America—was at its height, both on and off the field.

One of the countries that had taken the war from playing field to battlefield, El Salvador, finally arrived in the place it had long dreamed of reaching, with neither shame nor glory. It lost its three games (against Mexico, Belgium, and the Soviet Union), didn't score any goals, and had nine goals scored against it. Consequently, Group 3, which took place in Mexico City, was easily resolved: Mexico first, USSR second.

Group 2, in Puebla and Toluca, had Italy and Uruguay as its stars, surpassing Sweden and Israel respectively. For the Italians, this was to be the Cup of the "vendetta," after the embarrassment suffered in England 1966 against the North Koreans. But it was not easy to unite Italy's internal forces. As is the case to this day, that attempt to come together was more dramatic than amusing. On the one hand, there was the side of Moratti and Helenio Herrera's *"nerazzurri,"*[1] personified on the national team by Sandro Mazzola: extreme defensive tactics, with strategy and planning above all else. On the other hand, there were the lovers of a new line, which favored showmanship and beautiful play: the line led by Gianni Rivera, already christened "The Golden Child," wearing the colors of AC Milan. It was a public battle and, given the unresolved internal tension, it was a miracle that the team passed to the next round. In fact, it scored only one goal, and tied its other two games 0–0, getting to the next round with those four points. It wouldn't be the last time they would advance with such a bad performance; they would do so again in 1982.

In Group 3, taking place in Guadalajara, there was another home team. I'm talking about Brazil, full of brilliance and charm, which easily qualified for the next round, accompanied by England.

After Brazil's loss in 1966, Vicente Feola had been replaced by the controversial and surprising ex-journalist Joao Saldanha. His greatest contribution was not paying too much attention to Pele's repeated absences (his publicity engagements and his matches around the world with Santos increasingly required his presence), and replacing him when necessary with another Brazilian-style "ten": Tostao, from Cruzeiro. Moreover, in best-case scenarios, he played the two together, breaking an unwritten rule that one shouldn't use two players of similar characteristics. However, in

---

[1]*Nerazzurri* means "black-blues" in Italian. The term refers to Internazionale (commonly known as "Inter"), a Milan club whose players wear a striped black-and-blue jersey.

spite of hitting the bull's-eye with that move, poor Saldanha did not last long. He was replaced by a man who was starting to become unmatched as far as collecting championships was concerned: Mario Lobo Zagallo.

Zagallo took his predecessor's idea even further and put a revolutionary theory into practice: "What is a national team? The grouping of the best . . . therefore, let's let the best play." So he sent five "number tens" onto the field! Pele, from Santos; Tostao, from Cruzeiro; Jairzinho, from Botafogo; Gerson, from São Paulo; and Rivelino, from Corinthians.

It was a dream quintet that began to captivate the world, a revolutionary offering that further separates today's soccer from that of the past.

In Group 4, played on the fields of Leon, another battle of styles made the game irresistible: the disciplined power of the German "panzers" versus the reckless talent of the Peruvians. Fortunately, they both qualified. I say fortunately because the great diversity of soccer is shown in their clash of styles.

Peru debuted on June 2. One day before, their delegation received some terrible news: An earthquake had terrorized the country, claiming the life of a relative of backup goalkeeper Goyzueta. For that reason, everyone thought that the men coached by Didi, who had been World Champion as a player with his native Brazil, would enter the field unfocused. That's not the way it went. Spectacular performances by Chumpitaz, Sotil, Teofilo Cubillas, and Ramon Mifflin took them to a 3–2 victory, causing a journalist to tastelessly title his story: "Watch Out, Peru Can Shake the Ground Under Anyone." Afterward, the Peruvians danced past Morocco, which represented Africa, in the continent's return to the World Cup.

When the quarterfinals came, a colorful, unforgettable, euphoric feeling ran through Mexico, from one end to the other. Mexico had gotten to this stage for the first time, and the people were as elated as the team. Their advance to the semis had included the ever-present controversial play of every World Cup, especially where the home team is involved. Mexico defeated Belgium by the narrowest of margins on a penalty kick called by Argentine referee Norberto Coerezza that the Belgians disputed vociferously. So much so that it provoked one of the most ill-mannered protests in history, with the eleven Europeans cornering the referee inside the goal. The penalty itself arose from a loose ball in the penalty area, which defender Jeck and Valdivia got to at the same time. The powerful Belgian managed to clear the ball, but also caught a piece of the Mexican's leg. For those who were there, it was a play that could have gone either way, but for others it was a clear case of favoritism toward the host country.

Mexico has always prided itself on its celebrations, and just as it would later invent the popular "Mexican wave," that victory over Belgium transformed the Angel of Independence monument in the middle of Paseo Reforma into the favored spot for public celebration. But let's get back to soccer.

Just as in Chile 1962, it was Italy that had to face both the home team and the wave of euphoria surrounding it. In Chile, the Italians had been beaten by intimidation. This time around, the European team was able to overcome the daunting climate in Toluca stadium and come back after being down 1–0, thanks to a gutsy decision by coach Ferruccio Valcareggi, which ended the internal disputes that were tearing the team apart. While Italy was still behind, he took Mazzola, leader of one of the team's two fronts, out of the game and replaced him with Rivera, leader of the other. It paid off. The "Golden Child" provided the surge the team needed, waking up scorer Gigi Riva. The game ended with a convincing 4–1 win for the Europeans and respectful applause from all sides of the stadium.

The rest of the field also gave dramatic shows that, when combined with the Cinderella story of Mexico and the Italians' redemption, wound up making this World Cup an unforgettable experience that surpassed the drama of almost every World Cup up to that point. Here is how it all happened.

Uruguay and the Soviet Union butted heads in a hard fought match, a description that goes beyond the teams' defensive tactics. In regulation time, it was one of those 0–0 games that is just as exciting as a game filled with goals, and in overtime they stayed so even that everyone thought referee Van Ravens would have to flip a coin to decide the match. But that's not the way it ended, of course. . . . Cubilla saved a ball that was going out of bounds and made a cross that Esparrago headed into the goal. The Soviets protested, demanding an offside call. They would repeat the act years later, in the same country, during another World Cup, with the same negative result. The Soviets had been jilted more than once in the history of the World Cup, and they never had enough clout to complain. Thus Uruguay became one of the four semifinalists, putting its faith in goalkeeper Mazurkiewicz, defender Matosas, and forward Cubilla.

The other dramatic game was in Leon, and it also needed more than ninety minutes to be resolved. It was a matchup with enormous tradition: no less than England and Germany, face to face, in a rematch of the final, four years before, that still stirs up controversy today. On that day, the past was fresh on everyone's mind.

This time, the referee was Angel Norberto Coerezza, who would be voted the best of the tournament. This time, there was little controversy, just a hellish back-and-forth pace, with England pulling ahead first (2–0) and Germany catching up (with goals by Seeler and Beckenbauer, no less). That's how they ended regulation, forcing thirty more minutes of pure soccer enchantment. The Germans had the first opportunity and they didn't squander it: The great Gerd Müller—headed toward lifetime supremacy amongst World Cup goal-scorers—was the final executioner, scoring the winning goal (3–2).

There was another act left to the quarterfinal stage, of course, in Guadalajara. Pedro Escartin, former Spanish referee, journalist, and witness to every World Cup since 1934, reported: "Brazil and Peru played beautiful soccer in Guadalajara. Perhaps the best of the tournament. They were two teams that permanently went to the attack, without worrying about defense. It was beautiful, beautiful soccer that day. Brazil shot on goal twenty-seven times to Peru's twenty-two. . . ."

It was truly a jewel. The brilliant Peruvians got ahead with goals by Cubillas and Gallardo, but twice Tostao and later Jairzinho and Rivelino registered a final 4–2 score to a game that could be described with one word: unforgettable.

Those days were perhaps the true golden age of international soccer. Big stars participated in big games, which deserve to be remembered as the ideal: a clash of styles; brilliant, emotive play; suspense transformed into glory and drama—the essence of soccer. The two semifinal matches were, perhaps, the climax of that essence. Moreover, the high quality of soccer was not incidental: Three of the four teams still in the running wanted the title because winning it meant keeping the trophy forever. Brazil, Italy, and Uruguay had already won the Jules Rimet trophy twice. One more World Cup victory would land it in their trophy case permanently.

Completing the four was Germany. What happened next, then, was no small affair.

Brazil–Uruguay was, along with everything else, a rematch of the 1950 "Maracaná shocker." The fans were seeing, once again, two very different styles on the playing field: The Brazilians had scored twelve goals in four games; the Uruguayans had scored only three, but had only one against them.

Uruguay's defensive style was quickly strengthened when Cubilla put them ahead after nineteen minutes. From then on out, it fell back to withstand Brazil's merciless attacks. The Uruguayans endured until almost the end of the first half. With one minute remaining in the half, Clodoaldo breached the Uruguayans' defense and would later penetrate it two more times, but not until the end of the game, when it seemed the Uruguayans were going to be able to prolong the suspense. If ghosts can be buried, the ghost of 1950 was buried under the field at Jalisco stadium.

I now turn to the other semifinal, a game that will always be cited whenever one seeks to explain the beauty that is soccer. I suggest that, after reading this book, anyone who wants to understand this game should get a videotape of that Germany–Italy match, remembered as the game of the century.

The majestic Azteca stadium was full. The Germans (perhaps because the opponent was Italy, which had eliminated Mexico) were rooted on by the Mexican fans, but they were coming off an exhausting battle against the English. The Italians had easily resolved their internal conflicts, but the full proof was yet to be seen on the field. Neither one had the advantage then as the teams went head to head. After seven minutes, Boninsegna beat Maier to open the score for Italy and set the stage for the rest of the game: Germany to the attack and Italy on the counterattack, in a soccer battle played at full intensity. The German siege finally yielded results at ninety minutes! As fate—or soccer magic—would have it, the scorer of that stay of execution was a German who was an idol of the Italian league: Karl Heinz Schnellinger, star of AC Milan. It was a scene that would be repeated over and over again as a consequence of soccer's universalism. (For example, the Bulgarian Letchkov, a star for German club Hamburger SV, would eliminate Germany from USA 1994, bringing on accusations that he was a traitor against those who paid him. Incidentally, Schnellinger, in 1970, would admit that his life was a living hell after returning to Italy, where he couldn't even go out on the street without being insulted.) In any case, on that day, he opened the floodgates for an overtime that would be anything but run of the mill.

At 94 minutes, Müller scored for Germany. At 98, Burgnich for Italy. At 103, Riva's goal made the score 3–2. At 109, Müller made it 3–3. What more could you ask for, besides a winner? It was Italy, thanks to the triumphant play of Rivera. Germany was also a winner, in its own way: Franz Beckenbauer, with his shoulder bandaged from an injury, deserved kudos as well. But soccer is like that. All-embracing.

The final, like the rest of this excellent World Cup, once again put two different schools—two different ways of expressing the same idea—face to face: Brazil versus Italy. A decisive match that would be repeated twenty-four years later in the United States, under different circumstances. In 1970, Brazil played artistic soccer and Italy played practical soccer. In 1994, both would curiously attempt a role reversal. Were they successful? That will be seen later. For now, imagine a full Azteca stadium with the *azzurri* and the *verdeamarelhos* about to take the field.

How did Italy play?

After all the discussions, their style seemed set. In the back, they kept a trio from the last World Cup: goalkeeper Albertosi and backs Burgnich and Facchetti. In the middle of the defense, Cero, who had helped Cagliari to the *scudetto*,[2] played the role of sweeper, and Rosato, a man-to-man specialist, was the stopper. The midfield included the playmaking skill of De Sisti and the energy of Bertini. Further up was Domenghini, complemented by Rivera or Mazzola, leaders in the fray. When the former played, the team got an extra dose of rich skill and offensive capacity. The latter added self-sacrifice and defensive skill. With the hindsight the tactical revolution has allowed, it is easy to think they could have taken out some other player and played Rivera and Mazzola together. Perhaps Valcareggi could have changed history. After all, Rivera was the one who worked best with the surefire starters up front—Riva and Boninsegna—who didn't get along very well off the field, but on the field they were a fearsome duo. In the end, the coach decided in favor of Mazzola . . . and that's how they lined up to face Brazil.

And how did Brazil play?

[2]*Scudetto,* meaning "badge" in Italian, is the common name given to a victory in the Italian league championship. Therefore, saying "Juventus won the *scudetto* in 1995" has the same meaning as "Juventus was the 1995 Italian league champion."

Argentine coach Cesar Luis Menotti, World Champion in 1978, once wrote:

> Everyone talks about the revolution brought about by Holland in 1974. People keep talking about England's ultradynamic soccer in 1966. The dazzling Brazil in 1958 and Hungary in 1954 are still remembered. But the great revolution, one that no one talks about, was the one brought about by Brazil in 1970. In the Mexico World Cup, Brazil presented a team with five "number tens," five giants who simultaneously steered their club: Pele, Tostao, Gerson, Rivelino, and Jairzinho. That was truly revolutionary. At a time when, thanks to the success of England in 1966, the collective value of a team seemed to overshadow the importance of individuals, Zagallo gathered the best players he had, without taking into account the positions they played or the role they filled in their club. Individual talent once again became the deciding factor. They were the best players and, because of that, they had to be there. Where would they play? With what plan? It would be shown on the field of play. And it was shown in a way that the world would never forget. . . .

Of course old Lobo, Mario Zagallo, had a plan for them. And that was what was truly revolutionary: They weren't just thrown on the field and told to play.

Under that plan, the brain was Gerson, whom nature had blessed with a formidable and accurate left-footed shot. Pele was his companion and, more important, the finisher. Tostao moved like a center-forward, pivoting and distributing the game. Rivelino had the job of occupying the left wing of the attack, and Jairzinho the right. That's how Zagallo divided up the roles from midfield forward, and the rest was the work of the combined magic of these talents. From the back, Carlos Alberto, right back, advanced with the class and soul of an attacker, and Piazza, a midfielder turned central defender, became the leader. Little can be said about goalkeeper Felix: Rarely did his opponents get the ball and, when they did, the ball rarely made it to him.

At exactly noon on June 21, as befits a Mexican World Cup, the final started in Azteca stadium, filled with 105,000 fans rooting for Brazil.

Quickly, the field was covered with individual duels: Rosato and Tostao; Facchetti and Jairzinho; Burgnich and Rivelino; Bertini and Pele. It was Pele who began to confuse his defenders by retreating to midfield, only to suddenly be found at the head of his team's attack, deep in enemy territory. It had been eighteen minutes since the East German referee Glockner had blown the starting whistle, when one of the legendary images of World Cup history was first frozen in time: Pele suspended in the air, at an indeterminable distance from the ground, easily beating the best Italian jumper, Burgnich, in his fantastic flight to a header that made it 1–0. That goal opened the road to the victory expected by almost everyone. A mistake by Evaraldo, less than twenty minutes later, returned the story to its starting point. With the score tied 1–1, the first half ended.

Everyone expected to see substitutions made at halftime. Especially the Italian fans, who wanted to see Rivera come out and assault the Brazilians. But Valcareggi made a common error that more than a few coaches have committed in the World Cup: he gave in to a whim. Perhaps it was a refusal to agree with the majority of the people. What is certain is that he didn't put Rivera in at the half, or even later after sixty-five minutes, when Gerson tipped the scales in favor of Brazil. At seventy minutes, Jairzinho extended the difference with his seventh goal in as many games—a record that still lives on. By the time the "Bambino" finally came on the field, it was already too late. Rivera arrived only in time to get a closer look at Brazilian captain Carlos Alberto's final goal, giving Brazil a 4–1 win. Then, the party started. . . .

Few World Cup titles were as indisputable as that one was. When Carlos Alberto lifted the Cup toward the sky, the entire soccer universe gave a standing ovation. For Mario Lobo Zagallo, it was the third consecutive success, with the first two coming as a player, this one as coach, with one more reserved for him in 1994 as an assistant to coach Carlos Alberto Parreira, his trainer in this tournament. It is remembered by all as the ultimate triumph of pure artistry. This was the World Cup of beautiful play, with looser defense and no tie-ups, where they played rather than fouled (it was the only World Cup without any ejected players). Four years later, as we shall see, soccer began to change, both on and off the field. The incredible success achieved by the Mexican company Telesistemas, which provided the television signal for the entire world at an amazing financial gain, drove FIFA to forever after control transmission rights, which would become the biggest prize in the communications market.

GERSON
(Brazil)
Mexico 1970

In those days he was already bald, giving the impression of an old, wise man who deserved the utmost respect. Nothing has changed, even as we approach the year 2000. Gerson is still Gerson, one of the five fantastic "number tens" who delighted the world defending the colors of Brazil in Mexico 1970. Gerson is still Gerson, and because of that he characteristically maintains a low profile, responding to questions with humility and simplicity, and even putting himself under the microscope, twenty-five years later. He was the real driving force behind that team, even though he'll never admit it.

A.C.: Gerson, were you guys the epitome of freedom on the field?

G.: Not quite. Mario Zagallo, as a coach, had very clear concepts and was really a stickler for detail. For example, he wanted to play with a retreated left wing, and because of that Rivelino became a kind of fourth midfielder. . . . In truth, it was all planned for one of us to get to that open space in the left sector of the field ready to surprise. That's how it was done then.

A.C.: Was it difficult for all those stars to live together, especially considering that many of them shared the same position?

G.: No, precisely because the most experienced players made sure it was not a problem. Pele, Alberto, Felix, Jairzinho, and I decided to unite the team. Literally. We got all the players together and talked to them about the importance of unity—that we had no alternative, only the choice between winning and winning. We, the oldest players, were deeply aware that it was our last chance, our last World Cup. And we knew that we had a team ready to compete for the top spot, especially since we had Pele.

A.C.: Obviously, people remember that team for its virtuosity, its beauty; but it was also practical. How was it that Wilson Piazza, a midfielder, was placed as a central defender?

G.: During a training session in the Maracaná, the starting defender, Joel, wasn't feeling well. His natural replacement, Fontana, was injured. Therefore, Zagallo asked Piazza, who backed up Clodoaldo at midfield, to momentarily cover that spot. He did it so well, he never left the starting lineup. . . . Of course, it wasn't planned. It was total coincidence . . . helped, of course, by the skill of every player.

A.C.: The passing of time has made that team look invincible, as if they had won all of their games by being infinitely superior to all their opponents. Was that the case or, at some point, did you think that things were going out of control?

G.: We played the most difficult game of the Cup against England. I didn't play that day, but those who did were very nervous and, instead of winning by four goals—which was the logical difference between the two teams—we barely won 1–0. Afterward, the situation also got complicated in the game against Uruguay, but for other reasons: We were haunted by the ghost of 1950 . . . besides, they scored the first goal, and we had to resort to our experience to turn the game around. We did it and then calmed down.

A.C.: The final saw you speeding down the last stretch to the Cup, all systems go.

G.: Exactly. Besides, Italy played predictably. They had played all of their games the same way and continued to do so. They made the fatal mistake of defending us man-to-man. We had too many options, we found the holes, and we gave them a beating to the tune of four goals.

A.C.: How has soccer evolved from then to now?

G.: I don't think that any tactical explosion has come about. From 1970 to today, the only team that has really stood out has been the 1982 Brazil team, with Zico, Socrates, Falcao, Junior, Leandro. . . . But, in general, I really think it's gone downhill. What has changed is the physical aspect. I think Brazil's win in USA 1994 was based on that. . . . In general, the level of play in the last World Cup was very low, although not as bad as in Italy. Considering the low quality of the others, our team stood out and could continue to do so if Zagallo works on thinking ahead to France 1998 and the Olympic Games in Atlanta. In my opinion, those should be our main objectives for now.

Germany 1974

If you really analyze the tenth World Cup, you'll see that there were some big changes taking place; changes that brought soccer to its present incarnation, ideologically and stylistically. That is basically what this chapter is really all about.

Because the Jules Rimet Cup was now permanently in Brazil's hands, a new trophy was needed. That's how the FIFA Cup, the work of Italian sculptor Silvio Gazzaniga produced in the workshop of Bertoni of Milan, came about, chosen from among fifty-three candidates on April 5, 1971. The sculpture, the same one that is still in use today, is a representation of two stylized athletes trying to hold up the Earth. The five-kilogram, gold cup with a material value of twenty thousand dollars, is the permanent property of FIFA, which gives custody of it to the champion every four years and then leaves them a smaller permanent replica as an eternal reminder of their victory.

Moreover, as Sir Stanley Rous's reign had come to its end, a new president elected by the international soccer association, Brazilian Joao Havelange, became the first South American or non-European to take office. Twenty years later, it was apparent that he had been willing to face any odds and overcome any obstacle to achieve his ultimate goal: to "sell a product called soccer."

Also the interest in participating in this party-turned-big business was increasing; the number of countries signing up for the qualifying rounds hit an all-time high: ninety-four. This time, the sixteen teams that made it premiered a new format for the competition. In the first round, there were four groups of four teams each, with the top two from each group qualifying for the next round. In the next round were two new groups with four teams each, with the top teams in each group matching up in the final and the two second-place teams in each group playing the consolation game.

Every single one of the games was transmitted via satellite. Technology had finally taken the World Cup to every house in every corner of the world. This included Argentina, of course, where I was able to escape my scholastic obligations to sit down in front of the television and see live what was happening on the playing fields, on the other side of the ocean, in the far away and unknown German stadiums.

That Germany had been selected is no coincidence. Just as the previous Cup had followed the steps of the Olympic Games (Mexico 1968 and 1970, respectively), soccer once again took advantage of the infrastructure created by that other athletic mega-event. However, that's where the similarities ended. The grave events of Munich 1972, with the terrorist attack that ended the lives of eleven Israeli athletes, made security a priority from that day forward. It all happened on the night of September 5, 1972, when Palestinian guerrillas invaded the Israeli training camp. Afterward, the conflict in Fürstenfeldbruck military airport left eighteen dead (eleven Israelis, five Palestinians, and two agents).

The eyes of the world were now focused on the World Cup, so more machinery was put into place: publicity, sponsors, and big business. Clothing manufacturers that suited up the teams were, without a doubt, getting involved, and the German company Adidas was surely not going to lose out on this golden opportunity of having a World Cup at home. The final designation of Germany as host surprised no one then, and there weren't many who put up resistance.

The seventies had started and with them came a new approach to life. . . .

The world was in turmoil when Richard Nixon came to office, and was shaken by his resignation after Watergate. A military coup led by Augusto Pinochet ended the leftist government of Salvador Allende in Chile, where poet Pablo Neruda had died. Nearby, just across the Andes, Argentine president Juan Domingo Perón was also dying. In the soccer world, the commotion was caused by the European clubs: most of all, the Dutch clubs Feyenoord and Ajax. Pele was no longer around to defend either Brazil's *verdea-*

marelha[1] shirt or South America's power, and the same Edson Arantes do Nascimento prepared himself for a titanic and almost quixotic endeavor: to introduce football—soccer, of course, not the American variety—to the United States, no less. On July 18, 1971, he had defended the colors of Brazil for the last time, and a few years later, the New York Cosmos would welcome him with open arms. The best player in the world's dream of establishing soccer in America started with several million dollars in his pocket and ended abruptly, the day of his permanent retirement on October 1, 1977. Pele said goodbye to soccer, and soccer said goodbye to the United States. At least until 1994.

For different reasons, when the tournament started on June 14, people were already taking sides and predicting the winner: Germany, because they were the home team, and because they counted within their ranks a brilliant generation of soccer players, headed by Franz Beckenbauer; Brazil, because of tradition and because, even without Pele, they kept many bright stars on their team like Jairzinho or Rivelino; Italy, the runner-up of the previous event, because they appeared to have learned the lesson of Mexico and combined experience (Rivera, Riva, Mazzola) with youth (Causio, Benetti, and Capello, who is today coach of super-champion Milan); and, finally, Holland, because . . . well, that will soon be seen.

The tournament began with a new twist: The opening game no longer featured the home team. Instead, the defending champion played. In this case, Brazil played against Yugoslavia, but the result did not change with a third straight score of 0–0 in opening games.

The kickoff also saw the problems of Germany versus Germany. In those days, the Berlin Wall had still not come down (that would happen in 1989), and the drawing determined that visitor East Germany and the home team, West Germany, would face each other in Group 1. The visitor won, in a game charged with tension and closed with a goal by Jurgen Sparwasser. Although the game decided the final standings of the group, it would ultimately have positive side effects for the West Germans. It delayed a face-off with Holland until the final. On the other hand, it brought to light team problems that had to be resolved: Beckenbauer wanted Overath on

---

[1] *Verdeamarelha:* "green and yellow" in Portuguese.

the team, but coach Helmut Schoen preferred Gunter Netzer. In the end, Beckenbauer got his way.

They were internal problems that, in spite of the Germans' harsh discipline, would always be repeated as, for example, in Mexico 1986.

In the same group, Chile and Australia did not contribute much except the curious circumstances of their qualifications to the World Cup. In the qualifying rounds, the Chileans did not play the second leg of their play-off, because the Soviet Union refused to fly to Santiago as a reprisal for the dismissal of leftist president Allende in Chile. After having tied 0–0 in the first leg, the Chileans qualified automatically. The Australians got to the World Cup for the first time, representing Oceania, and providing a universal touch, although not much more than that. Something similar was happening with the Africans of Zaire, indirect participants of Group 2. There, Brazil, Yugoslavia, and Scotland finished with practically the same points and the same goal difference, with everyone's game against the Africans deciding their pass to the second round. The Scots made three goals, the Brazilians made three (strangely the only three goals made by the Brazilians in the first round), and the Yugoslavians made nine. Brazil advanced with Yugoslavia since they had no goals against Scotland's one.

In Group 3, played in Düsseldorf, Hannover, and Dortmund, Holland was the clear standout. They turned away a Uruguayan team that still featured Mazurkiewicz, Rocha, Cubilla, and the up-and-coming Fernando Morena. They also blew out Bulgaria, 4–1. Only Sweden (0–0), which would accompany them to the next round, was able to (partially) block their path. The Uruguayans finished last in their group, with their only point coming from a tie against the Bulgarians, who were also eliminated.

Group 4, finally, was the most disputed. That was the one with Argentina, Italy, Poland, and Haiti, each with their own story. For the Italians, getting to that stage was simply a result of an amazing winning streak, which had started in 1972 and included a spectacular period following Dino Zoff's goal, when the team went 1,097 minutes with no goals scored against it in international matches. For the Argentines, it was the coming together of their stars, who had come from all corners of the globe. As we'll see, however, this would not be enough to make up a great team. For the Poles, it was the opportunity to make themselves heard, especially after the two great campaigns that had brought them to an unprecedented place in their history: First, the qualification to the World Cup, after having eliminated the English, in Wembley, no less; later, the Olympic title, achieved right there on German soil. The Haitians, in their debut in the World Cup, just tried to lose by as little as possible. For them, it was an honor just to be there. They had beaten Mexico, which for the first time lost the CONCACAF qualifiers.

In the start of the group, Poland's organized play beat Argentina's improvisation. The game showed the best characteristics of a team destined to make history. Security was guaranteed by goalkeeper Jan Tomaszewski, who had already won fame in the legendary qualification match at Wembley. The leaders of Poland's solid defense were Zmuda, Gorgon, Szymanowski, and Musial. The midfield had the aggressive playmaking of leader Kazimierz Deyna and the energy of men like Kasperczak and Maszcyk. Up front were the final ingredients: all the power of Gadocha, who many went so far as to compare in style to Garrincha; Szamarch, a born scorer, with all the tools; and Gregorz Lato, who was headed for supremacy among goal-scorers. He would achieve it with the excellent mark of seven goals.

Argentina had resorted to its expatriate players for the first time— players like Carnevali, Perfumo, Heredia, Ayala, and Yazalde—and even arrived as a favorite to take the Cup, but its own disorganization proved to be its most difficult opponent. Its three coaches (that's right, three coaches), Vladislao Cap, Jose Varacka, and Victor Rodriguez, made too many changes in the lineup, never allowing the players to gel, as one example shows: At the last minute, an injury to Roque Avallay, a striker, brought about the emergency callup of Carlos Babington, a creative midfielder, but who had just joined the team when it was already in Germany. For the first game against the Poles, Babington, with whom no one had played, was situated as the playmaker!

By now, you can probably guess who won: Poland, 3–2.

For Italy, the other favorite, everything *seemed* to start more easily. I emphasize *seemed*. The ghost of North Korea once again crossed the minds of the "azzurri" when Sanon put Haiti ahead in both teams' debut. With great effort, the Italians turned it around (they wound up winning 2–1), but an anecdote serves to illustrate their spirits from there on out. Old Ferruccio Valcareggi, the same coach who had faced all of the problems in Mexico 1970, ordered Anastasi to go in to the game in place of Giorgio Chinaglia, and received a stream of insults from the outgoing forward as he left the field. Once again, the Italians played in the midst of controversy, and it is worthwhile to point something out: That is how they played in their first World Cup games in 1934 (those in the presence of the all-powerful *Il Duce*) and in all those that followed—with fights over the *oriundi* in Chile, the humiliating loss in England, and the conflicts over style in Mexico, and beyond. Theirs was a style that, even with all their internal conflict, didn't impede them from almost always being near the top of the heap.

In Germany, they never stopped suffering. Against Argentina, they tied 1–1, but the South American team was more deserving of the win. Houseman's goal is remembered by everyone because of the beauty of the shot: With his left foot, he kicked the ball over Dino Zoff, who had already had his shut-out streak snapped by the Haitians. The Argentine striker turned out to be one of the big stars of that Cup. They called him "El Loco,"[2] and he lived up to his name with the skillful, creative plays he invented. Later, many would ask themselves, "What could this player have done had he had more order around him?" In terms of talent, he was comparable to any of the best in the world. The tying goal was, strangely enough, made by another Argentine player, the great Roberto Perfumo, into his own goal.

At the same time, Poland swept to victory against Haiti (7–0), leaving the matchup between the two Europeans to decide the group. A tie would send both teams to the next round.

Part of the legend of that game is the first suspected incentive scheme in World Cup history. Legend states that Argentina offered the Polish money to go all out for victory against Italy (it's assumed they were supposed to anyway). Many players including Enrique Wolff, now a journalist, spoke of a suitcase full of dollars that ended up in Polish hands.

What we know for sure is that the Poles won, Argentina defeated Haiti, and both of the winners qualified. Italy went through another frustration, with players like Rivera and Riva watching from the stands. For them it was time for a new generation. For the rest, the World Cup continued.

It was here that the competition's new format began to differ from the old. It was a clear ploy to pull in more money. Goodbye to the quarter-final knockout stage, hello to a semifinal round con-

[2]El Loco: "the madman" in Spanish.

sisting of two groups of four teams each: more games, more money grossed. As will be seen, the new way of playing the quarterfinals turned out to be a huge success.

On one side, Group A: Holland, Brazil, Argentina, and East Germany.

The Dutch simply glided to victory: three victories in three games, with eight goals for and none against! The names that had promised so much in the first round finally appeared in the headlines: Johan Cruyff was the centerpoint of the spectacular, well-oiled machine that was Holland. Neeskens, the other Johan, became the top scorer after his goals started off the wins against Argentina and Brazil (4–0 and 2–0). The Dutch team beat its two big rivals with authority and prepared itself for the final, leaving the Brazilians, who had come to defend their title, the small consolation of the chance at third place. And already in those days, the game for the bronze medal had become no big deal.

On the other side, Group B: West Germany, Yugoslavia, Poland, and Sweden.

It has been said that the home team, West Germany, was dragging over an internal conflict ever since its loss against its cousins from East Germany. But the conflict had left a clear winner: the team itself. To start, Overath, chosen by Beckenbauer, was already on the field in place of Gunter Netzer and with new men behind—Herzof, Bonhof, and Holzenbein, who ran more than Hoeness, Grabowski, and Cullman. Perhaps it was because of that that Overath was one of the catalysts of the initial win against Yugoslavia (2–0). Despite these positives, the restructuring also produced a clear loser: Netzer, who was left out of the starting eleven, was also left out of a big endorsement deal. Where did that endorsement money wind up? In the hands of Beckenbauer and his men.

No one was thinking about that when, after the win against the Swedes (4–2), the time came for the decisive game. It would be against Poland, which had also won its two games, the first against Sweden (1–0) and the second against Yugoslavia (2–1). Rain was also present and the field at Frankfurt's Waldstadion was almost flooded. The grass endured in the best German style, and the two sides offered a soccer duel, in the best European style, showcasing great physical effort from the German side and fast, precise passing from the Poles. It was a memorable duel, which was symbolized in the head-to-head confrontation of two men: Gadocha and Vogts, who alternated victories in each round of their duel. The scales were tipped in favor of the Germans by Gerd Müller, thirty minutes into the second half and, even though the pace of the game didn't slow and the Poles had a final chance to tie the score with a penalty kick (which was saved by Jan Tomaszewski, dispelling any remaining doubts about his greatness), no one could change the score.

So even though Poland was the big surprise of the tournament, the final would be between Holland and West Germany.

The last time the Dutch had participated in a World Cup had been in France 1938. Thirty-six years later, they arose as the defining factor of the tenth World Cup. In fact, by the time they reached the final they had become more of a revolution than a revelation: a revolution known as *total football*. Under that system, everyone covered for and covered everyone, in a circular movement without fixed positions, which served to disorient the opponent while allowing the Dutch total control over the field. That is why they were known as the "Clockwork Orange."

A Brazilian journalist defined it as "controlled chaos," but coach Rinus Michels knew exactly what he was doing. Making his job easier were accomplices such as the incomparably intelligent Cruyff who led the Dutch attack, supported by Neeskens, Van Hanegem, Resenbrink, and Rep. From behind, if one can even attempt to speak of this team in terms of positions, were Haan, Suurbier, Hansen, Rijsbergen, and Krol. Like the great Brazilian teams that preceded them, the Dutch could afford goalkeepers who were less than brilliant. In this case it was the chubby Jongbloed, who used contact lenses to correct his vision problems, almost always tended goal without gloves, and wore the number eight on his back. Enrique Wolff, the Argentine right back who had himself been left dizzy by the "Clockwork Orange" described them like this: "Individually, they had no advantage over us. Every time I sprinted against my man, I always had the impression I was faster, but he always had teammates nearby to help him . . . they beat us because of their team play." Cruyff, who conducted them from the inside, said, "Holland does not have one style of play; it has many and applies the one appropriate to the needs of the game. It is important for us to know how our opponent plays, their strong and weak points. But more important, we think about how we can frustrate and confuse our opponent. Every player knows what he has to do in every instant of the game, be it on defense, in the midfield, or on the attack. We play with total freedom but never do we feel as free as when we are doing something to help the team. . . ."

And so they lined up before the always solid Germans, who must have been asking themselves, "Doesn't this Dutch team look suspiciously like the Hungarians we faced in Switzerland 1954?"

Everyone went to the stadium to see whether or not it was true, including local politicians Walter Scheel and Helmut Schmidt, Prince Bernard of Holland, and United States Secretary of State Henry Kissinger, perhaps the person most associated with soccer in the United States. Germany sought to avenge the events of eight years before, when they were left with the silver medal and an axe to grind in England 1966. Holland left nothing to chance—it was not their style—and coach Michels started playing mind-games, a habit that would become a leitmotiv: "Don't give anything for free." Before the match he let it leak out that he would not start Neeskens, a key player, for the decisive match and that the striker Resenbrink would be replaced by Keizer, a player with less ball-controll. However, these changes never went into effect, and on July 7, both teams went onto the field with the very best that they had.

The officiating was left to the Englishman Taylor who, in the very first minute of the game, dispelled any doubts the Dutch may have had about his performance. From the moment the game started until sixty seconds later, the Dutch had the ball; the possession ended with Cruyff being brought down in the penalty area and the referee calling for a penalty kick. Before the astonished eyes of the world, the inventors of *total football* gained a quick 1–0 advantage, because when it came to penalty kicks, Neeskens never failed.

We are perhaps dealing here with one of the most legendary scenes in World Cup history. Only this time, unlike when Uruguayan Obdulio Varela, ball under his arm, silenced the Brazilians in the Maracaná in 1950, television was there to capture everything. And so we have irrefutable proof of the greatness of that German squad, solid as a rock. Today you can actually see the skill of Sepp Maier, one of the most important goalkeepers of all time; how the "Kaiser," Franz Beckenbauer, organized his team from the back, complemented by "the brain," Wolfgang Overath, up front with the relentless Gerd Müller. Surrounding them was the talented guarding of Paul Breitner and the aggressive energy of Bernd Holzenbein and Rainer Bonhof. Names so legendary it's almost frightening. But across from them was the "Clockwork Orange" ready to face their fear. And that's what soccer is all about.

It was the West German Holzenbein who got free and entered the enemy area. And it was Jansen who had to detain him with a foul. At twenty-six minutes and by way of a penalty kick, West Germany equalized the score. Everything started anew.

On the field, the battle between two different styles could be summarized with two names: Berti Vogts versus Johan Cruyff. The German was on the upswing when, one minute before the end of the first half, the great Gerd Müller turned around at the penalty spot, found space for his right foot to strike the ball, and made the score 2–1. The Germans won it definitively when the Dutch couldn't equalize before the second forty-five minutes were up. Holland's *total football* would become legend, still in use today— an example of what soccer is all about. In the meantime, Germany, with its practical style of soccer, celebrated its second World Cup, the first with the new trophy. . . .

Franz Beckenbauer's memories would lead us to conclude that this was not just any World Cup: "Everyone talked about Cruyff, but in the end he was unable to beat an exceptional defender like Vogts. Had we played ten games against Holland, we would have certainly won at least seven. We were the champions because we managed to forget the criticisms, the tensions that the long concentration produced in us, and we had the spiritual strength necessary to correct our mistakes in the middle of the tournament. . . . That's why I don't doubt that we were the best." It's true, the best won even though today, in hindsight, everyone remembers the loser more as would happen eight years later with Brazil in Spain 1982.

JOHAN CRUYFF
(Holland)
Germany 1974

He was the star of the brilliant generation which, under the leadership of coach Rinus Michels, gave birth to a tactical revolution in Germany 1974. The Dutch national team was known as the "Clockwork Orange," and its new, revolutionary style was known as total football. On the field, the team counted on a different kind of player. With a body so slim it bordered on frail, Cruyff was not a center-forward, but rather a player of the entire field. Skillful, intuitive, intelligent, and electrifying, he came to World Cup 1974 considered the best player in Europe. He was also champion with his club, Ajax Amsterdam, who won both the European and the World Club Cup.

Nowadays, this successful coach of Spain's FC Barcelona seems to want to be at the vanguard of today's soccer, in which no one risks anything and nothing changes. . . .

A.C.: Johan, what did the 1974 World Cup mean to you?

J.C.: Speaking only for Holland, it meant the introduction of what several Dutch clubs had been showing at the national team level. What the clubs had achieved in different competitions was perfectly translated to the national team stage by the performance of the "Clockwork Orange."

A.C.: What else can you say about that team?

J.C.: It's not easy to say, because it surprised everyone so much that its appearance left the whole world flabbergasted. Except for us. The players, as well as the coaching staff, knew that we were a team that could make history, and we did. As we won games and advanced in the World Cup, we were cool, calm, and collected. I'd say we were a great team in every way: both collectively and individually. I've always said that everything starts with great players. Not only did that Dutch team have them, but they were all at their peak, forming a solid, coherent machine, with its own unique style.

A.C.: And how did you take having been one of the best teams, only to return home empty-handed?

J.C.: It wasn't easy, but everything got better for us when we returned to Amsterdam and found ourselves basking in the love and gratitude of a whole country convinced that what we did was very well done, regardless of the final score. There is no doubt time has shown that the 1974 World cup had two champions, although I am among those who believe it definitely matters who the actual winner on the field is.

A.C.: How many elements of that World Cup are still in effect in today's soccer?

J.C.: There are national teams that have fallen with time, others that have risen, and still others, like the Germans, which keep showing why they will always be in the race, because they are united and·organized. If there is something that World Cup 1974 deserves to be remembered for, it is the respect for a style of play. We were very faithful to a style of playing, a way of thinking and feeling about soccer, and that took us to the highest level.

A.C.: Is Holland's case the same as Ajax Amsterdam's, which also made history?

J.C.: Ajax was responsible for the real revolution. They changed soccer for themselves as well as for others. Today, they continue to be a model to emulate. The names change, but the philosophy is always the same. Ajax started the trend for everyone else to follow. It was something that I, of course, caught on to as well. As a player and now as a coach.

A.C.: And what stands out most for Cruyff the coach?

J.C.: Above all, a few of the things I consider unalterable are ball control; the obligation to take the initiative against any opponent, no matter where we play; making sure I have the best players I can; and a religious belief in the importance of ball possession. I can't forget that every kid who comes to Ajax wanting to be a star is given a ball to write his name on and keep for the rest of his life.

To think that one day, many years ago, while walking his Dobermans through the streets of a Los Angeles neighborhood, he signed his name on the ball of another kid who wanted to be a star and never missed a single one of his games. Even with his years weighing on him, he was still as classy as ever wearing his signature number fourteen on the back of his Los Angeles Aztecs uniform. Intuitive, fast, and skillful, he took his soccer to the fields of the United States before his final goodbye as a player. Those who saw him play in the twilight of his career knew that this thin guy with a penchant for complaining to the refs, a bohemian look, and the soul of a sandlot player had deservedly won a privileged place in soccer history.

Argentina 1978

For me—up until this point—the history of soccer's World Cup had been the result of study and passion. Reading contemporary articles, secondary sources, and personal narratives of those involved; viewing existing footage; interpreting all that and comparing it to the present . . . from here on, in addition to all these, I can now add the unique and incomparable feeling of having lived it, of having been there in body, mind, and soul.

It's no accident that this new journey begins in a place called Argentina 1978.

I have already told how I got there there; this chapter calls for a look back, through time and space, in order to reconstruct what actually happened.

It was—and this is a memory that expresses the feeling of the time and place—the last cold World Cup, with the dominant gray of a Southern Hemisphere winter seeping into everything. After this, soccer's international gala would take place every four years in a setting—Spain, Mexico, Italy, United States—under a summer sun. . . .

It was—and this is a feeling that grows in intensity with the passage of time—a sad reprise of those old images of *Il Duce* controlling the victory of the Italian players in 1934, with the members of the military junta that had taken charge of the government in 1976—Videla, Massera, and Agosti—lodged in their VIP box, an image repudiated by the world, but one that still leaves an inescapably bitter taste in one's mouth.

It was—and this is not related to the above, although some people tried to use it to soften the country's terrible international image—a month-long soccer celebration, with people pouring into the stadiums, providing the warmth that the weather and political climate could not supply.

Hosting the World Cup had been promised to Argentina—perennial contender since the beginning of this history—during the Congress that took place in England 1966 and finally assigned at Mexico 1970. When the coup took place on March 24, 1976, not a finger had been lifted with respect to the coming event. . . . On December 3 that year, the EAM 78 (Autonomous Entity for World Cup 1978) was formed, and this brand-new body, functioning as an organizing committee, spared no expense, in compliance with orders received directly from the government. The order came for three stadiums to be remodeled (the legendary Monumental of River Plate, Velez Sarsfield stadium, as well as Rosario Central's Gigante de Arroyito), and for another three stadiums to be constructed in the country's heartland (the chosen venues were Mar del Plata, Mendoza, and Córdoba) at an estimated cost of $700 million. Also under way was the construction of a communications center, Argentina Televisora Color, which initiated a color-TV signal—until then the only one possible was black-and-white—with an estimated investment of $60 million. Strategic sites such as airports were also modernized. All this resulted in a World Cup site that was aesthetically impressive, with modern, up-to-date, functional venues.

On June 1, 1978, facing the skepticism—as well as the resentment—of the world, everything was ready for the start of the eleventh World Cup. Taking its international image into account, Argentina's opening ceremony was designed to tug at the heartstrings, and so it featured a lot of young children. Unfortunately, the opening match did not have the same effect: The first game pitted the most recent World Champion—in this case West Germany—against the scheduled opponent—Poland—and this unimaginative, tedious game ended with a score of 0–0. The brand new soccer ball, christened the "Tango" by Adidas and designed especially for the occasion, was booted futilely from one side of the field to the other.

In any case, most eyes were centered on Group 1, in which Argentina—playing in Buenos Aires—was facing some very tough opponents: Italy, France, and Hungary. This would be the last World Cup to have sixteen representatives, divided into four groups of four teams, with the top two qualifying . . . and none had any guarantees of success.

The first obstacle for Cesar Luis Menotti's Argentine team was Lajos Baroti's Hungary. There was nothing simple about it. Ten minutes into the game, Csapo put the visitors ahead, and a dead calm swept over the crowd that filled the renovated Monumental stadium. But it only lasted a moment. . . . Immediately, that same crowd became a factor: pressuring, encouraging, with the chants that would become famous; with their joy, in spite of everything; and with their incessant flag-waving. All of a sudden, Leopoldo Jacinto Luque, Argentine center-forward, scored the equalizer. From then on, the game went back and forth. On one side was the tension of the Argentines, who could not execute the game-plan that their coach, Cesar Luis Menotti, had so vehemently stressed. On the other side was the calmness of the Hungarians, whose ranks included such skillful players as Nyilasi or Torocsick—who would end up being suspended from the tournament—rightful heirs to the throne of Puskas and company. . . . Finally, the tension overwhelmed the calm: Seven minutes from the final whistle, Norberto Osvaldo Alonso—a much-loved player for River Plate who was added to the roster at the last minute—teamed up on a play with Ricardo Daniel Bertoni, who scored the goal that decided the final score. Perhaps it's enough to sum up the feeling about this victory with the headline used by *El Gráfico,* a local sports magazine of international renown: "IT HAD TO BE WON AND IT WAS." Certainly, the drama and the title could be traced from there right through to the final.

In the same group, Italy advanced quickly, with a squad composed basically of Juventus players: eight of the eleven starters. The manager was Enzo Bearzot, and the majority of his stars—Dino Zoff, Gaetano Scirea, a fellow named Paolo Rossi, and Roberto Bettega, who is now president of Juve, no less—were preparing themselves for the victory lap they would take . . . four years later.

Maybe because it was in their nature to do so, the Italians recovered right away, after receiving a tough blow at the outset: thirty-two seconds into the match—still a record—Bernard Lacombe gave France the lead. The game was played on a damp Mar del Plata field, which became famous because of a landscaping defect: Divots (loose pieces of turf), something new in that era, were kicked up by the players as they ran.

The two winners repeated their successes in their second matches: Italy, without problems against Hungary, which was already weakened by the suspended players; and Argentina, again experiencing anguish and misery early, against France. Another great goal by Luque—this time scoring from outside the penalty area—and one by Daniel Passarella (after a handball) finished off a team managed by Michel Hidalgo and led on the field by a fellow named Michel Platini. Many good things would later be said about the French. As for Argentina 1978, they left only an odd, unpublished anecdote: During their final game against Hungary, which was played without much fanfare, they realized too late that the only shirts they had were the same color as their rivals': white. Saving the day, a local team—Kimberley of Mar Del Plata—lent them theirs (alternating stripes of green and white), and France became the only team in history to play a game without their original colors.

What remained was the final game of the first stage, a spectacular duel to decide first place: Argentina versus Italy. The visitors won 1–0 with a goal by Roberto Bettega, off a heel pass from Paolo Rossi.

That result, and its consequences, give rise to a current thought of mine: If the Argentineans benefited so much from the referees and the atmosphere—as many revisionist detractors now assert—then how is it that they suffered such an important loss, transferring them from Buenos Aires to Rosario for the second round, where they would have to face Brazil, no less? It is a question that answers itself.

Of course, in those days, my mind was far from pondering those questions. Instead, my big worry was whether I'd be able to find Italian tourists with whom I could trade second-round tickets. It had seemed set in stone that Argentina would win their group and continue playing in Buenos Aires, and that Italy would come in second, sending them to Rosario. But reality threw all my plans down the drain.

Germany headed Group 2 in Córdoba, but was unable to come out on top in the end. After their lackluster debut against the Poles, the Germans—just as they did four years earlier, coached by Helmut Schoen—demolished Mexico (6–0), before running into an opponent from a continent that always brings them bad luck: Africa. It was Tunisia, which played Germany to a tie, relegating this team that mixed experience (goalkeeper Sepp Maier, defender Berti Vogts, and midfielder Rainer Bonhof) with youth (Hansi Müller, Karl Heinz Rummenigge, Klaus Fischer) to a second-place finish, a point behind Poland. Many people speculated that the Germans were better off that way: Had they beaten Tunisia, they would have had to play in the difficult second-round group filled with South Americans (Argentina, Brazil, and Peru). By losing, they would face opponents they knew well: Holland, Italy, and Austria. But as we'll see, speculation—like a dark cloud covering the field—would be the order of the day.

The Poles, on the other hand, were in the midst of the greatest decade in their history: third place in World Cup Germany 1974—they would also get the Bronze in Spain 1982—and with the men to make a mark on Argentina 1978. Their coach, Jacek Gmosh, was a man with an elastic face and clear ideas. His strategy was fortified by goalkeeper Jan Tomaszewski and defenders like Szymanowski, the fighting spirit and solid play of midfielders Gorgon and Zmuda, the clairvoyant playmaking of Deyna, and the power and scoring ability of Lato.

Tunisia and Mexico were left, respectively, with a smile and a frown. Although they didn't qualify for the next round, the Africans were left with the pleasure of having tied the defending champions and a clear victory (3–1) against Mexico, displaying players of surprising skill, like Temine, in all of their games. The Mexicans, on the other hand, disappointed, especially after having arrived with a young Hugo Sanchez and a hyped Rangel. It would be a while until they would get another chance.

Because of the way the competition was set up, the teams chosen as top seeds of their group were given the advantage of playing all three of their first-round games in the same place. In Brazil's case (Group 3) more than one supposed benefit turned into a disadvantage. Mar Del Plata's cold, humid climate was nothing like what Pele's successors were used to. Moreover, since 1970, the quality of Brazil's players had decreased as much as the temperature they had to bear, and the new ideas of coach Claudio Coutinho did nothing more than make things worse. With Roberto Rivelino as the holdover from the glory days and Zico as the chosen one to fulfill the prophecy—the appearance of a "white Pele"—the team advanced by way of fights and stumbles. They debuted by tying Sweden before tying Spain in their second game, thanks to what can be remembered as a goal by Cardenosa that, paradoxically, was not a goal. All alone in front of the empty net, he delayed his shot for so long that he gave his opponents enough time to block the ball. Afterward, the Brazilians beat Austria (1–0), which had already qualified for the next round and, therefore, put up almost no resistance. Austria's attitude was, at the very least, suspicious. It would be repeated four years later, when the same Austrian national team gave Germany a helping hand in their quest to make the next round. These moves dirtied the image of a team that should have shone since all its stars were at their peak: goalkeeper Koncilia, midfielders Pezzey and Prohaska, and forward Johan Krankl. Somehow, they would wind up paying. . . .

Four years earlier, there had been a champion—Germany—and a revolutionary team—Holland. This time, the "Clockwork Orange" sought to put the final jewel in their crown: to win the title. But it was no longer the same: Their roster no longer included the incomparable number fourteen, Johan Cruyff. His absence was felt from the very beginning.

In Group 4, centered in the city of Mendoza, Holland qualified for the second round only because they had a better goal difference than Scotland. In the head-to-head matchup between the two teams, Dutchman Robby Resenbrink entered the record books by scoring the thousandth goal in World Cup history.

The real stars of the group were the Peruvians. The team led by the talented foot of Teofilo Cubillas played by far the best soccer of Argentina 1978's first round. Around Cubillas' "number ten" orbited—in the traditional Peruvian style—virtuosos like Cesar Cueto and Juan Carlos Oblitas. In that first round, after an honorable tie against the defending World Cup runners-up (0–0) and before destroying Iran (4–1), they would delight the public, by supplying the tournament's greatest show, against Scotland. After falling behind 0–1, Peru played flawlessly with spectacular finishes—as was their style—to win 3–1.

Holland showed barely enough to make the next round. With several hold-overs from the 1974 team (Krol, Rep, Neeskens, and Van Hanegem were the most important examples) as well as some new faces (the Van der Kerkhof twins, Willy and Rene, leading the charge), the Dutch beat Iran, tied Peru, and lost to Scotland. Even though they beat the latter out of a space in the second round, it was only because of goal difference, and because the Scots had been hit by something worse than a loss: Willy Johnstone, one of their most important strikers, had already gone back to his country, because his drug test after the game against Peru had come out positive.

That's how the second round was set up. It would be the last time the round would be played with two round-robin groups of four teams.

In Group A, played in Buenos Aires and Cordoba, all the participants were Europeans: Italy, Germany, Holland, and Austria. In Group B, Rosario and Mendoza hosted Argentina, Brazil, Peru, and Poland.

Just as in the beginning of this World Cup, the second round began as cold as the weather. It is worthwhile to go team by team. . . .

First, Argentina. Up to that point, it had gotten by on the security of Fillol under the goalposts, the energy of Ardiles at midfield, and the power of Luque up front. When the time came to play in Rosario, in the Gigante de Arroyito—that hot cauldron—some of the players confirmed their star status while other new faces joined them. Among the former was Fillol who, thirty-seven minutes into the game against Poland, blocked a Deyna penalty kick and, in doing so, should have ended—but didn't—all of the suspicions that clouded Argentina's path. Swedish referee Fredriksson, who would later figure in two very controversial plays (Belgium's offside goals against the Soviet Union in Mexico 1986 and Maradona's handball against the same Soviets in Italy 1990), didn't hesitate to make the call. Mario Kempes finally came out of his shell by scoring two amazing goals. The first was a header in which he beat the entire Polish defense to the ball and, in the second, he scored after eluding two defenders, giving the Argentines some hope to nourish them.

Of course, Brazil was also charging forward. Two things—one traditional, the other contemporary—made the *verdeamarelhos* the main obstacle to the home team's dreams: first, simply the fear that the green and yellow jerseys evoked in opponents; second, the relationship between goals for and goals against. Coutinho's Brazilians beat Peru 3–0 and Poland 3–1. Menotti's Argentineans beat Poland 2–0. The head-to-head match between the two teams ended 0–0. The equation was simple and was made even clearer because the Brazilians had already finished all of their Group A games. Argentina entered its last game of the group, against Peru, knowing it needed at least a difference of four goals to reach the final.

So the historic game started. Both Oblitas and Muñante hit the post for Peru before the onslaught of Argentine goals suffered by Oscar "Chupete" Quiroga, the Peruvian goalkeeper who was born in Argentina, but had become a Peruvian citizen. He was beaten by Kempes, Tarantini, Kempes again, Luque, Houseman, and Luque again for a 6–0 final score that brought back the clouds of suspicion—suspicion of things that were never brought to light, never backed up, and certainly never proven. So, suspicion or no, Argentina was in the World Cup final.

The other group featured the European battles. Italy–Germany ended in a 0–0 draw, but Bearzot's men, with their ambitious and consistent play, ended up looking better. Holland–Austria showed the definitive reappearance of the heirs to *total football,* with a convincing 5–1 win. Germany–Holland was an honorable rematch of the 1974 final, although the Dutch couldn't totally shake off the ghosts of four years before: The 2–2 final score left both teams unsatisfied. Italy–Austria announced to the world the take-off of an irresistible goal-scorer, Paolo Rossi, as well as the elimination of the Austrians, who showed very little. Now the truly decisive games could begin.

Holland–Italy had all the ingredients of a final. Played in the Monumental stadium, it was jam-packed with soccer lovers, even though the game didn't feature the home team. It did, however, have the suspense the fans deserved. Twenty minutes in, the youngest player in the World Cup, Brandts, in an unfortunate play, sent the ball into his own net and put the Italians ahead. From that moment on, the Dutch went into all-out attack mode against an opponent that could barely defend itself. Then, the tying goal came, scored by the very same Brandts. That's soccer—constantly providing these wonderful little dramas. Finally, Ari Haan, taking advantage of veteran Italian goalkeeper Dino Zoff's lack of movement, put the icing on Holland's comeback. Once again, the "Clockwork Orange" would play in the final against the home team.

The Italians would be left with the chance at a consolation prize, while the Germans would hit rock bottom in one of their most criticized World Cup appearances in history. They fell against Austria, giving Italy a chance to play Brazil for third place.

Ultimately, the Bronze would go to the South Americans, because of their strength and their opponents' weakness. Two long-range bombs by Nelinho and the late Dirceu, both specialists, surprised Zoff.

In the meantime, the moment of truth had come for Argentina— the chance to make its dream a reality. So many times they had been "moral" champions, at least according to their own fans, and with an unquestionably rich history, finally—at home, forty-eight years after the first tournament—they had their best chance ever to lift the Cup.

In truth, the World Cup had started for them in the first months of 1976, when national team coach Cesar Luis Menotti managed to get AFA officials to agree to new rules which, for the first time in history, put the needs of the national team above those of the clubs. From that moment on, the national team was a model of coherence, order, and seriousness. Until then, the national team had meant little more to Argentine players than a waste of both money and time. Menotti changed these attitudes so much that putting on that striped light-blue-and-white shirt became an uncontrollable desire. Many years later, with Argentine players dispersed throughout almost every league on Earth, the words of an Italian journalist summarized this feeling: "No player in the world loves his national team as much as the Argentinean . . . they are capable of doing almost anything to be there when the call comes."

That feeling was already embedded in the heart of Diego Armando Maradona. Only seventeen years old, he had gone through the team's training camp until the very last moment. When Menotti had to cut two men in order to trim his roster down to the final twenty-two, one of the players released was Diego, who many years later, in the height of his glory, would say: "That was the most bitter moment in my career . . . I cried, and I still cry when I remember it." The coach, however, never regretted the decision: "He was still too young." No one will ever know what would have happened if he had been present at the final that year—the same age as Pele in Sweden 1958.

What is certain is that, at that time, no one protested the decision.

Tactically, even though there were no major innovations, there wasn't a lull either. Menotti's game plan was one that emphasized the aesthetic aspect of the game, with specialists in every position who could control the ball well, playing with team spirit, unity and with these words as his maxim: "I think that the most important concern of any coach is choosing the right players. If he chooses badly and gives the player a role that doesn't jive with his skills, and it doesn't work out, one can't blame the player. If I ever hesitated in doing anything at the start of this process, I wasn't hesitating when confronted with the choice between athleticism and talent. I've always preferred talent. If a talented player works hard enough, he can become an athlete. From an athlete who works hard, you'll just get an athlete in even better shape. But you'll never get a soccer player out of him. . . ."

With that concept in mind, the Argentine team counted on the ideal man for each role. Its goalkeeper was full of thrills and quick reflexes: "el Pato,"[1] Ubaldo Matildo Fillol, the best of the tournament. Its zone defense possessed right and left backs with the souls and ball control of forwards (Olguin and Tarantini), and two central defenders who complemented one another. One of them, Galvan, was calm, with exquisite skill; the other, no less than the "Great Captain," Daniel Alberto Passarella, was overwhelming and powerful. In the midfield stood Ardiles, an energetic playmaking machine; Gallego, a classic defensive midfielder, in front of the central defenders; Larrosa, a link to the attack, capable of both robbing from opponents and feeding his teammates; and a man with as much offensive sense as destructive power—Kempes. Way up front were Leopoldo Jacinto Luque and Ricardo Daniel Bertoni, with Houseman or Ortiz as alternates. The list was not too shabby; far from it. So far, in fact, that Menotti wrote the following in his book, *How We Won the World Cup:*

The most important thing in the entire process before the World Cup was learning to always respect, under any circumstances, our convictions, our ideology of the game and the show. By the time we got to the competition, we all knew that the most important thing was to play ninety or one hundred twenty minutes of soccer that was both hard-fought and well thought out, striking the perfect balance between the show we owed to the public and the desire to fight on the field for our ideals. That's why I always remember that, before going out on the field to play the final, I got the players together, and told them: "I can forgive you for anything: for making a mistake in the defensive switches, for giving the ball away and having a goal against us as a result; I'll even forgive you for forgetting the game plan. What I won't forgive is you guys lacking the character to be faithful to a style of playing. I've always told you why and for what purpose I have called you to the national team, and I will not let you betray the calling that made you soccer players." Everything else was said and understood: We had to impose our game on the Dutch, play them tit for tat. If they tried to jam us, we had to jam them even harder; if they pressed us, we had to press them twice as much; wherever there was one of them, there would have to be two of us. That's how they went

[1] "el pato": "the duck" in Spanish.

out to play: convinced that the game could make us rule over international soccer, helping us start a new age of games played cleanly for ninety minutes. It was a tribute to that old, loved Argentine soccer, which had been betrayed for too many years. It was also a response to those who thought that style—our style—had failed worldwide. What had failed was the lack of seriousness in acquiring what was necessary to add to ability and natural talent. . . . I think I had been dreaming of that game against Holland for a long time before. It formed part of a series of soccer and human convictions that I held. Holland was a team with character, that never betrayed their soccer, no matter where or against whom they played. I felt the same way about Argentina. Holland had two things that demanded special attention: their press and the spaces on the field that they constantly created. Their press could only be broken by ability, with ball control. It's well known that the press is based on giving the attacking player less time and space in which to move. Therefore, the only way to break that pressure was to play the ball quickly and as precisely as possible. If an Argentine player found himself with three Dutchmen on him, he had to make them pay by playing the ball with one touch, through the only little hole that they left. I was sure that we would surprise them because we were showing something different. I asked myself, "What surprise could I give them by defending Resenbrink man-to-man? In playing with a sweeper and a stopper? Where's the novelty if they have been playing against those strategies their entire life?" Instead, we would play a zone defense and pressure them when they brought up the ball. We would give them a taste of their own medicine, but would add skill and creativity. That was what was new. And history would agree with me. . . .

In the end, history did agree, but not before making him suffer first, on that unforgettable day of the final, June 25, 1978. The crazy desire to see that game, to be present in Monumental stadium, drove people to all kinds of acts, both moving and strange. For example, it was not uncommon to see ads in the newspapers of the time offering a car in exchange for a ticket. . . . Fortunately, I already had mine. Ironically, my seat, even back then, was right next to a television camera. Of course, I was in the general admission bleachers—the western ones, to be exact, with my back to the River Plate—and the camera didn't capture my play-by-play, but rather was there to replay the most important plays of the game. I can still feel the cold of that day, overshadowed by the euphoria and emotion of being there.

The Dutch team facing Argentina was not the "Clockwork Orange," but it was a difficult team, led by the late Austrian coach Ernst Happel who is memorialized by a stadium in Vienna that bears his name. He rigorously guided Cruyff's orphans, the World Cup 1974 holdovers. Even before starting, the game presented some hazards: one of the Van der Kerkhof twins, Rene, came onto the field with a cast on his right wrist. The Argentine players protested, and Italian referee Sergio Gonella threatened to delay the game until the situation was resolved. Van der Kerkof placed an elastic bandage on top of the cast, allowing what would be an emotive, hard-fought final to begin. Happel, realizing that his opponent was not characterized by solidity, opted for an aggressive strategy—attacking and surprising. So the game became a fast-paced back-and-forth, with scoring chances on both sides that kept the fans on an emotional roller coaster. Fillol responded brilliantly on a shot by Rep, but Jongbloed was helpless before Kempes. The unstoppable midfielder finished a play started by Luque and Ardiles, putting Argentina ahead 1–0. That's how the first half ended, under a cold, gray sky, but surrounded by a feverish, light-blue-and-white crowd. . . . It would hold until the end of the game . . . almost. While Argentina was satisfied with the score, Holland was unable to tie until nine minutes from the end, Nanninga—who had replaced Rep, perhaps to take advantage of his large frame in the penalty area—found a ball lifted into the air by Rene Van der Kerkhof and, from the middle of the penalty area, headed it into the goal, totally freezing the atmosphere. It was 1–1 and the Argentines would have to start all over again. Or maybe not. The history of soccer—and particularly of the World Cup—always leaves a surprise for the end. After ninety minutes of play, Resenbrink—who had been totally invisible for the whole game—won a ball near the Argentine goal line, and took a shot which . . . . it rebounded off the post, unleashing a huge sigh of relief from the eighty thousand fans, every single one of them on the verge of fainting! The Argentineans had gone from imminent victory to the verge of defeat, all in the span of nine minutes. The only thing left to Menotti's team was to start all over again. The overtime would give them their chance. Let's hear how the Argentine coach himself described the feeling:

It had been dramatic: With only nine minutes left, victory had escaped us. When Gonella blew the final whistle, I approached the players. I couldn't believe how they wasted their energy, fighting like madmen. They all lined up to criticize Larrosa because, when Van der Kerkhof launched the ball, the team tried an offside trap, and Omar, who had dropped back to help the defense, had not gone forward with his teammates. They didn't let me say a word. They were wasting the few minutes of rest they had. I almost die of laughter when I remember it . . . Fillol huffed and puffed as was his custom, going back and forth like a caged lion, repeating, "Nine minutes. Right? There were nine minutes left. . . . Can you believe it, Cesar?" He looked everyone in the eye and, totally pissed off, went on about the nine minutes. Fillol was always like that. It was hard for him to accept that goals could be scored against him. I had to shout for anyone to listen to me. Those men had become kids clamoring to get their hands on a toy that kept escaping them. But we couldn't lose because we had too much energy.

Evidently, that's the way it went. Against all the doubts, against all the shadows, against all the clouds, against everything that was said and will be said, Cesar Luis Menotti's national team showed, in that thirty-minute overtime, why it deserved to be World Cup Champion for the first time in its rich history. First, Bertoni assisted Kempes. Then, Kempes assisted Bertoni and, with goals after 104 and 114 minutes, the final score of 3–1 was sealed. In regard to these two last stars, here's some statistical data and a little more: Mario Alberto Kempes was both the tournament's best player and its top scorer, with six goals (two goals scored in three different games); Ricardo Daniel Bertoni made a dream come true, which he had shared a year before: "I will be a World Champion," he had said, "and I'll score a goal in the final." The players were showered with glory. Argentina was rewarded too: A soccer team with that much tradition behind it could not go on without its name inscribed on the golden Cup.

I remember that, on that afternoon, I had been one of the first fans to enter Monumental stadium, and that night, I was one of the last to leave. My joy, like everyone else's, knew no bounds: because of my country's victory, and because I had seen the sport that I loved—the sport that would change my life—up close and personal. That night, on the way back home, my still-adolescent mind swore never to miss another World Cup.

Pablo Dorado opens the scoring for Uruguay in the final of the first
World Cup, in Centenario stadium, Montevideo, Uruguay. Uruguay beat
Argentina, 4–2.

Jules Rimet, FIFA's first president, presents the winner's trophy to Raul
Jude, president of the Uruguayan Football Association.

Belgian referee John Langenus and his peculiar choice of attire for the first final.

3

The first World Cup champions: Uruguay, 1930.

4

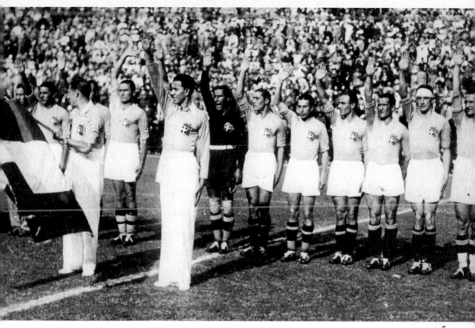

A sign of the times: Before the 1934 final, the Italian team pays homage to Benito Mussolini with the traditional fascist salute.

Italian coach Vittorio Pozzo with his players after capturing their second consecutive World Cup, this time in France, 1938.

Larry Gaetjens scores the lone goal that gave the United States the upset over England in the 1950 World Cup.

Obdulio Varela, Uruguay's legendary captain, in 1950. His team's championship victory over Brazil, know as the "Maracanazo," was the greatest soccer upset of all time.

The final whistle sounds in the Maracana. Uruguay is champion!
Schubert Gambetta goes after the game ball while the defeated Brazilians
look on in disbelief.

Alcides Ghiggia's shot beats Brazilian goalkeeper Barbosa, giving
Uruguay the win in the 1950 final.

The captain of the former West Germany, Fritz Walter, holding the Cup his team earned by beating Hungary in 1954.

11

Pele in his first World Cup. Only seventeen years old, he scored in the final against Sweden and Brazil became world champion.

12

Brazil, champions in 1958 with the young Pele and Zagallo.

A rare save against Frenchman Just Fontaine. Fontaine scored thirteen goals on his way to becoming goal-scoring champion of the 1958 Cup.

15   "Because we have nothing, we will do everything." The immortal phrase of Carlos Dittborn—father of the 1962 World Cup in Chile—defined the spirit of that tournament.

"Mane" Garrincha celebrating after a goal in the 1962 World Cup.

One of the most memorable games of the 1966 World Cup: England versus Argentina in Wembley, featuring the controversial ejection of Argentine captain Antonio Rattin.   16

17

Everybody's out to get Pele. The Portuguese accomplish that objective and a badly injured Pele is taken out of the 1966 World Cup.

Yet another controversy for the English: The infamous "phantom" goal of the 1966 final. It would be proven years later that Hurst's shot never crossed the goal line.

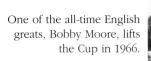

One of the all-time English greats, Bobby Moore, lifts the Cup in 1966.

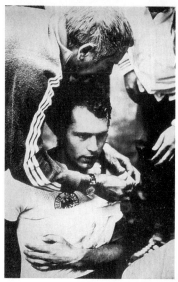

In one of the most emotional games of the 1970 World Cup, Germany beat England and Franz Beckenbauer played with a separated shoulder. This improvised sling allowed him to finish the game.

21

Pele, in all his glory, taking a victory lap after winning his third World Cup in Mexico, 1970.

22

Dutchman Johan Cruyff is tackled in the penalty area during the final
against Germany in 1974. Germany would emerge victorious.

Mario Kempes of Argentina not only scored two goals in the 1978 final
against Holland but was also the leading scorer of the tournament. 24

The culmination of a work of art. The most beautiful goal ever scored in the history of the World Cup: Diego Maradona's second against England in 1986.

Diego Maradona's finest hour, 1986.

Germany's 1990 victory lap, led by their great captain Lothar Matthaus. Germany beat Argentina 1–0 in the final.

Diego Maradona cries upon receiving the second place medal after the 1990 final.

Brazil's Romario, the best player of the 1994 World Cup, battles Franco
Baresi, one of the greatest Italian players of all time.

Diego Maradona, all smiles, being led to the doping control center after
Argentina's match against Nigeria in the 1994 World Cup.

Those damn penalty kicks! Baresi of Italy missing his shot. Brazil won the shoot-out and became World Cup champion in 1994.

A young Andrés Cantor and his encounter with Dutch great Johan Cruyff on the streets of Pasadena. The author was playing for his high school team while Cruyff was heading the Los Angeles Aztecs of the North American Soccer League.

An unforgettable moment! The author kisses the coveted World Cup statue during the raffle in Las Vegas before the 1994 tournament.

33

Andrés Cantor and David Letterman yell "Goooal!" together during the author's visit to *The Late Show with David Letterman*.

34

MARIO KEMPES
(Argentina)
Argentina 1978

It's amazing. Now more than forty years old, Mario Alberto Kempes still maintains many of the features that made him famous, different, and unique: his long hair, for example, topping his tall, elongated body. His passion as well, because he always keeps putting off his definitive retirement from soccer, leaving the impression that it will never take place. His strength isn't the same, of course, but that's what matters the least. The "Matador," that relentless goal-scorer who became known worldwide after "his" World Cup, Argentina 1978, takes soccer one day at a time, and it seems that it will be that way forever. At least that's what's implied by his own profound words: "The World Cup? The World Cup doesn't last forever."

A.C.: In any case, that surely must be the best memory of your soccer career.

M.K.: Of course. That 1978 Argentine national team reached the peak. There was a lot at stake, and the mission was completed. I'm not talking about politics, because I've never been interested in politics; I'm speaking only of soccer . . . and that was a serious, responsible, ordered process.

A.C.: What was the influence of coach Cesar Luis Menotti?

M.K.: He turned out to be the ideal coach for the group. Not only because he was a great motivator but, more than anything, because he had great character. He was one of the best coaches I've had in my career, and remember that I haven't been coached by just anyone: Alfredo Di Stefano, Helenio Herrera, Carlos Griguol. He was the one who created balance in a roster full of stars, of amazing individual talent. Cesar was very clear. For example, the talk before the game against Holland only lasted four minutes. He gathered us around him two hours before in the training camp; he told us to think about our fans, that the only ones who had to worry about anything were our opponents, and that was it . . . on to the game.

A.C.: In light of that, we should talk about some related things. Some people, for example, talk of the six goals made against Peru with a certain amount of irony. . . .

M.K.: Had we needed ten or twelve goals, we would have made them. No one understands that we weren't afraid of anything, that, for us, nothing was impossible.

A.C.: Did you also feel that way before the final against Holland?

M.K.: It was different, but also life or death. We had gotten there taking the tournament one game at a time. Never did we count our chickens before they were hatched. It's probably because of that that we came back so well after the loss against Italy, which made us have to go play our second round games in Rosario.

A.C.: There weren't even any doubts when Dutch forward Resenbrink hit the post in the last minute of regulation?

M.K.: It was a paralyzing moment, which we instantly recovered from.

Among the other traits that haven't changed, there is also his simplicity, which fame has not altered. His original accent, from his native Córdoba, in the center of Argentina, long ago made way for his typical Spanish way of speaking, which he picked up in his adopted country. On his return to South America, he settled in the Argentine South, in beautiful Mendoza. There he organized a soccer school with another big star of 1978, Leopoldo Jacinto Luque, and every now and then he crosses the border into Chile where he indulges in his vice of kicking a ball around.

A.C.: Mario, was that the peak of your career?

M.K.: Maybe, but in my career as a player for Valencia, I had periods as good as that one. In truth, it all had to do with confidence: I knew that when I faced my opponents, I would beat them. I felt indomitable. Although no one remembers it now, I began Argentina 1978 playing badly, out of position, not having any contact with the ball. I talked it over with Menotti, and we came to the conclusion that I was playing out of position. I was too advanced, I needed to accelerate from further behind, to be able to beat defenders with my power. In the first game, against Hungary, he had put me as left wing. I didn't play well, so against France I played as a classic "number ten": That's when everything changed for the better.

A.C.: So you were champion and leading scorer. Was it just the way you had imagined it?

M.K.: No way! Never! I only wanted to play. And I'll tell you even more: I didn't even know I was the top scorer until later in the hotel. I didn't even keep count of the goals I was scoring!

A.C.: You must have seen it a thousand times since. . . .

M.K.: Never. I don't even have a videotape. I have them all taped in my head. It all hit me a month later, after I returned to Valencia. It was then that I understood that we had paved the road for the birth of Argentine soccer. All the victories that came after can be traced to that title.

A.C.: It's true, Mario, although you also lived through the disappointment of Spain 1982, your third World Cup, only four years later.

M.K.: Of course, and I think that that's the saddest memory of my career. We thought we were the best without having to show it on the field. We lacked professionalism, and it showed. I hope no one gets offended, but it's the truth. We weren't able to focus like in 1978 when we were really hungry for glory.

He once said: "I don't need to go out in the street with a name tag on my chest that says 'Mario Kempes.' I don't want it, and I don't need it because I've always wanted to keep some anonymity. It's something I have to have."

He once expounded on his soccer philosophy: "Its essence lies in its boldness, in not holding back, in prioritizing, in listening to the opinion of the fan, who is the one who has to put up with this whole soccer thing. I don't want to preach reformism—nothing of the sort—I'm just saying what I think. Most people think that if you play beautiful soccer, you play well. I don't agree, because if I don't win, I'm not playing well. You know what I mean?"

The past will always give way to the present, but when it comes to soccer, Mario Kempes seems more at home in the past than anywhere else.

Spain 1982

At this point, the big soccer show had also become big business, and it was treated as such. In truth, this is what FIFA's ambitious officials seemed to be after, instead of the ideal that Jules Rimet had dreamed of. The twelfth World Cup combined both—business and the ideal of soccer.

Of course, the choice of venue helped quite a bit. World Cup Spain was a party—as their style dictated—and also a financial success as a consequence of the new way of playing. This Cup had it all: from the warmth of its streets and its people, to the heated competition; from the rush of the crowds to enjoy a show that had become universal, to the increased number of participating countries attracting their fans to this beautiful spot on Earth.

It just so happens that this favorite European summer spot, which is the Iberian peninsula, had to stretch itself to the max to become a host worthy of this milestone World Cup: No longer would there be only sixteen teams competing for the prize in the final round; now twenty-four would be admitted. Soccer's map would expand, following the wishes of FIFA's president, Joao Havelange, who happily gave in to pressure in exchange for the votes that kept him in office. Thus, two Asian representatives, two African representatives, and two CONCACAF representatives would boost the presence of continents with weaker soccer teams while also increasing the political leverage of Havelange throughout the world. On the other hand, Europe did not lose out either. After reappraising their situation, they demanded—and got—fourteen spots. They all got there, of course, because the limit had been expanded.

In South America, Argentina was being bled almost to death in an absurd war against England, but not even this could keep the champion of the last tournament from competing in the Cup, to which it automatically qualified thanks to its title of defending champion. In Europe, the unpleasant aftertaste of the Italian soccer scandal for match-fixing in the Italian league championship, which led to the exemplary suspensions of star players like Paolo Rossi and Bruno Giordano, sent shock waves throughout the entire continent.

The world was utterly dismayed by two unsuccessful assassination attempts—against the lives of United States President Ronald Reagan and Pope John Paul II—as well as one that hit its target, costing Egyptian President Anwar Sadat his life. Color television had reached all corners of the world, and big networks fought over a new market: television rights. For millions of television viewers, the main attractions were in South America, which possessed a matchless constellation of stars: Zico, Junio, Socrates, and Toninho Cerezo for the Brazilians; Maradona, Ramon Diaz, Kempes, and Passarella for the Argentines. These names were an invitation to dream, even though the beginning of the tournament produced nightmares.

Few World Cup competitions generated as much controversy as Spain 1982, and one needs to focus only on the first round to find out why. The twenty-four teams that made up the tournament were divided into six groups of four each, with the top two of each group qualifying for the next round.

Group 1, playing in Vigo and La Coruña, on Spain's Atlantic coast, gave rise to the first suspicions. Poland emerged as the clear-cut winner, grabbing the top spot of the group after one victory (5–1 against Peru), two draws, and a show of talent from a giant who had already filled soccer fields all over Europe: Zbigniew Boniek. Peru also remained outside the controversy, but for other reasons: They were above suspicion, given that Cubillas, Cueto, and Oblitas could not perform as they did four years before, leaving Peru with a lackluster showing in Spanish lands. But dark clouds of suspicion enveloped Italy and Cameroon: Neither of them had lost, but they hadn't won either; and they had finished with an identical goal difference. The group standings showed an identical three draws for each, but a slight difference tipped the scales in favor of the Europeans: The scoring of one more goal gave them their pass to the next round. With the World Cup barely over, two Italian journalists wrote a book, *Mundial Gate* (World Cup Gate), which disclosed the fixing of the final match, against the Africans. Keeping in mind the Italians' prior history—the soap opera that they had recently gone through—things didn't look very hopeful. But in soccer nothing is ever carved in stone until the referee blows the final whistle. As it were, those Italian players, which included the reappearance of Paolo Rossi after his long suspension, resolved to take a drastic step. With all the rumors circling, they decided not to talk to the press. So what was to be known worldwide in its original Italian as *silenzio stampa* (silence to the press) was born.

Group 2 had Gijón and Oviedo, in North Central Spain, as its stage. There too, surprise and indignation mixed. But first things first: Algeria beat Germany and provided the resounding upset present in every World Cup. The team that included Madjer and Belloumi showed the best in African soccer, which was, of course, positively influenced by South American soccer. Good play and an attacking game, coupled with a cool "nothing to lose" attitude, were the reasons behind a victory widely celebrated throughout Spain, like every victory of an underdog over a favorite. Afterward, Algeria lost against Austria, but beat the Chileans—who left the tournament with three losses—making the final game of the group, between Germany and Austria, decisive. If the Austrians were to win or, if the game were to end in a draw, the Africans would automatically pass to the next round. Unfortunately, that game between those two European teams is now remembered as one of the most embarrassing moments in the history of this great sport. Ten minutes into the game, the gigantic Hrubesch put the Germans out in front. After that, the game died. And with the game, a bit of soccer also died. All three teams finished with an equal number of points and, because of a better goal difference, the two Europeans advanced to the next round. They left the Gijón stadium accompanied by the boos of the spectators, who threw white handkerchiefs in the air, in protest. As a result, FIFA would make rule changes to ensure that this would never happen again.

Group 3, set in Barcelona, Elche, and Alicante, started with something like a surprise, and then nothing happened beyond the expected. The days of the Dutch "Clockwork Orange" were over, but Belgium's "Red Devils" were in full swing, with the splendid Jean Marie Pfaff guarding the goalposts, Eric Gerets in the back, and Jan

Ceulemans on the attack. They beat the Argentine stars, among which was one who shone more brightly than the rest in the eyes of the public: Diego Armando Maradona.

This "number ten" had already been bought by powerful Barcelona in a $7 million transfer, and an incredible amount of pressure was placed on his young shoulders. His fame required him to play better than anyone and was also a warning light for his opponents: They began to guard him like no one else. The Hungarians, true to their style, didn't and paid the consequences: The Argentineans won 4–1, displaying brilliant soccer, with two goals by Diego. El Salvador opted for a more violent defense and, even with the limitations inherent in that approach, at least got to lose by a smaller margin: 2–0. Perhaps the game served to make the Argentineans' opponents pay attention and see how to defend the men guided by Cesar Luis Menotti. Moreover, the Argentine team seemed to have a built-in advantage: Most of the starting lineup was the same as four years before, making the relationship between players and coach more like that between friends and the hunger for glory (except among the younger players) no longer the same.

The Hungarians won a place in the record books for making more goals in one game than any other team in World Cup history, in a 10–1 win over El Salvador, but were left with the pain of being unable to advance to the second round, even after tying the group leader, Belgium.

Group 4 was centered in Bilbao and Valladolid. It fell to the Basques to deal with a task that was starting to be problematic for everybody, and that would be repeated in the next few tournaments: receiving the English fans. The now-famous "hooligans" were capable of engaging in all kinds of mischief, consuming alcohol, and provoking violence. The team of the eternal masters passed through the first round without any problems, scoring three wins in three games. The great duel was with France, in a clash that seemed to go beyond the playing field. As sometimes happens, the anthems sung before the commencement of the game smacked of false patriotism—beyond mere emotion—which resulted in mixed feelings. What is certain is that the soccer battle left a clear winner: England. That team included the natural heir of Gordon Banks in goal—Peter Shilton—and men from midfield forward who knew how to play . . . and think: Glenn Hoddle, Trevor Francis, and Raymond Wilkins. Unfortunately, as often happens because of the timing of the World Cup, the big star of English soccer in the 1970s,

Kevin Keegan, was already on the decline and could only put in a ninety-minute appearance.

The French, before tying with the Czechoslovakians, whose team appeared far from the glory that had made it a World Cup finalist, experienced one of the unique moments of Spain 1982. It represented the universality that the event was beginning to acquire. France, with the great Michel Platini among its starting eleven, faced Kuwait, coached by Carlos Alberto Perreira, in Valladolid. A win for the Europeans was what had been predicted, but then the play happened: Platini himself played the ball to Alain Giresse—that small giant—who took advantage of the distracted rival defense and scored. Immediately, the Kuwaitis complained to the referee because, according to them, they had heard a whistle and thought the ball was dead. The referee, Stupar, paid no mind to the protests, until he saw a man wearing a turban and a tunic enter the field. It was sheik Fahd Al-Ahmad, president of Kuwait's soccer federation. He then took the lead in protest against the referee, and the Russian official responded with an unprecedented action: He took back his call, canceling the goal. In spite of this, France won 4–1, and Stupar was later ousted from FIFA.

Group 5, stationed in Valencia and Zaragoza, was the luckiest draw a host team could hope for. Spain's rivals were Yugoslavia, Northern Ireland, and Honduras, all of them beatable on paper. But, once again, soccer showed that it is the least predictable of sports. With the crowd (and the referees?) favoring them, the home team suffered incredibly on their path to the next round. "They aren't even furious," said a witty journalist, alluding to the classic characteristic of Spanish teams. What is certain is that Argentine referee Arturo Iturralde had to call a penalty so Spain could score its equalizer against Honduras, twenty-five minutes before the final whistle. The Central Americans were reaching the pinnacle of glory in their soccer history, aided by the spectacular work of a man who would later emigrate to European soccer: Gilberto Yearwood. Afterward, against Yugoslavia—coached by Miljan Miljanjic, who had occupied the same post at Real Madrid—Spain fell behind once again on a tenth-minute goal by Gudelj, who would later star at Deportivo La Coruna. Spain then equalized on a strange penalty, called by Danish referee Lund Sorensen, even though the foul took place almost a full meter outside the penalty area. It took two tries for the kick itself to enter the goal. Spain ended up winning that one, only to lose (1–0) in its final game of the first round, against the winner of the group: Northern Ireland, which advanced with headers, in the classic British style. Within their ranks was the youngest player in the tournament, the eighteen-year-old Norman Whiteside.

Group 6 featured a team that could count on an instant fan base as soon as it touched the soil of beautiful Seville: Brazil. The Brazilians also saw their debut assisted by favors from the referee—in this case, a Spaniard named Lamo Castillo—and the victim was a national team that would have to get used to the injustice: the Soviet Union. What was also clear was that the Brazilians didn't need anyone's help. Even with the traditional advantage they offered by handicapping themselves with a terrible goalkeeper—this time Valdir Peres—they could still outplay anyone who crossed their path—the Soviet Union (2–1), Scotland (4–1), and New Zealand (4–0)—with the accuracy of their splendid play, headed by Tele Santana and executed by Leandro, Junior, Falcao, Socrates, Toninho Cerezo, Zico, and Eder. In a comparison of questionable taste, he was nicknamed "The Exocet" (after a missile used at that time in the Falkland Islands War) because of the power of his shots. In spite of the loss, the Soviets beat out Scotland, for a spot in the second round, on goal difference (they were both tied with three points), helped by the fact that they claimed the best goalkeeper in Europe within their ranks: Rinat Dassaiev. Mindful of that, one of the clubs from the city in which the goalkeeper shone—Seville—acquired his services. Today, however, Dassaiev walks through the capital of Andalucia without much fanfare, since his performance in the Spanish league was a true fiasco, and he never again felt welcome back in his country.

These things happen in the World Cup, where the most powerful clubs allow themselves to be dazzled blind by the fleeting brilliance of a star. Dassaiev is just one example out of many, showing why players aim for the World Cup as their top career objective: There is no better, bigger showcase for one's talents.

The results of the first round left ten European and two South American teams in the race. These numbers reflect the reality of the situation: South American teams were in the minority, something that will not change even by the time France 1998 comes around with its thirty-two participating nations.

But let's go back to 1982. The second round was set up as four groups of three teams each. The first team in each group would be a semifinalist. The format was profitable, but suspect. It was clearly ripe for negotiations, which had already begun.

In Group A, played in Barcelona, the main encounter occurred between Poland and the Soviet Union. The Belgian "Red Devils" had almost totally faded, as if they had used all their strength to relegate Argentina to second place in the first round. Both Eastern European teams beat the Belgians before tying without score amongst themselves, causing the Poles to break into the semifinals (they had beaten Belgium by more goals than the Soviet Union had). Once again, Boniek stood out among the rest. It was the only noteworthy thing in this group . . . the best action was elsewhere.

In Group B, set in Madrid, Spain could no longer fool anyone. Germany advanced true to their style: After heating up the motor, they stepped on the gas, beating Spain decisively and playing England to a scoreless tie. It was enough to place them among the four best in the world.

Group C was the "group of death" that every World Cup is lucky enough to have. There, three memorable games took place, which are all worthwhile reliving.

Argentina–Italy. Once again a clash of different styles. The Argentineans arrived amidst a storm of rumors that they weren't completely focused on the business at hand. Menotti employed the same defense that had helped him to the title four years before, but the years had passed in vain. Fillol in goal, Olguin and Tarantini guarding each flank, and Galvan and Passarella in the middle. Except for "the Great Captain," Passarella, they were simply not the same players they had been four years before. And Maradona was there. . . . The Italians arrived more silently than ever, because of all the criticisms they had received—justly since, until that point, Italy and Spain were the worst teams still in the tournament. So the Italians were continuing their vow of silence as far as the press was concerned. It was their fourth game, but there was still no sign of Bruno Conti's feats or Paolo Rossi's goals. The encounter could therefore be summarized, like so many others, as the duel between two men: Maradona and Gentile, talent at its peak against systematic guarding. Guarding won, although it wasn't limited to normal defense: Bumps, slaps, and systematic fouls took Maradona out of the game while Tardini gave Italy the lead, and Cabrini increased it. Passarella, with a greatness that knew no bounds, narrowed the lead six minutes from the end, but his pride was not enough. The Argentine national team went on to face Brazil, no less.

Brazil–Argentina. The only two South American teams prepared to eliminate each other, and one did so in a game that maintained the South American touch. It was a very well-played match, with many scoring opportunities and a great deal of emotion. Zico tipped the scales in favor of the Brazilians twelve minutes in, but it was necessary to wait another hour until Serginho increased the lead. That's when Argentina broke down.

Junior made the game 3–0 and Ramon Diaz, showing his talent in what would be his last World Cup, narrowed the lead one minute from the end. For Argentina, an adventure marked by controversy was over: Diego Maradona had been ejected, after reacting unprofessionally to a foul on his friend and teammate Juan Barbas. That was the ending of what was supposed to be "his" World Cup. Right then, as he left the field with his head down, consoled by Tarantini, he must have sworn to himself that he would have his revenge. . . . Meanwhile, I was in the midst of a battle myself: the battle between the fan in me and the journalist in me. On that hot afternoon in Sarria my passion took control over my objectivity, and I almost traded fists with those who made fun of Diego's sadness, which was my sadness, too.

For Brazil, it was another win in their march toward the title. Judging by what they believed and what had been seen on the field until then, everything else was little more than nominal. In their way was Italy, with their eternal internal conflicts.

Italy–Brazil. This was the true duel of the championship. Soccer with a smile against soccer with a frown. *Jogo bonito* (beautiful play) versus *catenaccio* (defensive tactics). Five minutes into the game came a goal by Paolo Rossi, the man in whom coach Enzo Bearzot had placed his faith, even after his long inactivity due to suspension. The king of rebounds was beginning to try on his crown. To show how much he deserved it, he responded in his own way to two Brazilian masterpieces: Twelve minutes in, Socrates tied the game; at twenty-five minutes, Rossi again tipped the scales in favor of Italy; at sixty-eight minutes, Falcao evened the match again; at seventy-five minutes, Paolo closed the score to complete the upset. Brazil continued its streak as "moral champion," since its last true championship, Mexico 1970, was already in the far reaches of memory. The 1982 team played so well that, even before the game against the Italians, the players' main concern was what part of Brazil they would land in after their World Cup win. For their part, the Italians brought about a change: They were no longer considered the worst.

Group D, in Madrid, was the most uneven. France was too much for Austria (1–0), which was now paying for its first-round sin, and for Northern Ireland (4–1), which had gotten to that stage only because Spain had been in their first-round group. That French team was at the peak of a golden generation. They played in the Brazilian style in almost every sense: They had a weak goalkeeper, Ettori, and great talent from the back line to the front line; Amoros, a back with the class of a midfielder; Tressor, the Black central defender who played like a gladiator; and Giresse, Tigana, and Platini, the creators. They deserved to be in the semifinal and were poised to play one of the best games in history.

Germany–France was one of those games that exemplifies why soccer arouses such passion. It had it all, good and bad. It was played in Seville on July 8, 1982, and it is necessary (now more than ever) to go into specifics, so it can be seen as the historical milestone that it was.

On one side, the French "champagne" game was rich in refined skill. On the other side was the machinelike game of the Germans, with an overwhelming display of physical strength and endurance as well as a precise tactical plan. On one side: Ettori; Amoros, Bossis, Tresor, Janvion; Genghini, Giresse, Tigana, Platini; Rocheteau, Six. On the other side: Schumacher; Kaltz, Stielike, Karl-Heinz Foerster, Briegel; Bernd Foerster, Breitner, Dremmler, Magath; Littbarski, Fischer.

Littbarski put Germany ahead eighteen minutes in, and Platini equalized nine minutes later, on a penalty. With that same score, they got to the end of regulation after ninety minutes of soccer played at a hellish, back-and-forth pace, with no sign of either giving in. Once again, overtime would be necessary. Wasn't that ideal for the supreme physical condition of the Germans? No. France surprised them. First Tresor and then Giresse charged forward to put the French ahead 3–1 to the devastation of the Germans. Game over? Not quite. Remember, the French were facing Germany and, if World Cup tournaments teach us anything, it's that the Germans give up only after the referee blows the final whistle, and Dutch referee Corver had not yet done so. Fischer first and then Rummenigge made the game 3–3, leaving the fans in the Seville stadium and millions of television viewers with their mouths hanging open, awaiting a penalty kick tie-breaker that would have the same dramatic tone as the first 120 minutes. But before that, there was a shameful incident: Just past the ten-minute mark of the overtime, Frenchman Battiston—who had just come in—went for a ball that was falling like a bomb onto the German penalty area. Schumacher went off his line and intentionally crashed into his opponent, knocking him unconscious. Battiston had to be carried away on a stretcher before the unremorseful perpetrator, who was not even booked. Later, however, he would get another kind of punishment: Back in Germany, he was scorned by the public and even lost out on huge endorsement deals that he had signed.

The other interesting case is that of Karl-Heinz Rummenigge. The top star of his country's soccer struggled through the World Cup but, at crucial moments, he always responded in the most welcome way, with goals. That's how it went in Spain 1982, and that's how it would go in Mexico 1986. But would that be enough for Germany?

It was the first penalty kick tie-breaker ever. At that time, it seemed like the best answer. The "golden goal" or "sudden death" had not yet been invented. The debate as to whether penalty kicks are a fair way to decide a game or whether it is just all luck was just starting. Yet, no matter where one stood on the issue, it was hard to deny that they were exciting. . . . When Stielike's turn came to kick, his shot was saved by Ettori. The Germans were left kneeling on the ground, holding their faces in their hands, crying for their pass to the next round, which seemed to be gone. But it didn't go that way. Immediately after Stielike, the Frenchman Six also missed his opportunity as did his compatriot Bossis, sending Germany to the final.

In the other semifinal, Bearzot's Italy easily defeated a conformist Poland. After having beat the Brazilians, everything else seemed perfunctory to the *azzurri*, who forced a definitive change in the way they were described: No longer was the Italian press begging their national team to return home to avoid being embarrassed.

And so, as it sometimes happens in the World Cup, the two teams that had played the best soccer—Brazil and France—were out of the race for the title; the two teams for whom the first round had been a nightmare were to fight for the Cup. It had only been a month before, but it seemed like ages since Italy made it to the second round thanks to making one more goal than Cameroon with suspicions of foul play to boot. Also only one month previous, Germany had lost to Algeria, before beating Austria in a shameful game.

Italy had been the worst but, little by little, it transformed itself into the best. It played with a style that its men had known almost since birth. It was called "the module." It was based on the following outline, naming both its positions and players. A sweeper would sweep away anything that got through the defense (known as a *batidore libero* in Italy, and as *libero* worldwide). This position was filled by Gaetano Scirea, maybe the best of all time until the appearance of Franco Baresi. In front of him were three defenders, with one guarding the most dangerous enemy striker man-to-man, as a "stopper." This job fell to Claudio Gentile, Maradona's nemesis in the game against Argentina. Midfield was composed of two enforcers (among whom Tardelli stood out the most): a playmaker or *regista*—Antognoni until his injury, and Oriali afterward; and an *ala tornante*[1] who would be a key to the team's collective play—Bruno Conti. In front of them were two classic strikers, one of whom was an insatiable goal-scorer: Paolo Rossi.

That system failed in the first round because terrible individual play could not effectively support it. It was successful after men like Tardelli, Rossi, and Conti returned to form. Yet to be fully successful it would have to pass one final test against the German "panzers" with their historic character and chronic internal conflicts, always concealed behind their classic organization. Coach Jupp Derwall had lost his authority, and those on the field were boss. An unusual final . . .

In a head-to-head encounter between two Europeans, it was easy to read the strategies. Bearzot sent Scirea as sweeper, and Bergomi—a young Inter star who would later symbolize the *calcio*—would guard Rummenigge, with whom he would later play at Inter. Gentile was placed on Littbarski, and Collovati on Fischer. Cabrini, a defender who controlled the ball well, was given more freedom to move up his flank while midfielders Tardelli, Oriali, and Marini were mobilized, although without fixed positions. Bearzot could no longer count on Antognoni, tragically injured. On the other side, Derwall attempted to take care of Rossi by putting in Karl Heinz Foerster—a player reminiscent of a German guard dog—and reserved what was at this point the toughest job, guarding the tireless Bruno Conti, for Hans Peter Briegel, a true tank. With things arranged in that way, the game started almost like a chess match. Seven minutes in, a Breitner tackle took Graziani, Italy's "other" striker, out of the game. Right away, the incomparable Conti was tripped by Briegel,

[1]*Ala tornante:* "a wing that goes back and forth" Italian.

and Brazilian referee Coelho—the only South American participant left in the tournament—made the obvious call: penalty. Everyone expected Rossi to take it, but Cabrini did so instead. Everyone awaited a goal, but the defender got more grass than ball, and it went inches past the post. No one expected Italy to recover, but it didn't go as expected.

With Italian president Sandro Pertini looking on from the royal box, sitting next to King Juan Carlos and Queen Sofia as just another *tifoso*,[2] and with thousands of Italian fans spurring their team on from the stands, Rossi opened the score at fifty-seven minutes, to crown himself top scorer of the World Cup and to finish a story that seemed made for TV: dead yesterday from a terrible, if deserved, suspension; resurrected today like a good kid in the movies who learned from his mistakes. Eleven minutes later, another magic scene: a goal by everybody's partner and laborer, Marco Tardelli, made it 2–0 and his emotional celebration became yet another illustration of the passion that soccer awakens. Finally, at eighty-one minutes, Altobelli caused a delirium that not even Breitner's late goal could overshadow.

Spain's World Cup ended in full Italian style. Like a dramatic opera, it had an unexpected finale: Those who once had been considered an embarrassment were now the heroes, and they returned to their country in the presidential jet. Once again, the reality of the score had made its mark. Once again—like Holland in 1974—the best memories were provided by a loser: Brazil. It was a fact that didn't bother the Italians, who became the second national team—after Brazil—to claim a distinguished title: three-time World Champion.

---

[2] *Tifoso:* "fan" in Italian.

PAOLO ROSSI
(Italy)
Spain 1982

Soccer changed his name. His parents had named him Paolo but, after the world had seen his goals, he was rechristened Pablito. This change is among the best World Cup memories of Paolo Rossi, who at the age of thirty-nine is no longer living a life dominated by a soccer ball. Paolo has many businesses; among them a custom jewelry store in his native Vicenza. He only thinks about the ball when tribute games are organized or during the World Cup . . . for seniors.

My best World Cup memory? Well, there are many. Needless to say, the win in Spain 1982 is unforgettable: champion, leading scorer. It's crazy. But casting aside the results, which rule our world, I can say that the most pleasant memory for me was the training camp before World Cup 1978, the one in Argentina. In those days I was twenty-one years old, I had just played my first Series A game and knew the world more by way of the geography classes I took in school than by my own travels. The very act of traveling opened my mind. I remember how fascinating it was to be located in the Hindu Club, and, of course, I remember the first goal I scored for the national team. It was in Mar del Plata city stadium, after France got ahead 1–0, fifty seconds into the game, thanks to a goal made by Lacombe. A half hour passed and, thanks to a rebound as would happen many times in my career, I made the tying goal . . . me! A kid who had replaced an Italian soccer legend like Francesco Graziani. Finally, we won 2–1, and the World Cup continued as if it were a dream: beating Argentina, no less, and in Buenos Aires! I participated in the decisive play, giving a heel pass to Bettega, for him to put the ball in the net. . . . Losing the semifinal to Holland was a shame. But I knew it was only a matter of time, that "my" World Cup was yet to come.

Although it may seem contradictory, "Pablito's" worst memories deal with Spain 1982.

> It's that, when it started, I was a disaster. I'll go even further, I deserved to be left off the team. . . . But what hurt me the most was an article that was published in Italy, in which something strange was insinuated about my relationship with Antonio Cabrini, with whom I shared a room. Afterward, although a bit too late, the journalist attempted to clear up the misunderstanding: it so happened that all the wives of the players had arrived at the training camp, except for ours, who had decided to wander around Spain a little more. Therefore, the journalist had nothing better to do than to write, "Poor Pablito had no other option but to console himself with Cabrini." And whoever titled that article added a bit too much . . . color to it. I threatened to sue, but then everything was resolved.

It resolved itself so well that the World Cup that began as a nightmare ended up being a dream come true. The headlines of the Italian newspapers that read VERGOGNA ("Shame") at the beginning now screamed out CAMPIONI ("Champions"). It was almost like the personal history of Paolo Rossi, "Pablito," who, besides leaving behind more than one rival defender, left behind the unavoidable pain of a match-fixing suspension and the doubts surrounding his infrequent participation in the team's play. . . . It wound up being infrequent, but not ineffective: Whenever he touched the ball, it went in.

Soccer, pure and simple. And the soccer of tomorrow?

> I don't think it will change much in the future. Of course, there are improvements, in strategies and in rules, but soccer—and even more so in the World Cup—goes on like nothing ever changed. Sure there are some trends: an upsurge in African soccer, speculations about the Japanese or perhaps now the United States . . . but the fact is that the traditional big teams have made it to the finals of the last four World Cups: Italy–Germany, Argentina–Germany, Germany–Argentina, Brazil–Italy. Without a doubt, the more things change, the more they stay the same.

Mexico 1986

Sixteen years later, soccer returned to a previous venue for the big international show. Mexico proudly stood up to say that it was the first country to host the World Cup twice. Last time around, in 1970, it had crowned Pele as king; this time, in 1986, it prepared itself to anoint his successor.

When Mexico took over as organizer of the tournament after Colombia's withdrawal, no one could have predicted the tragedy that would befall them. One and a half years before play was scheduled to begin, Mexico suffered the wrath of nature: An earthquake opened up huge gashes in its land and was particularly merciless with Mexico City, home to Azteca stadium, Mexico's soccer temple.[1]

Everyone contributed to the effort to forge ahead, and that smog-ridden city managed to lift its head and lead the rest of the country, from Toluca to Puebla, from Neza to Guadalajara.

The Mexicans were ready to receive, for example, World Champion Italy. But Bearzot had repeated the mistake made by almost every past world champion: clinging to the past, keeping the men who had attained yesterday's glory . . . while today called for something else. They were also prepared to receive France. In the highest splendor of their generation and with the championship of Europe around their waist, Michel Platini and his teammates arrived to finish their cycle by placing the last, most important jewel in their crown.

[1]Azteca stadium, site of the 1970 and 1986 World Cup finals, is home to Mexican clubs America, Cruz Azul, and Necaxa.

From the other side of the world came the three giants of South America. Argentina, Brazil, and Uruguay arrived with big names and changes under way. While Carlos Salvador Bilardo's innovative ideas raised dust clouds of controversy in Argentine soccer, he silently awaited the final results of Mexico 1986 to speak for him. What he proposed was simple yet revolutionary for a country that carries this sport in its blood: Add order and tactical discipline—European characteristics—to natural talent, leaving not even the most minor detail to chance. The Brazilians—"moral champions" four years earlier—kept the leadership of a Tele Santana, still surrounded by controversy. The torcedores[2] were not satisfied with their team playing as well as the best; they wanted them to be the absolute best and to bring back the World Cup as proof. The Uruguayans also presented a golden generation of players, led by Enzo Francescoli, the brightest star in the Argentine league, playing for a River Plate on its way to world soccer supremacy.

In truth, almost everyone was there. Almost, because Holland, now far from the glories of "total football," was missing its second consecutive World Cup. North America was represented by Canada, as well as Mexico, the host country. Asia, by South Korea and Iraq. Africa, by Morocco and Algeria. Soccer had reached the four corners of the world, and was by now a huge multinational business.

So much so that the competition's structure was again changed. Like in Spain four years earlier, the teams were divided into six groups of four teams, with the top two teams of each group qualifying for the next round. Joining these teams in the second round would be the four best third-place teams of the first round. From the second round on, the tournament would go back to being direct elimination. The new system prevented the possibility of match-fixing—the memory of West Germany–Austria four years earlier was still damaging—and it increased both interest and the number of games, because that was what it was really about: making it attractive for television, which also set the game times. That is why in Mexico, under a scorching sun and at 2,224 meters above sea level, soccer was played at noon. That way, people in Europe could watch it comfortably on TV, nice and cozy at dinnertime. It was—and still is—business. In response, a certain Diego Armando Maradona—joined by another Argentinean, Jorge Valdano, and a

---

[2] *Torcedores* is the common name given to the fans of the Brazilian national team.

Brazilian, Socrates, among others—initiated a protest that would not be listened to by FIFA officials, who were unmoved by their complaints. But Maradona was already at center stage though not because of his words.

Democracy had returned to Argentina, with Dr. Raul Alfonsin as president. The United States had invaded Grenada and its embassy in Beirut had been destroyed. The Challenger had exploded in the air, televised by satellite to the entire world . . . and in Mexico the party was starting.

The first round provided no surprises, but it did give a glimpse of those projecting themselves as contenders.

In Group A, played in Mexico City and Puebla, South Korea was eliminated while Argentina, Italy, and Bulgaria went to the next round, although each with different stories.

Carlos Salvador Bilardo's Argentineans advanced in magnificent form, led by their superb "number ten." They angrily flattened South Korea, whose main resistance was cunning tackles. It was not enough, although Maradona was fouled as much as when he was guarded by Italian defender Gentile four years earlier. The referees continued to ignore him, but the structure surrounding him allowed him to take advantage of his great talent more forcefully: He joined up with Burruchaga to create the plays, and Valdano would join in for the finish. They achieved an important tie against Italy, after falling behind early because of a childish penalty committed by Garre, six minutes into the game. Half an hour later, Maradona completed his first work of art on Mexican soil. Receiving a long pass from Burruchaga that came in from the left, he raced Scirea to the ball and, when everyone thought he would wait for that high ball to drop from the sky to the ground, he did something different, something unusual, something magnificent: He jumped to meet the ball, kicking it at a higher level than any normal soccer player would have, surprising his defender and the goalkeeper, who remained frozen as he watched the unexpected shot enter meekly into the far side of the net. Diego jumped again, but this time in celebration. Later, the *albicelestes*[3] landed two punches on Bulgaria and went on to the second round with ease.

Italy's case was different. The old champion was . . . old. The Ital-

[3] *Albicelestes*, meaning "white and light blues" in Spanish, is a popular nickname given to the Argentine national team, after their traditional shirt—alternating vertical stripes of white and light blue.

ians suffered through the inaugural match against the Bulgarians (1–1), respecting the parity that was beginning to characterize the opening match of the Cup. They tied Argentina by the same score and narrowly defeated South Korea (3–2), which at some point had threatened to do to Italy what their cousins to the north had already done in 1966.

Group B, also in Mexico City as well as in Toluca, had all the local color. Under the guidance of their coach Velibor "Bora" Milutinovic, Mexico had prepared like never before. Its big star—Hugo Sanchez, leading scorer of the Spanish League—was joined by valuable men such as the goalkeeper Larios, defensive marshals Quirarte, creative midfielder Negrete, and popular hero *el Abuelo*[4] Cruz. They were all supported by amazing fans, which showed the world something new: The wave, that coordinated movement that ran through the stands, was the trademark of this World Cup. Things went better for Mexico than for Spain in its World Cup, but don't think it didn't struggle. When the Mexicans won, they won narrowly. They defeated Belgium 2–1 and Iraq 1–0, and tied Paraguay 1–1.

In Group C, set in Irapuato and León, France and the Soviet Union tied each other, but finished off the others. From the outset, the French felt the pressure of being heavy favorites. They never had been, nor would they ever be, ready for that role. It was noticeable in their initial match, against a weak and naive Canada. A super-young Jean Pierre Papin—favorite target of Platini's passes at that time and later a big star at Olympique Marseilles—missed several chances, but converted one, twelve minutes from the end. It was enough to let the French exhale and face with relief—after the tie against the Soviets—a faded Hungary that had nothing in common with its glorious forebears. Mercilessly, they blew them out, 3–0.

The true leader of the group was the Soviet Union, which scored six goals against Hungary and two against Canada. It still had Rinat Dassaiev between the goalposts, men of Kuznetsov's caliber on defense, Zavarov and Alenikov generating its attacks, and Belanov and Protasov providing goals. It was a great team that knew how to enchant the public and surprise it with its austere and restrictive play. It wasn't long after the Cup that, with the opening of political

[4]*El Abuelo* means "the Grandfather" in Spanish.

doors, the majority of those players would spread throughout Europe, with few positive results despite their unquestionable caliber. Their inability to adapt to a different world caused their play to suffer immeasurably.

In Group D, in Guadalajara, Brazil once again played as if it were at home as it had done sixteen years earlier and as it did anywhere in the world. The Brazilians' particularly good diplomatic skills were continued by their new crop of players. Pele, Gerson, Tostao, Jairzinho, and Rivelino were no longer there, but their intermediate stars—Socrates and Junior—were. They were joined by newcomers like Alemao, Careca, and Julio Cesar. Almost as a rite of passage, those who put on the *verdeamarelha*[5] had to respect a certain standard of playing style. For example, they once again played with a mediocre goalkeeper—Carlos; right and left backs who had the soul and characteristics of forwards—Josimar and Branco; central defenders with the ball-control skills and style of midfielders—Julio Cesar and Edinho; midfielders with the spirit of jugglers—Elzo, Alemao, Socrates, and Junior; and forwards who were slaves to the artistic goal—Careca, Muller, and Casagrande. They beat Spain (1–0); they beat Algeria (1–0); they beat Northern Ireland (3–0); and they had a feeling they'd be champions for sure. But that remained to be seen.

Group E, centered in Querétaro and Neza, was called the "group of death." In fact, a name having to do with life would have been more fitting, since we're talking about the opening round's best soccer. In that group three giants would conquer and one giant would fall, because all four teams deserved that description: Denmark and Scotland, because of their recent rise to prominence; and Germany and Uruguay, because of their tradition of excellence. But the competition ended up being less close than people thought it would be. . . .

Denmark's stars shone brighter than any of the others. They were guided from the back by the commanding presence of Morten Olsen, a veteran central defender, who was joined by the spirited play of Soren Lerby, one of the best players of his time. They also had the power of Preben Elkjaer Larsen and the subtle touch of a very young Michael Laudrup, who was just starting on his path, even though he was already a star in the Italian League, defending

---

[5]*Verdeamarelha:* "green and yellow" in Portuguese. It refers to the Brazilian national team jersey, which is comprised of those colors.

the colors of Lazio. Denmark destroyed Uruguay, putting on a spectacular and effective soccer clinic. That 6–1, which exposed the tactical backwardness of the Uruguayans, showed the Danes to be the practitioners of a new kind of soccer. With their flag waving high, they had advanced; with this same flag, they would fall. But more on that later. In spite of that loss, Uruguay joined Denmark in the next round as did Germany, with more shame than glory. It's a fact worth keeping in mind, to see how history repeats itself.

The Germans were now guided by the great Franz Beckenbauer from the outside and by Lothar Matthaus, just starting out, from the inside. In the Mansión Galindo—a Mexican dreamhouse—a place the Germans shared with journalists during press conferences, they once again suffered internal crises. But as is well known, the Germans don't give up until the fat lady sings . . . and there was still a lot of time left until that would happen.

Group F in Monterrey was the only one that took a detour from the predictable. It could have been one of the best . . . instead, it was the worst. It had its favorites . . . but the results reflected the exact opposite. Some of the most passionate fans in Mexico, who expected to see world-quality soccer, remained unfulfilled, because Morocco, England, Poland, and Portugal—the order in which they finished, after one win each and a tie that tipped the scales in favor of the North Africans—showed nothing. The English, always stingy in their contribution to the history of the World Cup, only contributed a smile: that of Gary Linaker, who greatly helped his own cause in search of the Golden Boot, scoring a hat-trick against the Poles. The Poles fielded a sleepy team; not even Boniek managed to wake it up, although it managed to tie the Moroccans and beat the Portuguese. The most pleasant surprise was the performance of the North Africans, who bettered Algeria's record of four years earlier and paved the way for Cameroon four years later. With the talented left foot of Timoumi as the playmaker and the spectacular interventions of Zaki in goal, they took first place in a group that surprised everyone.

The time had come for the changeover. The round of sixteen once again implemented direct elimination, and the spectacular quality of each one of the matches ended up proving that this system was better. Each game had its own special character, and each one was truly memorable because of one particular scene or another. Let's look at them.

Mexico–Bulgaria was the game remembered for Negrete's spectacular goal—perhaps the best goal in the history of the Mexican national team and surely one of the best of that World Cup. It was a scissors kick from the penalty arc, almost two meters off the ground, that rocketed into the near-post corner. Bulgarian goalkeeper Mikhailov had been beaten thirty-five minutes into the match, opening the door to what would be the host's most celebrated victory.

Belgium–Soviet Union was a show-stopper filled with controversy. In fact, it had everything. In terms of play, it was almost entirely dominated by the Soviets, who took the lead on a goal by Igor Belanov—a small, effective striker—at the twenty-eight-minute mark. They suffered a controversial goal by Scifo, fifty-six minutes into the match—Scifo appeared to have been offside but the Soviets recovered with another blast by Belanov after seventy minutes. Then, the Soviets were victimized by another questionable goal— this time by Ceulemans, seventy-six minutes into the game. If Swedish referee Fredriksson's mistakes served any higher purpose, it was to give the world thirty more minutes of the highest-quality soccer. In the overtime the Belgians turned the game around, no longer needing questionable goals: First Demol, then Claesen made Belanov's last effort—a score-narrowing penalty kick—futile. The final score read 4–3, and it is remembered as simply a great game, for better or for worse.

Brazil–Poland . . . could hardly be called a game. With authority, just as in their prior matches—one had been the light of its group, the other the shadow—the South Americans thrashed the Europeans convincingly, 4–0. That Brazilian team put their fullbacks, Josimar and Edhino, in goal-scoring positions as well as their midfielder, Socrates, and of course their forward, Careca.

Argentina–Uruguay was the duel between the two nations of the River Plate—the hour of revenge. Fifty-six years after the battle that decided the 1930 World Cup, the Argentine team finally cashed in on what they were owed. It won in style, with a goal by Pasculli and wonderful performances by Maradona and Valdano. There was some difficulty at the end, when Uruguayan coach Raul (Omar) Borras remembered he had Ruben Paz on the bench and sent him onto the field to complicate matters . . . but it was not enough. Bilardo's men were already well on their way to avenging themselves.

France–Italy was the striking point for two European schools. Michel Platini, who sparkled at Juventus, the reigning monarch of

Italian soccer teams, defended the French colors and took no pity
on his Juventus teammates. He opened the door to victory for the
French and closed it for the Italians, who went home without the
glory or the title they'd won four years earlier. The contribution of
the youngest members of the team—Bergomi, Galderisi, De
Napoli—had not been enough. The French moved on to the next
round.

Germany–Morocco was a match with the only goal scored at the
bitter end. The North Africans were on the verge of performing an
enormous feat, obliging the Germans to go into overtime . . . when
Matthaus proved his ability to score from far out and showed that
the excellent Moroccan goalkeeper Zaki was fallible. It was a goal
one minute from the end, and it was the Germans' pass to the next
round. They were advancing almost by inertia, still with internal
conflicts and an unacceptable game. But they advanced all the
same.

England–Paraguay was an excuse to reconfirm England's position as masters of the game. The British finally demonstrated on the
field the reason for their fame. As the game progressed, their
team—managed by Robson—showed some of the power of the
English clubs: the security Shilton offered in goal, the talent of Hoddle and Beardsley, and the voracious goal-sense of Lineker. It
ended 3–0, and Lineker added two goals to his personal collection.

Spain–Denmark confirmed that, in soccer, there is always a surprise. When Jesper Olsen put the Danes ahead 1–0, thirty-three
minutes into the match, anyone could have predicted what was
coming next. When this same Jesper Olsen made a mistake ten
minutes later deep in his own territory—where every mistake ex-
acts a high cost—by giving the ball to Emilio Butragueño, "the
Buitre" did what all vultures do and evened the score, throwing all
predictions into the trash.

No one could have foreseen that the game would end 5–1, with
four goals scored by that very same Butragueño and Spain's best
collective performance in memory.

Neither could anyone have foreseen that nine years later, this
amazing Spanish striker would once again step on the grass of the
same stadium—La Corregidora de Querétaro—but this time defending the colors of the local Mexican team, Atletico Celaya, in the
twilight of his career.

The new system had paid off. Unlike the previous World Cup,
where the South Americans were outnumbered by the Europeans,

this time things looked more even by the quarter finals. It was three against five. A place in the semifinals was at stake. . . .

As in Spain 1982, France stepped forward to fight a memorable duel. After ninety minutes of stylish soccer, it was tied with Brazil. There was stylish play from both sides and performances of the highest level from men like Tigana, Fernandez, and Platini on the French side; Socrates, Alemao, and Junior on the other; and two identical endings for the two stories. Zico, who had gone into the game after seventy-two minutes, still had the opportunity to put the Brazilians ahead, but before the Romanian referee Igan had whistled the end of the game, there was a penalty for Brazil . . . but the shot was missed by the "white Pele." Then, in an overtime period, the playing continued at that same level, both teams as high as they could go in soccer heaven. Then on to the penalty kick shootout, to decide once and for all . . .

The history of soccer is reserved only for those very special achievements. One always imagines that the greatest players of all are the ones who step up to decide these issues, but in this case Platini on one side and Socrates on the other missed the penalty kick from 11 meters, facing a goal 7.25 meters wide, with only a small part of it blocked by the goalkeeper. Julio Cesar also missed, but there was no mistake from Luis Fernandez, who must still be running through the streets of Paris celebrating that decisive score that placed the French among the four best teams in the world.

For Mexico, the dream ended here. Playing in front of the most fervent crowds in the country—those of Monterrey—and against the tough Germans, the Mexicans managed to keep their opponent scoreless until the overtime, even through to the penalty shootout. That's when Harald Schumacher, until then the best goalkeeper of Mexico 1986, entered the limelight. He stopped four penalty kicks and showed that as long as this kind of tie-breaker exists, it's important to work on it. His saves allowed Germany to advance—but staggering and without a clear game plan.

Mexico's consolation was a best-ever sixth-place finish as well as introducing to the soccer world a man who would later receive the nickname of "Wizard of the World Cup": Bora Milutinovic, still a Yugoslavian citizen then and just beginning to be respected.

Belgium was another of the ghosts in this tournament. It started quietly in the first round and won that spectacular, if scandal-ridden, match with the Soviet Union; then once again it surprised everyone with its game in the quarter-finals. The veteran Jan Ceulemans put the Belgians in front at the thirty-four-minute mark. Spain's persistence—these players were indeed "furious"—was rewarded five minutes from the end, when the prayers of the Spaniards were heard and Señor evened the score. As in the other two matchups, the outcome once again was decided by penalty kicks. Jean Marie Pfaff, until then the other great goalkeeper of the tournament, rose to the occasion, and the Belgians won the shootout 5–4 (the game had ended 1–1). The Spaniards were beginning to sense that being eliminated in the quarter-finals was their eternal fate. They would live that fate again in USA 1994, when Roberto Baggio's Italian team would knock them out at the same stage.

The only team that didn't need penalty kicks to decide the game was Argentina, playing against England, no less. The War of the Falklands was still an open wound, but participants in this confrontation struggled to keep it untainted by anything that didn't have to do with sports.

In the soccer battle the winner was Argentina, with two goals by the man who, by this time, was the undisputed best player in the world: Maradona.

Those two goals with which he won the game have gone down in history, and each deserves its own chapter.

The first. At the fifty-one-minute mark, Valdano chipped the ball from the penalty arc toward the penalty-kick mark. Diego went for the loose ball as did Peter Shilton. The two—goalkeeper and striker—jumped at the same time. Shilton couldn't reach the ball with his hands, but Diego reached out with . . . "the hand of God." It was a handball, it's true, but the Tunisian referee Bennaceur did not call it. Diego looked at the referee from the corner of his eye and saw that he was running toward midfield—traditional signal that a goal had been scored—so he jetted toward the corner flag, suddenly thrusting his fist up again . . . this time in celebration. The sandlot player in him had come out, revealing that even in great soccer duels you take what you can get. To make things worse, the English were a team used to getting things their way. Whatever the case, this now famous goal would go down in soccer lore as the one scored by "the hand of God."

Of course, so that no one would be left with any doubts or complaints, four minutes later Diego pulled off a work of art that upstaged everything: not only his own clever move of a few minutes earlier, but also any goal ever achieved in the history of the World

Cup. It was fifty-five minutes into the game in an Azteca stadium surging with 104,000 souls. Diego received the ball from Enrique at midfield and turned around, leaving two defenders behind him; he faced his target, the opposing team's goal. His thick thighs pushed like they never had before, demonstrating one of the chief traits of this genius: a sprint that could upset the balance of any game. He beat one rival player, then another. When he got to the penalty area, he broke inside, faking Butcher out and evading Reid's block. In front, Fenwick waited. Another break, this time to the outside, and the fifth man was left flailing. He entered the goal area with the ball on his foot and his head up. In front of him was Shilton; on one side, Butcher. With a fake to the right, the goalkeeper was left sprawling. Butcher attempted the final block, from the outside, but Diego defended the ball with all his body and moved it so he could kick it with his left foot into the empty goal, one meter away from the goal line. He withstood the final attack and gave the ball a touch with his golden leg. He then ran to the corner flag where he had run four minutes before, but this time he didn't need to look behind him. He was aware, with his usual intuition, that he had pulled off the most beautiful goal in the entire history of the World Cup. A goal which has still not been surpassed . . .

Valdano, Diego's teammate and one of soccer's great analysts, would later say:

In that play, I trailed him because it was my job, and I ended up trailing him because of my fascination. When I reached the goal line I was no different from the more than one hundred thousand fans in that stadium. So much so that I didn't want to celebrate it with him. . . . It seemed to me that that goal was all his and had nothing to do with the team. I had trailed the play, but I didn't in any way feel like a participant of the spectacular adventure that Diego had undertaken. In time, that goal became the hallmark of world soccer. . . . What is interesting is that, in the showers, when Diego still had not seen the goal on television, he came up to me and said: "During the whole play I was looking for an opening to pass you the ball, since you were coming toward the far post. . . . If I had found it, I would've passed you the ball, the goal would've been yours, and the play wouldn't have been so complicated." That was too much. I mean, he had actually seen me, when the play itself was so difficult. You would think that the only thing he had time to do was focus on the play itself; but no, on top of all that he had been looking to pass me the ball. . . . It seemed superhuman; it made me feel like less of a soccer player.

I lived that goal like no other. I remembered how, as the play developed, from the press box of Azteca stadium all of my Argentine colleagues exclaimed, "It can't be!" every time Diego beat another defender. But it was true, and by the end we were all entranced, with tears in our eyes. It was the most beautiful, most harmonious, most spectacular goal I'd ever seen in my life. At the time, I was still writing, not broadcasting. So today, when I look at soccer stars for the joy of soccer and do not find it, I load up the VCR and do a play-by-play alone in front of the screen. After I shout my longest and most beautiful "goooal," I have the same feeling I had when I saw it years ago and said: "It can't be!"

By that point, only four teams were left in the race, but one had the advantage: the only South American team, the one that had Maradona. Three Europeans—France, Germany, and Belgium—aimed for something none had achieved: a title in the stadiums of the New World. The first two matched up in Guadalajara, each one bearing its own burden. The Germans bore the burden of having gotten there without having shown much, except the strong, innate will to overcome any obstacle; the French bore the burden of their own talent and the pressure to perform in order to reach a final that had eluded them four years earlier. Under the watchful eye of the great Italian referee Luigi Agnolin—a believer in officiating with a smile—willpower achieved more than talent and, with goals by Brehme and Voeller, Germany won 2–0. France repeated a historic weakness: Their goalkeeper Joel Bats—in fact, one of their best ever—gave away the first goal on a predictable free kick; and although he went on to stop some great German opportunities, his fundamental error had decided the match.

Argentina, in the other semifinal, didn't need to count on the other team's errors. In fact, they took advantage of their own skills and ended up crushing Belgium. Two goals by Maradona would have ended up in the running for the most beautiful in history, had the previous goal against England not happened. Diego humiliated Pfaff and the entire Belgian defense, but he was not alone: Alongside him glittered Jorge Luis Burruchaga, his squire, and a team that was playing exactly as their coach Carlos Salvador Bilardo had dreamed and planned.

The final match featured teams that had been there before: on one side one of the lead actors in the drama of 1978, Argentina; on the other, one of the standouts of 1974 and 1982, Germany. The past decade of international soccer would culminate in this game . . . and not for the last time.

When Carlos Salvador Bilardo proposed changing the face of Argentine soccer, he must have known he would be facing a lot of criticism. He was hindered by journalists who criticized his principles; by some players, who were incapable of doing what he asked of them; and by a shortage of the time needed for the players to practice what was asked of them. But he was too self-confident to change his game plan. His changes were so controversial, in fact, that he had to put up with a political power struggle that threatened to remove him from his post just days before the start of the World Cup, after an embarrassing defeat by Norway in a preparatory match.

Was what the popular *Narigón*[6] proposed so complicated? In theory, no. He operated with a few basic precepts such as these: a European-style defense, with a sweeper and two stoppers, each stopper guarding the rival's respective strikers; the conversion of the right and left backs into "wing-backs," adding them to the midfield; executing the game plan at midfield with five men, all sharing offensive and defensive responsibilities; and, finally and most important, not tying anyone down to fixed positions, with a constant movement and shifting and responsibilities.

Finally while the World Cup was in progress, the results of his work began to show on the field. A strange illness sidelined Daniel Alberto Passarella, who played sweeper, and Bilardo was forced to replace him with Jose Luis Brown, a protégé of his who knew exactly what he wanted. Another fortuitous event—the suspension of Garre after receiving a second yellow card—removed a classic left back from the scene and permitted the entry of Julio Jorge Olarticoechea, a prototypical defender with the ability to play as a midfielder and even an attacker. With the stoppers, Bilardo never had problems: They were Oscar Alfredo Ruggeri and Jose Luis Cuciuffo.

In the midfield, the coach first decided on Giusti and Batista, defensive midfielders, and Maradona and Burruchaga, offensive midfielders. He achieved perfect equilibrium when the missing ingredients, Hector Adolfo Enrique and the aforementioned Olarticoechea, were added. With them in the lineup, Maradona and Bur-

---

[6]*Narigón,* meaning "big nose," is a popular nickname in Argentina.

ruchaga were free to join up with another giant who mixed tactical knowledge and talent to the maximum: the super-intelligent Jorge Valdano.

With that roster, Argentina fielded a spectacular new formation: the 3–5–2. This formation sustained itself defensively by using a suffocating press from all eleven players. That European discipline was seasoned with a unique ingredient, the classic Argentine game. Bilardo's old dream was now put into action on the playing field: individual, natural talent governed by discipline and organization. All of it was made easier with players like Burruchaga, Valdano and, of course, Diego Armando Maradona.

In his moment of greatest splendor, at twenty-five years of age, "number ten" Maradona was part of a system that defended him and, at the same time, gave him the freedom to perform his unmatched, inventive plays.

It was perhaps a bit much for a German team that had reached the crucial stage more through its tradition than through the quality of its game.

"Sorry, Bilardo. Thank You." The banner appeared the day of the final, June 29, 1986, hung behind one of the goals of Azteca stadium. It reflected the feelings of millions of Argentine fans who during four years had doubted the national team coach. With results—his best weapon—the now popular *Narigón* had answered his critics.

The Mexican midday sun fell like lead on a field located 2,200 meters above sea level. As usual, the businessmen were not concerned with those little details: The important thing was that television could air the game at the right hour for those who had bought the rights. The merchandising was aimed at more than two billion television viewers, a number impressive enough to overshadow the protest made by Maradona and Valdano, attempting to defend the rights of the players. Without a doubt, the true heroes of this show were condemned to suffer, playing at an hour that was physically punishing even for someone taking a leisurely stroll. In any case, the Brazilian Romualdo Arppi Filho gave the order to start at exactly noon that day. And Argentina came out like a whirlwind.

Lothar Matthaus—a player who would show his versatility playing in all positions of the field—this time took over the man-to-man guarding of Maradona, undoubtedly the key player for Argentina. Bilardo had foreseen this: Burruchaga was in charge of creating plays from the midfield forward. In back, Brown swept away the

German attacks with the confidence that playing in a World Cup had given him while Cuciuffo dealt with Alloffs and Ruggeri handled Rummenigge. In the middle, Sergio Daniel Batista played the pivotal role of center-half.

After twenty-two minutes, Maradona burst through on the right flank and, when he got twenty meters from the goal line, Matthaus had no choice but to foul him. The German won himself a yellow card and Burruchaga took charge of the free kick, setting in motion one of the many set plays they had practiced: His cross, with the right foot from the right side of the field, curved perfectly, from the outside in, to find itself right in front of the attackers. The goalkeeper Schumacher was fooled and caught in no-man's-land, unable to intercept the ball that was curving away from him. The sweeper Brown received it perfectly and headed it into the goal to make it 1–0. For a long time after, the goalkeeper was strongly criticized for that excursion, but Bilardo always preferred to attribute it to a cross kicked the way it should be.

That's how the first half ended, and because of that the second half started differently. The German coach Franz Beckenbauer—whose debut at the head of the national team had come two years earlier in a loss against Argentina—attempted to change history: He sent Rudi Voeller to the field, where Cuciuffo stood ready to defend him.

Argentina went on with its game plan, and at fifty-five minutes scored another goal . . . as if trying to provide material for another chapter in Bilardo's imaginary book: *My Soccer*. Valdano started the play from right back position, snatching the ball away from Hans Peter Briegel. He crossed the field diagonally and, at midfield, passed to Enrique. *El Negro* took a moment to pause perfectly, then turned and returned the ball to Valdano, who was finally in his natural zone, the attack. Valdano continued with the ball in front of him, his eyes fixed on Schumacher, who failed to cut off the angle in time. It was fatal. Valdano set up his shot with as much skill as he had time for and put the ball where he wanted it, to seal the 2–0 lead. What was not sealed yet was the final score.

An eternal truth: The Germans should never be considered dead . . . unless you can't get a pulse. And there were definitely still signs of life. Rummenigge first and then Voeller took advantage of their team's own greatest strength: their skill in scoring on dead-ball situations. Nine minutes from the final, the game was 2–2. Paradoxes of history: There were also nine minutes left in 1978 when the Dutch forward Nanninga scored and made it 1–1 in the Monumental and momentarily threatened the dreams of the Argentineans.

It is easy to imagine the Argentine response upon discovering new flaws in Bilardo's team. But that group of players had already suffered too much, and there was no longer a question of giving up, especially with victory so close within their reach. That's what Diego Maradona was certainly thinking. He received the ball from Enrique, got free from Matthaus for the first time and saw clearly and perfectly how the field opened itself up for Burruchaga's sprint. He then gave him the perfect pass: clean, pure . . . Burruchaga ran and ran, followed by "the tank" Briegel. Each yard seemed like a mile, desert miles. The only reference point was ahead, Schumacher's goal. Schumacher was late again in coming off his line as if it were too much trouble to leave home. It cost him dearly once again. With class and delicacy, Burruchaga tapped the ball inside the far post and went to celebrate . . . with his arms and shoulders so wide open he seemed to be hugging the entire world. That same world, with unanimous and absolute admiration, gave in to the overwhelming evidence. Argentina was the greatest team on the planet, and it had an extraterrestrial in its ranks. In the reign of Diego Armando Maradona, everything shone brighter than ever.

Perhaps the best summary comes out of FIFA's technical report, presented a short time after the World Cup:

> This Cup showed that individuals can once again shine within the context of a soccer that's becoming more and more collective. A brilliant, individualistic player led his team toward achieving the title of World Champion: Diego Armando Maradona. He had perfect ball-handling skills, explosive runs, and a mixed role: He was both playmaker and finisher. Bilardo's victory is explained not only in the tactical aspects; he also got Maradona—that genius who can also be an egocentric artist, characterized by his constant propensity to make individual plays—to transform himself into a player who suddenly inspired team play as well as deciding games by his own penetrations into the enemy defense. That is Bilardo's great achievement. He was the one who definitively helped Maradona become the star he is today. In him, world soccer has a new idol. . . .

The report did not include, of course, the fact that the world now also had the biggest standard-bearer against the mandates of FIFA itself. But that's another story.

DIEGO MARADONA
(Argentina)
Mexico 1986

Few times in the history of the World Cup has a man distinguished himself so clearly. In Mexico 1986, Diego Armando Maradona was crowned the new king of soccer and turned a page that had before only been written by Pele. In the ultraselect gallery of "best players of their time," the undisputed Alfredo Di Stefano and Johan Cruyff were two players who were never given the crown that goes to those who finish a World Cup as champion. The Argentine who later became a Spanish citizen never even got to play in a World Cup; the Dutchman came one step closer, losing the final against West Germany in 1974.

In contrast, Diego was, according to many, even more important than Pele himself. He was the playmaker and finisher, the unquestionable key to every victory of Carlos Salvador Bilardo's national team. He was more than a World Champion: he was the embodiment of soccer itself.

A.C.: What I'm here to ask you about is World Cup Mexico 1986. What's the first thing that comes to mind?

D.M.: The first image that crosses my mind is the goal against the English . . . but that's nothing new, it's always been like that. More than anything, it was like beating a country, not a soccer team. Even though it's true that before the game we publicly declared that soccer had nothing to do with the Falkland Islands War, within the group we knew that many Argentine kids had died there, shot down as if they were birds.

A.C.: It's true, publicly it was declared that the two things shouldn't be mixed. . . .

D.M.: And it was a lie because, without trying, we were well aware of it, you know? So it was more than winning a game, more than eliminating the English from a World Cup. We transferred the guilt for everything that had occurred onto the English players. Yes, I know it is ludicrous, but that's the way we felt, and it was stronger than we were. We were defending our flag, the kids, and that's the truth. And my goal . . . my goal had an importance that . . .

A.C.: Both goals were important. . . .

D.M.: Both, both, it's true. The first was like stealing an Englishman's wallet, and the second one covered it all up.

A.C.: It is curious isn't it? The second goal was so amazing that no one rose up to accuse you of anything for the first. . . .

D.M.: It's that the first one had its own qualities. If Shilton doesn't find out, no one does. Fenwick, who was one meter away from me, didn't know what was going on. And Shilton found out because he practically had the ball in his hands, and I took it out. But that's just my take on it.

A.C.: Do you agree with what most people say, that that was your most glorious period?

D.M.: Yes, but I think it was more than just that moment. I had been playing very well in the Italian league, and I trained like never before. Professor Antonio Dal Monte gave us a plan, and I went forward with it with my personal trainer, Fernando Signorini. I remember that I trained in a gym that we had put together ourselves in our Naples offices. Even still I remember that no one thought we had a chance; in the preparatory friendlies we had been a real horror show. But afterward, my training paid off in the World Cup, which has an importance greater than any other soccer event. Afterward, I went back to Napoli and won the *scudetto*, but nothing compares.

A.C.: Also, great players who have been unable to emerge victorious in the World Cup are never as highly regarded as those who have. Look at the case of Van Basten, for example.

D.M.: Exactly, exactly . . . the motivation is great, but so is the pressure. It's easier to nutmeg[1] a player in the Italian league than it is to do so in the World Cup. You're being watched by the whole world.

A.C.: Since "your" World Cup, has soccer progressed or taken a step backward?

D.M.: I don't think it has improved as far as organization, and that has to do with the players' lack of say in the decision-making process. In Mexico, we played at twelve noon, under a blazing sun, and today, if television calls for it, that outrage repeats itself. It happened in the United States. If that's the way it is, how do they expect a player to excel? When one is playing in 120-degree weather or even in domed stadiums, how can they actually expect a player to give his all? Of course, much of the fault belongs to us for not demanding respect and the referee for not protecting us. No one thinks about the actual soccer, which, after all, is what brings people to the stadiums.

A.C.: No one worries about the essentials; the accessories are more important every day. Is that what you're saying?

D.M.: Exactly. Today the central issue to everyone who thinks they know something about soccer is physical training. "It's a physical game," they say. . . .

A.C.: That's right.

D.M.: But when are we going to touch the ball in this physical game? I want to bring that up . . . because if we don't, let's sign Carl Lewis, Pietro Mennea . . . please! All right, I agree that one has to be in good shape, but let's not let it surpass ball-handling skills and imagination! Because if everyone who gets the ball is going to go one hundred meters in nine seconds, then let's forget about this game, which is great for a reason. Let's see, why don't they just forget the ball altogether? Eleven against eleven, with the one who gets to midfield from the goal fastest wins . . .

A.C.: Are you the last soccer rebel?

D.M.: I don't know, I don't know. . . . The only thing I say is that in the last few World Cup games, the physical aspect is surpassing creativity in importance, and that's no good.

[1]Nutmeg: to put the ball through the legs of a defender.

A.C.: How can this be reversed in the future?

D.M.: I think that coaches have a lot to do with this. But many years will have to pass before things get better. Now we have the Cruyffs, the Passarellas, the Sacchis. All of them give a lot of importance to the physical aspect, and they limit the fantasy that the player can offer, understand? Maybe they don't do it directly, through orders, but the players are afraid. "If I don't do this, they might take me out," or "if I try a nutmeg, I might lose my spot."

A.C.: It's also the fact that coaches have become big stars themselves. Look at how it's very difficult to remember the names of the first coaches, and now they're more famous than the players themselves.

D.M.: You see? See? I always say it, and it's a sad fact. It shows that something is wrong. It's important to have respect for the coaches, but first we must give players the credit they deserve; because right now it's upside down. Let me make it clear: Games are won and lost by the players and even more so in a World Cup.

A.C.: By the way, and back to Mexico 1986, was it the happiest moment of your career?

D.M.: Yes, yes . . . for now . . . although the greatest happiness is still to come: at this age, to keep on having fun on a soccer field.

Italy 1990

Italian style, with a violent overture, magical nights, and everything seasoned with the purest passion: That defines the fourteenth tournament of the World Cup, played on that peninsula where people live and breathe soccer. For that, it deserved to be the site of the World Cup for the second time, joining Mexico as the only other country to host the tournament twice.

Mexico 1986 had proven that the competition's format was very efficient—if nothing else, it kept the price of the television transmission rights high—and because of that, no one had any desire to change it. The official sponsors were also all completely in place. They had slowly come to realize that the World Cup meant big business. In fact, the fighting between the big corporations was now just as intense as the competition between the national teams to win a spot at the starting gate.

Even though they were designated as host a long time before, Italy still got to the event in its customary style: arguing all the way. The first point of contention was the stadiums.

Five of them were partially remodeled: Rome's Olympic stadium, Florence's Stadio Comunale, Genoa's Marassi stadium, Bologna's Dall'Ara, and Milan's San Siro (which by then had already been renamed Giuseppe Meazza stadium). Two stadiums were built from scratch: Turin's Delle Alpi and Bari's San Nicola, futurist works with advanced designs, but lacking the warmth that only the greatest soccer temples could convey. This would be confirmed a few years later when the great Juventus, the most popular team in Italy, would relocate from Delle Alpi stadium, where they felt like a lonely old lady,[1] even with a huge crowd cheering them on.

The list of sites was completed by Naples's San Paolo stadium, Palermo's Della Favorita stadium, Verona's Marco Antonio Bentegodi, and Udine's Friuli stadium, all of them remodeled for the event.

Surrounding the stadiums were an almost infinite number of controversies, each with its own motivation: environmentalists attempting to defend nature from the attacks of modernity; traditionalists trying to keep their culture pure; politicians fighting to take advantage of the opportunities offered by the World Cup; plus many informed citizens concerned about the atrocities suffered by the workers. In the end, nothing was clear. No one would ever know the truth about the multimillion-dollar investment. FIFA, which had indirectly brought the effort about—thanks to its pressure—would forget about the requirements placed on the Italians when, four years later, it gave the United States the freedom to stage the World Cup in whatever way it saw fit. In Italy, however, the truth was buried by the time the ball started rolling.

Before the ball did start to roll, however, everyone had to put in their two cents on who they thought the candidates to the title were. Holland had just come from winning the 1988 European Nations Cup in Germany, and names like Ruud Gullit, Frank Rijkaard, and Marco Van Basten were an invitation for the Dutch to dream about staging a repeat performance of their 1974 "Clockwork Orange." From the other side of the Earth, the Copa America (the new name for the South American championship) had regained its competitiveness and prestige. The champion of the 1989 competition, therefore, also had to be considered a solid candidate to win the World Cup: It was Brazil, no less, with Careca and Romario (who would not make it to the World Cup because of off-the-field problems), among other stars.

These were the days that gave rise to one of the most controversial questions in modern soccer: national teams versus clubs. A question so controversial that, during the peak of his involvement with sports, Silvio Berlusconi—television magnate and owner of powerful AC Milan—said out loud what many had been thinking all along: "The truth is that the World Cup should be played by

[1] Old lady: Juventus is traditionally known in Italy as the *vecchia signora*, meaning "old lady" in Italian.

teams representing the leagues of each country rather than the countries' federations." In terms of business, a great idea. In terms of patriotism, treason. In terms of the sport, an injustice . . .

For Argentine players, for example, the national team had recently been a platform from which to launch themselves to all points of the world. To wear the *albiceleste* was a guarantee of their quality. For that reason, representing their country was, for them, almost a moral obligation as well as a great honor. Obviously, Berlusconi's idea had to do with the advantage it would give the Italian national team. In the Italian Calcio, the richest league in the world, the greatest stars from all points of the world gathered, lured by the power of money. Among them was, of course, Diego Armando Maradona, helping his club, Napoli—a symbol of poor southern Italy's fight against the opulent north—surge to unimaginable heights. That combination, by the way, of Argentina and Italy, would leave its own unique stamp on this Cup.

That the number of registrants broke the previous record, something that had become commonplace, no longer surprised anyone. Everyone wanted to join in the party . . . and in the business. The point is very clear: The days of Jules Rimet were long gone, and now every participating national team got four hundred thousand dollars for just stepping onto the field. If it got to the next round, the prize money would multiply itself many times over. That's why France, coached briefly by Michel Platini, must have been even more upset when left out of the final 24 teams, after the fight between the 112 that played the qualifying rounds.

To open the tournament, the Italians had sites galore to choose from for the now-traditional match featuring the defending champion—in this case Argentina. They decided on Milan's Giuseppe Meazza stadium, saving Rome's Olympic stadium for the final. After an exemplary opening ceremony—which achieved a difficult balance between practicality and show, spreading out the positive vibes of the local fans without taking too long—the time came to play. On that torrid, unforgettable June 8, Argentina, the champion, with Maradona, faced Cameroon, the rising African team. The first big surprise of the World Cup came in a game that included more than one preview of things to come. Cameroon won, with a goal by Francois Omam Biyik—who would later play for Mexico City club America. A disconcerted and disconcerting Argentina had perhaps too many younger players who were not yet ready to defend their country's colors in a World Cup. A semipublic harangue by

Maradona before the game while the team was lined up during the playing of the national anthems had not been enough: "We've got to play with balls, damn it!" screamed Diego, but the look on the younger players' faces showed a state of mind that would be difficult to change. Only the entrance of Claudio Paul Caniggia in the second half gave any hope to the World Champion. Controversial because of his life off the field and unpredictable on it, Caniggia left everyone unbalanced—even his own teammates—with his uncommon speed. In order to stop him, the African defenders had to resort to rough measures, which would be copied by other teams, leaving the sought-after and oft-repeated "fair play" far from true. But Caniggia's contribution was not enough, and the loss was a hard blow to Argentina: "It was the most bitter moment of my life," concluded its coach, Carlos Salvador Bilardo.

Of course Argentina made it to the next round, but not without struggling. It tied Romania and qualified for the next round as one of the tournament's four best third-place teams.

Preceding them in the standings in this competitive but odd group were Cameroon—even after losing to the USSR 4–0 in their last game—and Romania, which played as erratically as its big star, Gheorge Hagi.

For the Soviets, it would be their last World Cup with that name. Almost one year later, the iron curtain would disintegrate.

In Group 1, Italy started off its magic nights hosting Austria, Czechoslovakia, and the United States with the confidence of a team that knows they are better than the rest. In each game, they presented a new star. The World Cup started off belonging to Gianluca Vialli, but he then disappeared. At another moment, it was Roberto Baggio's, who made one of the most beautiful goals in memory against Czechoslovakia, dodging five opponents before driving the ball over the goalkeeper and into the net. Finally, the star became Salvatore "Toto" Schillaci, a typically Italian character—in a true dramatic comedy. Before the World Cup started, his name was clearly below those of Vialli and Carnevale when the starting lineups were penciled in. But seventy-four minutes into the first game, against Austria, Coach Azeglio Vicini put him in the game. Four minutes later, "Toto" responded by sealing the Italian victory and didn't leave the starting lineup for the rest of the World Cup. He would finish as top scorer, a lasting personal achievement. He was one of the miracles of that Cup. Everything he had done before (he was an irregular, unpolished goal-scorer who was transferred from Messina to Juve) and everything he did after (with more shame than glory he went from Juve to Inter, and from there to Jubilo Iwata in Japan's J-League) proves it.

The Argentineans were to embark on several trips through the Italian landscape that had nothing to do with tourism and everything to do with soccer. Their training camp—ordinarily the training camp of Serie A club AS Roma—was set up in Trigoria, just minutes from the city of Rome. From there, they had to go six hundred kilometers to the north to play the opening match in Milan. Afterward, they had to go 250 kilometers south of their training camp to play their two remaining first-round games in Naples.

In Naples, where they were top seed of Group 2 and where Maradona was more than just a mere idol, the Argentineans played the Soviet Union to try to come back from their bitter debut of four days before. The game went into the record books as a difficult 2–0 victory for Argentina (goals by Troglio and Burruchaga) and into history because of a second "hand of God." Swedish referee Fredriksson—the same man who ignored two offside positions in two Belgian goals against the same Soviets four years earlier—didn't see the second "hand of God," when Maradona, positioned on his own goal line, stretched his arm out to save a ball that was dangerously heading toward the net. The game also included a tragic injury that would later become a key in the tournament. Goalkeeper Nery Pumpido, who had been responsible for Omam Biyik's goal in the debut, but had also been a hero of a thousand battles in the Bilardo era, suffered a serious injury after crashing against teammate Olarticoechea. An exposed fracture in his right leg forced Bilardo to replace him. In his place entered Sergio Javier Goycochea, the team's third goalkeeper, who was without a club when he was called up and who was coming off a long period of inactivity. Some weaknesses in his game—hesitation when he went off his line to intercept crosses—would be forgotten after the quarter-finals, thanks to unforeseen circumstances.

In Group 3, played in Turin and Genoa, Brazil did what it was accustomed to doing: It won its three first-round games against Sweden (2–1), Costa Rica (1–0), and Scotland (1–0). In truth, not everything the Brazilians did followed habit. Their coach was Sebastiao Lazaroni, a man whose every decision sparked controversy. His plan was to "modernize" Brazilian soccer—a preview of what would be achieved four years later by Carlos Alberto Parreira (who was present in this World Cup as the head of United Arab Emirates, which would finish in last place)—but he never figured out how. While he tried, he clashed against the wishes of most Brazilians, who defended the traditional style. In that first round, they won, but they didn't play very well, with goals by Careca and Müller carrying them to the next round.

Behind them, in second place, was one of Italy 1990's pleasant surprises: Costa Rica. Coached by Velibor Milutinovic, the Costa Ricans achieved the best results in their sports history. In their first World Cup, they beat Scotland (1–0) with a goal by Cayasso and Sweden (2–1) with goals by Flores and Medford, turning the game around after having fallen behind. It was an impressive breakthrough by the Costa Ricans, who played with a captivating enthusiasm, motivated by a coach who stressed morale.

Those who were eliminated continued to reveal constant, almost emblematic defects: the coldness of the Scots, who never play up to their potential; and the inconsistency of the Swedes, who can lose every single game—and did in 1990 when they didn't get a single point—even when they have great talent in their ranks (in this case, a very young Tomas Brolin).

Group 4 was set in Milan and Bologna. There, Germany kept Franz Beckenbauer as coach, respecting a long tradition. In the forty years of post–World War II World Cup competitions, only four men have coached the Germans: Sepp Habberger; then Helmut Schoen, whose place was taken by Jupp Derwall; and finally Beckenbauer. With slight variations, all those who have coached the white-shirted team have proposed a similar system, based on tactical and physical solidity, plus the iron will to always go forward, never giving up. Another example of their continuity was Lothar Matthaus. Four years before, he had guarded Diego Armando Maradona in the final. This time, his role was to be his team's playmaker from the midfield. Four years later, he would play sweeper, guiding his team from the depths of defense. He was a great example of versatility, a truly modern soccer player. Joining the Germans in the next round were two teams that practiced the same kind of soccer, even though the players of the respective teams were born and raised on opposite sides of the world: Yugoslavia and Colombia. For the South Americans, the philosophy of Coach Francisco "Pacho" Maturana had successfully been carried out. With unprecedented discipline off the field and unrestrained freedom on it, the Colombians celebrated their tie against West Germany as if it were a historic feat. Thanks to that result, they qualified for the next round as third place in their group, demonstrating to themselves and everyone else that they could go head-to-head with anyone. And they could do it with their own style: a technically rich game that was appealing to the eye and an all-out attack, even with the risks that such a style entailed. The end of the game against the Germans was unforgettable: At eighty-nine minutes, Pierre Littbarski scored for the Germans—the only goal up to that point. But at ninety-two minutes—120 seconds into injury time—Fredy Rincon scored the equalizer, which was the most important goal in the history of Colombia's soccer. Also going to the next round was Yugoslavia, which was perhaps seeing its greatest generation of players just before the war that would divide the country. Four years later, by the time of USA 1994, Yugoslavia would no longer exist as a unified country. In Italy 1990, however, those who had exploded on the scene as World Youth Champion in Chile 1987 were now at their peak, led by Robert Prosinecki and including big stars like Dragan Stojkovic, Darko Pancev, and Dejan Savicevic. They all played the game the same way: without prejudices and almost irresponsibly. That style had gotten results, but it would later prove to be their undoing.

In Group 5, played in Verona and Udine, Spain and Belgium—fierce rivals ever since their quarterfinal matchup in Mexico 1986—met again. Completing the group were the Uruguayans and the running and slamming South Koreans, making their second straight World Cup appearance. The group's games were played at a less than brilliant level but, thanks to the group's parity, they were exciting nonetheless.

At this point in history, the Spaniards suffered from something similar to the British. They had great teams at club level and were always candidates to explode at the national team level, but they inevitably fell because of lack of chemistry and their inability to turn a game around. That's the only explanation for the negative results produced by a team with men such as Zubizarreta, Sanchis, Michel, Butrageño, and Martin Vazquez. They did, however, manage to get past the first round, dropping only one point, in their initial match against Uruguay. In that game, Ruben Sosa failed to take advantage of a great opportunity to score late in the game, when he sent his penalty kick over the crossbar, at a time when Luis Suarez's team would have had no time to react. Afterward, Spain easily defeated both South Korea and Belgium. In the game against Belgium, Michel, who was sick and tired of the jeers coming from his own fans, reacted by giving them the finger after scoring a goal, an act that was televised for the whole world to see. . . . The things one sees in the modern World Cup!

The Belgians advanced in their traditional style: silently. Within their ranks, certain key players made the difference: goalkeeper Preud'Homme, defender Grun, and the eternal Ceulemans. They finished second in their group, and qualified for the second round, just as they had in the two previous tournaments.

For Uruguay, getting to the next round was a struggle. Its 1986 team, with the brilliant Francescoli, Paz, and company, played with an internal enemy: the coaching mistakes of Professor Omar Borras. This time, the same foundation was enriched by the contribution of a new generation (including Sosa and Fonseca) as well as a coach with clear ideas, the "Maestro," Oscar Washington Tabarez. Even with all that going for them, the Uruguayans only managed to get to the next round by a goal in the last minute of their last first-round game, when a well-placed Fonseca header finally broke the Korean defense. In the end, Uruguay finished third in the group.

Group 6 was isolated in Palermo and Cagliari. Literally isolated. The first measure to combat hooliganism called for keeping the delinquents as far away and as enclosed as possible. Therefore, the peace-loving inhabitants of Sardinia watched in horror as those symbols of soccer violence—a stigma that has deeply rooted itself in today's soccer—disembarked on their shores. Moreover, whoever wanted to see the great soccer promised by the group's two main protagonists, Holland and England—not much was expected from Ireland, and Egypt was an unknown quantity—had their hopes dashed. It was the worst group of them all, with a game that symbolized them all: the English against the Dutch. Played in Cagliari stadium, in the middle of a besieged city, with incidents before and after the game, the score on the field was a big 0–0, thanks to deplorable play from both teams. Each with their own problems, the two European giants had a lot to make up for. In spite of it all, both teams made it to the next round, along with Ireland, whose performance was a good yard-stick for measuring the quality of the group: They finished second without having won a single game.

The constant fine-tuning of the tournament's format—always keeping in mind the competition and . . . finances—had left it at this point: Sixteen teams in the direct elimination quarter final; 90 minutes of regulation and, in the event of a tie, 30 minutes of overtime. If the tie persisted, the game would be decided on penalty kicks, a solution that, in this World Cup, would be more decisive than ever.

Cameroon–Colombia in Naples needed an extra half-hour to decide the winner. Face-to-face were two identical ways of playing the game, with artistry taking a lead role and defensive precautions taking a back seat. Strangely, there were no goals scored in the first ninety minutes. After 106 minutes, the legendary Roger Milla beat eccentric Colombian goalkeeper Higuita for the first time. Even though the African striker was approaching his permanent retirement, he was still in good shape physically, and his talent still made a difference. Two minutes later, the same face-to-face duel repeated itself: Higuita, far outside his area, received a pressured pass back from a teammate. Faithful to his style, he played the ball with his foot, putting himself at risk by trying to dribble past Milla. But the veteran Milla used his experience to steal the ball from the goalkeeper and put it in the open net, sealing the win, which still stood after Redin cut the African lead in half. Cameroon, the African power, the great surprise of the games, was now in the quarterfinals. In the meantime, controversy enveloped Colombia and spread throughout the soccer world. Was Higuita responsible for Colombia's elimination? The truth is that Higuita was Higuita. So often heralded for his style of play, the possibility that it would one day backfire was always present. Today, rule changes and the game's unstoppable evolution have made it necessary for goalkeepers to learn to control the ball with their feet as well as with their hands. If they don't, they will be giving their opponents an advantage. A good example is the case of Paraguayan Jose Luis Chilavert, goalkeeper of Argentine club Velez Sarsfield, 1994 Copa Libertadores champion. He both saves and makes goals, scoring on free kicks and penalty kicks as well as creating goal-scoring opportunities for his team with his long passes. With this in mind, Higuita was before his time and not responsible for his team's loss.

However, Higuita's errors off-the-field with the biggest Colombian drug-trafficker—Pablo Escobar, from the Medellin Cartel—would cost him a stay in prison and would make his name infamous. Only today as we approach the year 2000 is he again making news for the right reasons: because he is a unique player.

In this World Cup, Czechoslovakia returned to glories not seen since the 1930s. In large part, this was due to a giant with a heroic face: Thomas Skuhravy. In the round of sixteen, he scored three goals, all made easier by his ability to destroy enemy defenses with his headers. Crushed by three of his attacks was Costa Rica, which got to the game with a dream, but without injured star goalkeeper Gabelo Conejo. The feats of Costa Rica while in Italy reflected two months' work with a soccer globetrotter: Bora Milutinovic, who would next work his magic for the United States, no less. Costa Rica's return to reality, however, was not nearly as traumatic as that of Spain or Romania, which lost when they least expected it. Spain was left "fury-less" against the good play of Yugoslavia and ended up losing in overtime (2–1), thanks to Dragan Stoijkovic's inconsistent greatness. The Romanians tied Ireland 0–0 after a mediocre 120-minute long game, causing the first penalty kick tie-breaker of this World Cup. The last Romanian kicker on the list—Timofte— was unable to get his shot past Irish goalkeeper Bonner, and the Irish got to the quarter-finals with an interesting, yet unimpressive, twist: They had still not yet won a game.

In the meantime, Italy continued its magic nights in Rome's Olympic stadium. Its victim this time around was Uruguay (2–0), with the ineffable Schillaci again making his presence felt in the score and Serena making a contribution of his own. In those days, the home team tried to back its claims of being the best by way of the classic "module" Italian formation—a solid defense; a battle-hardened midfield; and that unrefined, yet irresistible, goal-scorer. The Uruguayans could only look back on a great tradition, because their present was awful.

England went to Bologna to match up with Belgium in a game that was very . . . British. The British played at a fast, back-and-forth pace, with long passes, speed, and strength. Yet, despite all this, no goals . . . until, in the last minute of overtime with the penalty kick tie-breaker looming, David Platt did something different. He received the ball in the heart of the enemy area, made a 180-degree turn, and volleyed it into the net, wounding Preud'Homme and giving England a ticket to the quarterfinals.

The quarterfinals included two main attractions, two duels between true greats.

Germany–Holland was one of them, even though the two teams had given much different performances up to that point. This time, Franz Beckenbauer's Germans unwaveringly exercised their authority, even though they were also helped by the uneven quality of their opponents. Leo Beenhakker's Dutchmen, on the other hand, came wrapped up in a series of long-standing internal conflicts and with certain players who had not demonstrated the potential they had shown on their club teams. Men like Ronald Koeman, Ruud Gullit, Frank Rijkaard, and Marco Van Basten—all of whom would, at some point, win the European championship with Barcelona or AC Milan—left their fans with nothing but disappointment. Germany defeated them in a fiercely fought game, in which one of the Dutchmen, Rijkaard, scandalously left the World Cup early. He got into a shouting match—in Italian, no doubt—with German striker Rudi Voeller. The Argentine referee ejected both players and as they left the field Rijkaard spit at Voeller's face, another gesture captured forever by television. It was symbolic of a deeper frustration: the hope of again seeing a "Clockwork Orange" was dashed.

Argentina–Brazil was the other starry clash. The game in Turin's Delle Alpi stadium had a clear favorite: Brazil. The Brazilians prepared to face an Argentine team that, four years earlier and coached by the same Bilardo, had successfully put in place what Lazaroni wished for his players. Days before, Maradona had said: "Let our opponents be the favorites." The beginning of the game seemed to confirm the predictions. Few times had a team dominated a game as much as the *verdeamarelhos* did that afternoon. Pushed by the strength of Dunga and Alemao, they attacked from all sides, besieging Goycochea's goal with crosses and bombarding it with Careca's precise and Müller's imprecise shots. Yet, in spite of all those efforts, they were helpless against Maradona's magic. At eighty minutes, Diego cleared the midfield, leaving behind Dunga and Alemao (both of whom would later be criticized for not having the guts to take down the "number ten"); he looked to his left and saw that Caniggia had gotten loose of his guard and gave him a perfect pass. Claudio got to the ball, remembered all the tips he'd been given about the best way to finish in a *mano a mano* situation against the goalkeeper and, after leaving Taffarel in the dust, put the ball into the empty net. It led Argentina to wild celebration, Lazaroni into the abyss, and Bilardo, who had once again led the Argentine march toward the title, into heaven. Nothing could have been more heroic given the condition that Maradona was playing in. His ankle was so swollen it looked like the soccer ball itself. After being given a local injection to reduced the swelling, he went on to play a decisive role, even though that play was one of the few he participated in that whole game. Put simply, it was magic.

The quarterfinals had taken shape, and the remaining four match-ups included no surprises: Argentina–Yugoslavia (0–0 and

3–2 in the penalty kick tie-breaker), Italy–Ireland (1–0), Germany–Czechoslovakia (1–0), and England–Cameroon (3–2 in overtime). As the results show, only two of the games left stories to tell.

For Argentina, it would be the first game won on penalties. And it would not be the last. Carlos Salvador Bilardo, asked about the issue a zillion times, never hesitated in giving his answer: "No, they aren't all luck. You have to be prepared to save them and to convert them." For one reason or another, the Argentine players seemed up to the task. Against Yugoslavia, after an even, emotional, 120 minutes of soccer, the time for the penalty kicks came. On that June 30, beneath the Florence sun, when everything seemed lost, the legend of Goycochea was born. Serrizuela and Burruchaga had converted for Argentina and Stojkovic and Prosinecki had converted for Yugoslavia, when Diego Maradona stepped up to take his turn. His weak shot to the right side of the goal was stopped by Ivkovic, the same goalkeeper who had previously stopped a Maradona penalty in a game between Maradona's Napoli and Ivkovic's Sporting Lisboa. Diego turned around and returned to midfield; as he was on the edge of tears, with his head tilted downward, he heard the words of his teammate: "Calm down, Diego. I'll just save two and that'll be it." They gave each other a high five; Maradona believed him. But *el Vasco*[2] wasn't able to immediately fulfill his promise as the next kick was converted by Savicevic. Making matters worse, the next Argentine to kick, Troglio, struck the ball against the crossbar. If Brnovic scored, Yugoslavia would be in the semifinals. But Goycochea saved the next shot and Dezotti converted for Argentina, setting the stage for Hadzibegic's decisive kick. Goycochea intercepted for the second decisive save. Argentina was still in the race.

Those who saw England–Cameroon in Naples's San Paolo stadium were blessed with a duel charged with beauty, a lesson in how to play the game. It went into overtime, extending the total minutes to 120, but even that seemed too short.

England got ahead first, with a goal by Platt after twenty-five minutes. But forty minutes later, Cameroon had already taken over the lead, with goals by Kunde (a sixty-two-minute penalty) and Ekeke (sixty-five minutes). There were only twenty-five minutes left, and all it had to do was hold on to the lead. But that game strategy

---

[2]*El Vasco:* "the Basque."

wasn't in any of the manuals given out by Cameroon's Soviet coach Nepomniacij. Cameroon continued its attack, exposing its defense to a relentless goal-scorer: Gary Lineker, a player who transcends time. Just minutes before the end, he equalized on a penalty kick. At the end of the first half of overtime, he gave the crowd an encore, again converting a penalty kick. Cameroon's exit was met with warm applause, because of the style of game it played, because of Africa's rise in the soccer universe, and because of the joy it showed on the field. The English, more practical than the Africans but just as spectacular, were left with the pride of showing itself off as one of the four best national teams in the world.

The other two semifinalists got there without so much as a flinch. Italy beat Ireland 1–0, with the now inevitable goal by a man already known as *Il Salvatore della patria*,[3] Schillaci. Germany successfully marked Skuhravy and thanks to their star player, Matthaus, they finished off Czechoslovakia.

After the semifinal matchups were set, a shiver ran through Italy from north to south. The home team had to face Argentina and . . . Maradona. In truth, it was part of a longer game that had been going on since the beginning of the World Cup. In the opening game, in Milan—home of the "powerful Northerners"—both Maradona's name during the announcement of the starting lineups and Argentina's national anthem had been met with jeers. Moreover, the crowd's cheering on of Cameroon had been obvious. On that day, Diego gave the first stab in a series of verbal attacks notable for their wit and sarcasm: "The people of Milan showed that they aren't as racist as their reputation; they cheered on the Africans." Now, the matchup would be head-to-head, but would it be in neutral territory? As soon as he knew the rival and site of the game—Naples—Diego made a public call for support: "Neapolitans, don't believe what they tell you. . . . With the Cup on the line, Naples is suddenly part of Italy, and all of the country begs it for support. . . . Don't forget that until yesterday, you were the *terroni*,[4] just like the Africans . . ."

The day of the game, a banner attempted to reflect the feelings of the impassioned Neapolitan fans, caught between two incomparable loves: "Diego, you are always in our hearts, but we are Ital-

---

[3]*Il Salvatore della patria* has a double meaning. In Italian it means both "the country's savior" and "the country's Salvatore," which is Schillaci's first name.

[4]*Terroni:* "Southerner" in Italian slang.

ian." The atmosphere in the stadium was not suffocating for Argentina and, for the first time, their national anthem wasn't met by a chorus of boos. In this "World Cup of Magic Nights," this night was more magical than any of the others. The country and a good part of the world was breathless, awaiting the match. It was Tuesday, July 3. That same afternoon, the new edition of the prestigious magazine *Guerin Sportivo* had come out, with a cover that defined the feeling as well as the expectations: "The real king," it said, with a drawing of Maradona kneeling in deference to an exultant Schillaci.

After seventeen minutes, the unstoppable "Toto" fulfilled the prophecy. Taking advantage of a rebound, he beat Goycochea.

However, on that night, the two teams seemed changed with respect to their previous performances: Italy was slower and less confident; Argentina was more solid and sure of itself. This change was reflected in the result. Sixty-seven minutes into the game, Olarticoechea crossed the ball into the area from the left. Caniggia met the ball in the penalty area and headed it in after Zenga's horrid attempt at intercepting the cross. It was a goal met by silence, although the silence was not absolute. That goal deadlocked the game through both regulation and overtime, resulting in the type of tie-breaker that the Argentines wanted and Italians feared: penalty kicks.

In the beginning of the series, every player converted: Baresi, Baggio, and De Agostini for Italy; Serrizuela, Burruchaga, and Olarticoechea for Argentina. When AC Milan's great player Roberto Donadoni went to the penalty spot, a terrible silence filled the San Paolo, with the moon rising behind the stands. He hit the ball to the left side, well placed; Goycochea flew to meet it, and deflected it, increasing his myth-making potential. The stadium was almost totally silent. It grew even more silent after Maradona converted his goal calmly striking the ball the way he liked it—softly, not too far to the side, but fooling the goalkeeper. Therefore, everything—glory or failure—was in the feet of one man or in the hands of the other. Serena versus Goycochea: a man under the pressure of a "do or die" situation versus the confidence of a man who felt the goal was too small for him. The feet didn't win . . . but neither did the hands. Goycochea's body got between the ball and the net, leaving the Italians' glory on the wrong side of the goal line. Then "the Basque," a man with a unique place in soccer history, joined his teammates in the center of the field which, on that magical night, was the center of the world.

Sergio Javier Goycochea, the Argentine hero of that World Cup, knew that all of this was his way of getting even, but he didn't show it. A year before, mention of his name prompted only malicious comments. It had all started in 1988, when he was transferred from River Plate—where, paradoxically, he was considered a star, but didn't play—to San Lorenzo de Almagro. He had been Pumpido's backup on a team that was champion of everything (Argentina, South America, and the world), and was famous for his looks, which entranced the ladies, as well as for his sporadic appearances in the starting lineup, which were always spectacular. The day he left his old club, he hit his shoulder against a goalpost and took his pain with him to his new club, San Lorenzo. The pain turned into an injury, and the injury turned into a mystery. The cure didn't come, and his recovery time lengthened. Therefore, it even occurred to someone to say that he suffered from AIDS, that terrible scourge of our times. "Goyco" went underground, until he caught the interest of the Colombian club Millonarios, where he played for a short time. Later, he was once again left without a club and without work. So, when Bilardo called him to the national team to be the third goalkeeper, he was coming off seven months of inactivity.

In Italy, he entered the starting lineup because of that terrible injury suffered by Pumpido, and he entered history because of his knack of saving penalty kicks. For the Italians, the World Cup ended on that night, even though there was still another semifinal to be played.

In a game that was a carbon copy of the other, although without the same passion surrounding it, Germany shook England off its back and marched toward its third consecutive final. After 120 minutes of sparkling play—in the best German and English style—it ended 1–1, with goals by Parker (on his own goal) and Lineker, forcing a penalty kick showdown. This stage was also a deadringer for the first game: Germany converted on all of its opportunities; Pearce and Waddle missed the last two for England.

Therefore, something even more important would repeat itself: Just as four years earlier, in Mexico 1986, the final would be between Argentina and Germany.

It was the same matchup, but a very different game.

Germany got there on a rose-covered path. In addition to the original roster that had sweated so hard four years before to make the World Cup final were fantastic players whose presence caused the team to improve. Germany had not hesitated to keep men like Thomas Berthold, Andreas Brehme, Pierre Littbarski, Rudi Voeller, and of course, Lothar Matthaus. This base was enriched by the addition of midfielders like Thomas Haessler and Olaf Thon, stoppers Jurgen Kohler and Guido Buchwald, and Jurgen Klinsmann up front. In spite of all the starry names, however, the World Cup was marked by the use of extreme defensive tactics, and it was a temptation that not even Germany escaped. The system imposed by Bilardo's Argentina four years before was imitated by most—even by Lazaroni's Brazil—and only teams that could count on a man with great creativity—Baggio's Italy, Gascoigne's England—had shown anything different. Of course, results told another story, and that's what Beckenbauer and Bilardo clung to in their defense.

The years since the 1986 title had not been easy for Argentina. Always an exporter of soccer players, it had recently been exporting them in even greater numbers. Consequently, the players the coach believed to be fundamental all played in different points of the globe. So much so that Bilardo coined a famous phrase: "It is very difficult to practice like that. Burruchaga crosses the ball in France and Ruggeri has to head it in Spain. . . . It's very hard." Moreover, injuries—and the incertitude that they caused when the time came to name the roster—undermined their previous work. Five 1986 World Champions were injured during Italy 1990: Maradona, Burruchaga, Ruggeri, Giusti, and Pumpido. Bilardo waited until the last possible moment to see if Hector Enrique, Jose Luis Brown (who was practicing with the team, until he finally had to go back to Buenos Aires, accompanying the injured Pumpido), and Valdano were fit enough to play the Cup, but he had to cut all three in the end. Most upset about this was Valdano, who had gone ahead with a personal training plan, trying to come back from a career-damaging bout with hepatitis. He was left off the team after he was already in Italy. In response, he said: "I felt like I had drowned on the shore, after having swum across a whole sea."

The truth is that after an unimaginably bad start (the loss against Cameroon), they had advanced thanks to Caniggia's sprints, some creative sparks from a half-fit Maradona and, more than anything, Goycochea's heroic interventions in the penalty-kick shootouts.

The final would be a reflection of all of this. Moreover, a big star would be missing—Caniggia, suspended because of an accumulation of yellow cards—and Germany's path was made all the more smooth. It was a game that would go down in history because of both teams' hesitation to attack each other and the feeling that whoever did not make a mistake would win. In that gutless, tight-fisted game, Germany squeezed out a narrow win. It put Buchwald on Maradona and quickly found that its opponent didn't have the manpower to attack; it had Klinsmann provoke the ejection of Monzon and breathed easy when Mexican referee Codesal didn't call a clear penalty—a Matthaus foul on Calderon. Germany emerged victorious when, six minutes from the end, Codesal called a penalty after a Sensini foul on Voeller; a foul that is still controversial to this day. This time, Goycochea's magic was not enough; he was outdone by the exquisite precision of ambidextrous German defender Andreas Brehme, giving Germany its third title in World Cup history.

That's how Italy 1990, the first World Cup I worked on for Univision, ended: It was a marathon of games—I worked forty of the fifty-two—and the first reverberation of my play-by-play. Of course, the only thing I tried to transmit was my passion . . . and feelings . . . and to reflect the sad faces of the Italians, who ended their World Cup run after that semifinal loss against Argentina; to depict the happier side of the third-place game, an insufficient consolation prize for the home team; and to transmit a clear concern—which would immediately be felt by FIFA, too, when it started to consider rule changes—for a game that seemed to be veering dangerously toward stagnation. Because of all of that, Italy 1990 made history.

CLAUDIO CANIGGIA
(Argentina)
Italy 1990

In modern times, Argentine soccer players are generally recognized as the biggest fans of their own national team. Usually contracted by big foreign clubs, they never hesitate to heed the call of their national team and are capable of foregoing huge sums of money in order to wear the albiceleste. Within that group of players, one has stood out in the last few years who, as he says himself, deserves credit for that very reason. In the words of Claudio Paul Caniggia: "Personally, beyond the final result of the team, I've always produced. . . . For me, the World Cup competitions—and I've played in both Italy 1990 and USA 1994—have always been something special." Without a doubt, he was something special to those two World Cup events, especially the first one in which he played. Carefully handled by the coaching staff led by Carlos Salvador Bilardo, he was kept under observation and safeguarded up to the very beginning of the competition, which he watched from the bench. On June 8, 1990, a black day in its great soccer history, Argentina's World Cup started in Milan with its surprising loss to Cameroon (1–0). That possessed, long-haired blond bird's[1] entrance was not enough to change history, but was enough to unequivocally state that he would be a part of it. With his blazing sprints, he provoked the expulsion of his defenders and affirmed that he would be one of the stars of the tournament. However, the World Cup had begun without him and would end without him: For that reason, though it may sound contradictory, he was one of its main protagonists.

[1]Caniggia's nickname is *el Pájaro*, meaning "the bird" in Spanish.

A.C.: Claudio, the years have passed, for the world and for you. Close your eyes, fly backward in time; what kind of taste did Italy 1990 leave in your mouth?

C.C.: A pleasant one, without a doubt. It was a very positive experience, one of the best. . . . In truth, I have good memories of both World Cup competitions. The same is true of the 1991 Copa America. But the 1990 World Cup was something special: because it was my first World Cup, because the national team wasn't playing well, and because I started off on the bench.

A.C.: But there was a disappointment.

C.C.: Yes, of course; not playing the final was frustrating. I'm filled with anger to this day, but I look at the positive side. For example, having made two goals—the two most important goals of my career—against the two most important teams in the world at that time.

A.C.: Against Brazil in the round of sixteen and against Italy in the semifinal.

C.C.: Exactly . . . they were even more special because we weren't favorites in either of the two games. Quite the opposite, in fact. No one could believe we were capable of continuing to advance.

A.C.: Do you believe that the goal scored against Zenga was in some way responsible for ruining your professional career in Italy? You had so many problems, including a suspension for drugs, that you had to leave Calcio behind.

C.C.: No doubt about it . . . I said it once, in the heat of passion, and I won't take it back now: For four or five years, the Italians made us pay for having eliminated them from their own World Cup. But I prefer not to talk about that.

A.C.: The other goal, the one against Brazil, also had a consequence: It dispelled the doubts people had about you that you didn't know how to finish, that you were an incomplete player because you hesitated when you got into goal-scoring position. . . .

C.C.: *Uuuhhh!* That I didn't know how to finish! That I didn't know how to finish! You know what the truth was? That I was never selfish when I found myself in front of the goalkeeper: I al-

ways passed the ball to a teammate for him to score the goal. . . .
That was always one of my strengths, but also one of my weaknesses.

*The exploits of Goycochea, the goalkeeper who saved the penalty
kicks in the ultra-suspenseful tie-breakers; the effect of a coach like
Carlos Salvador Bilardo, capable of conveying to his players the
greatness implicit in reaching a World Cup final; the mystique of
soccer propelled by its own tradition . . . Argentina was again one
step away from lifting the golden FIFA Cup. More than one person
couldn't believe it.*

A.C.: Claudio, why did Argentina make it to the final?

C.C.: Because we had faith, because of the group bond we
formed: We were convinced it was us against the world. For example, in the 1994 World Cup we started off well. Everyone counted
us amongst the favorites. . . . I'm not saying that it made us lose
focus, but in Italy it was all different: no one liked us, no one believed in us. . . .

A.C.: And what team do you think was the best of the 1990 World
Cup?

C.C.: I think it was Germany, even though they didn't outplay us
in the final, especially considering that we played without three important players. But taking the entire tournament into account, the
Germans were more consistent.

A.C.: In those days, and maybe even today, your image has
caused many to believe that soccer meant very little to you, that
you weren't passionate about it. However, having lost out on the
opportunity to play the final because of a yellow card against Italy
was one of the most bitter chapters in your life. Is that right?

C.C.: I was down, I was in bad shape. . . . As soon as I got to the
locker room while everyone was celebrating that victory in Naples,
I curled up in a corner of the room. I know it was an unfair thing
to do, because the whole team should have shared in the celebration, but I also didn't want to lie to myself: I was shattered. For
those who say I didn't feel or that I don't feel soccer in my bones,
that image is my best answer. Any of my teammates who were
there can confirm it.

A.C.: There are also those who say that had you entered the field of the Stadio Olimpico to play the final, the World Champion would have been Argentina. . . .

C.C.: Yeah, but you can't really say that. Soccer is always changing. It's a question that can't be answered. . . . What I know is that I was playing very well: I had just made goals against Brazil and Italy. Of course I would have also scored against Germany, so my arrows would have pierced all three giants, right? To make World Cup history. Although I guess I've already made it. . . .

USA 1994

Sixteen years later, the soccer party again came to my hometown. Before, I had felt that way about Argentina 1978; now, the same feeling came over me for USA 1994, the fifteenth World Cup.

But I can't deny that I was initially filled with anger when, on July 4, 1988, the site of the Cup was announced. "This country doesn't deserve a World Cup," I said, expressing my dissatisfaction with the choice. I was surely being affected by my own bitterness over the United States' general lack of interest in this sport, which so many of us carry in our blood. Instead of my beloved soccer, Americans prefer to watch baseball, basketball, ice hockey, and, more than anything else, American football, whose existence has forced the United States to rechristen what the rest of the world knows by only one name. Therefore, here in the United States, football is "soccer." After I cooled off and logic came back to me, it crossed my mind that this was a good opportunity to reestablish this most beautiful of sports in the country in which it is ignored. It would be a good starting point, since the United States professional league, the true heart of the sport in any country, had just become a reality. It was clear, then, that we would be watching a unique World Cup, different from all those that had preceded it. Until now, the organizing countries had always fought with all their heart to persuade FIFA to grant them the right to host the event. Here, it was the other way around. In fact, very serious polls taken hours from the starting kickoff gave some alarming results. . . .

"Are you interested in soccer?" was the first question. The answers: 50 percent "No;" 20 percent "Yes, but very little;" 20 percent "Somewhat;" 10 percent "Very much." Another question: "Will you watch the World Cup on TV?" The answers: 61 percent "No"; 28 percent "A little, but not much"; 11 percent "Yes." Finally, an essential piece of information: "Who is hosting the World Cup?" The answers: 66 percent "Don't know"; 31 percent "The United States"; 3 percent "Other countries." It was an uninspiring start.

Despite that disillusioning information, I still anxiously awaited the Cup. Not only professionally, but because of everything that was on the line. My objective was nothing less than to show Americans the beautiful side of soccer. Up to that point, they had only seen the negative side, such as tragedies in stadiums or suspensions of players due to drug use. Rather than sports news, any information about soccer that reached U.S. shores read like police reports.

Professionally, of course, it was the most important challenge of my career. So for four months, I killed myself getting ready: after all I was about to play with the best and I had to be in top form. I totally immersed myself, gathering information and statistics, and memorizing the correct pronunciation of every player's name. Unconsciously, all the stress and the enormous expectation was building up inside me. It finally manifested itself only sixteen days before the start of the World Cup. I was paralyzed, in bed, with sharp pains in my back. The diagnosis was a herniated disk and I was pumped full of analgesics and muscle relaxants.

On June 17, we kicked off our television coverage from a renovated Soldier Field in Chicago. Thankfully, our place for the opening ceremony was on the ground floor close to the production truck stationed next to the field. After that, I would somehow have to ascend to the broadcast booth—the highest point in the stadium. They had studied the possibility of taking me up in a wheelchair, because I could hardly walk. The producers had even taken the time to go up with an empty one to see how much time the trip would take.

The Univision team got to Soldier Field early and, seeing as I couldn't move, they parked in an illegal spot: right next to the press entrance. We rushed out, pressured by the secret service agents on watch for the imminent arrival of President Clinton. In all the commotion, I left my notes—the same notes that I had meticulously gathered for four mouths—in the van. Only minutes before the start of the game—Germany–Bolivia, the first game of "my" World Cup—I managed to get my hands on them, thanks to the skillful negotiations of a producer who, after battling it out with the secret service agents, managed to get to the van and my damned notes.

I remember that as soon as the opening ceremonies started, I was overcome with a strange euphoria. Objectively, what I was watching didn't have the emotion or the spontaneity that I would have liked, but at that moment it seemed to be the most beautiful opening ceremony ever. After all, there I was, the big day had finally come.

In the parade of participating countries, I announced the passing by of Romania and, for the first time, I had an experience that would be repeated throughout the competition, even when it conflicted with an essential part of my work: My voice cracked. Perhaps because hearing it reminded me of my mother, who was born there.

In general, tension accompanied my every move. That tension—normal—and the terrible pain in my back—circumstantial—left me a physical wreck. Still, I announced the first "goooal!" of the tournament with all my heart and soul. It was a work by German striker Jurgen Klinsmann, sixty-one minutes into the game, against goalkeeper Trucco, an Argentinean who had become a Bolivian citizen. It was the big debut—both theirs and mine but also a sort of confirmation, since, to my surprise, my first scream didn't hurt. It came from my throat, but it must have been born somewhere outside of my beat-up body, because it rolled out of me as effortlessly as ever. I was still drenched in sweat, and I barely had time to change my soaked-through clothes for dry ones . . . in the van on the twenty-minute ride from Soldier Field to the studio from which we were to televise the second game of the day: Spain versus Korea. It was just my luck that for the first time in history, the opening day of the World Cup would include *two* games, both for Group C.

Right after that tie (2–2) between the Asians and Europeans, we were to board a private airplane bound for Miami to begin the unforgettable marathon of games there. Before boarding at the Chicago airport, we saw how every television channel was broadcasting the now infamous O. J. Simpson car chase. All eyes were riveted to the spectacle of this American-football star accused, and later acquitted, of the killing of his own ex-wife. In the midst of all that drama on television, something that was clearly selfish crossed my mind, but forgivable given my priorities at the time. It was too ironic that this, of all things, was threatening to take interest away from a World Cup that already had more than enough stacked against it.

But by the next day, I was again immersed in my own world. The

United States made its tournament debut in the place that was most appropriate: in the most surprising stadium in the tournament, Detroit's, which was totally covered by a transparent roof, something unprecedented in World Cup history. That day I screamed out Wynalda's goal against Switzerland with all I had. That *"gooooal!"* startled a lot of people, but it meant many things to me: It was the tying goal for a team I loved deeply, and it was scored by a friend, the same one I met during my youth when he played for the San Francisco Bay Blackhawks; the same friend who I had been bold enough to predict that he'd one day be appreciated as a star in his own country. But right away, amidst all my elation, another feeling was rising, this time a cruel one: I feared I was going hoarse. This time, my voice had come out of my heart, and it was a warning sign to hold back a little bit. . . . I took note of the fact that I had another forty-nine games ahead of me—to complete the fifty-two—and that I could end up missing out on all of them if I didn't watch myself. Yet, that night when I tried to go to sleep—if you could call it that— my own nerves wouldn't let me close my eyes.

The Cup didn't give me a break. In Los Angeles, Colombia became its own worst enemy. Overconfidence, fed in large part by exaggerated praise and acclaim from the press and fans, led to their being derailed by the pragmatic Romanians. Radicioiu (twice) and Hagi were merciless, and they gave the Colombians a slap they wouldn't recover from. Colombia's big stars—Valderrama, Rincon, Valencia, Asprilla—were incapable of averting the approaching soccer catastrophe, and the first big surprise of USA 1994 was born. From here on out, Group A—formed by the United States, Switzerland, Romania, and Colombia—would turn out much differently than expected.

Led by the aforementioned names as well as by Dumitrescu, the Romanian team took the lead in the group, taking advantage of a less-pressured situation. Behind them came the Swiss, also under less pressure, with their publicized stars—Sutter, Chapuisat, Sforza— showing some sparks of talent.

In the most important duel, the scales were tipped in favor of the biggest underdogs. In their head-to-head matchup, the United States beat Colombia and earned a historic second-round berth. More than ninety thousand fans in Pasadena's Rose Bowl saw how Andres Escobar started off his team's loss with an unfortunate play, in which he slid the ball into his own goal. Countless soccer lovers throughout the world would be shocked a few days later, when they heard the tragic news: The same Colombian defender was assassinated in his country—perhaps because of that one error—a victim of insanity and irrationality.

In San Francisco, the Brazilians set up shop in their inimitable style: with diplomacy, happiness, good humor, and all of the other elements necessary to make them feel at home. Right away, the inhabitants of Northern California—with the Bay Area suburb of Los Gatos as the epicenter—knew what it was all about and who their illustrious visitor was. Their first step onto the field made one think that their path to the title wouldn't be one with many obstacles. With Romario's first goal, they beat Russia and heated up their engines. Also in that group (Group B) were Cameroon and Sweden, but neither of them looked like they could rain on the parade of the three-time World Champion.

The team coached by Carlos Alberto Parreira—assisted by "perennial winner," Mario Lobo Zagallo—began to put a new strategy into effect on the field, especially considering that it involved a Brazilian team: less boldness, more pragmatism; less showiness, more efficiency. With the goals and leadership of Romario and Bebeto, and the defensive ability of Dunga and Mauro Silva, they advanced easily, without a lot of fanfare. Behind them came Sweden, with standout Martin Dahlin, and Russia, which shone in only one game: a 6–1 win against Cameroon, in which Oleg Salenko scored five goals. With those five goals, plus one more in the game against Sweden, Salenko crowned himself one of the top two leading scorers of the World Cup.

The case of the Africans deserves its own paragraph. They had dazzled everyone in Italy 1990, opening up great possibility to the teams of their continent, and justifying the old protests against FIFA. But they disappointed everyone in USA 1994, falling prey to their own disorganization, and coming one step away from disappearing as a soccer entity.

Group C, which had started the World Cup, ended without surprises. The Germans went to the next round, showing little besides Klinsmann's power and with a fright at the end, when the tireless South Koreans almost rallied back from a 3–0 deficit, which finally ended 3–2. Spain advanced also, but without shining. Perhaps their controversial coach, Javier Clemente, preferred it that way.

Bolivia was left behind with the consolation of having scored its first goal in World Cup history—a work by Erwin Sanchez, sixty-seven minutes into the game against Spain.

In that first round, no team played as well as Argentina. Based in Boston, coach Alfio Basile's team started off by sweeping their way to victory. They flattened Greece (4–0), a team coached by Alketas Panagoulias (who previously coached the United States' national team), before patiently demolishing Nigeria (2–1), which later proved itself to be one of the big rivals in the group. Redondo's class, Balbo's excellence, Batistuta's power, and the touch of distinction given by Maradona were unstoppable qualities. Only a disgrace could leave Argentina out of the race . . . only a disgrace.

Playing against Argentina, Greece showed its incredible weaknesses while Nigeria and Bulgaria fought to be second best, each in its own way: the Africans, with their great strength and the quality of players like Oliseh, Finidi, Amunike, Yekini, and Amokachi; the Europeans, with the inconsistent talent of men like Letchkov, Balakov, Sirakov, and the infallible Stoitchkov. Both teams considered Argentina better than they were . . . that is, under normal circumstances.

Because of its teams, Group E could easily be described as the "group of death" always present in any World Cup: The group in which it's impossible to predict who will win and who will lose and in which every game is a battle. Ireland and Italy kicked it off with a battle between the big "hyphens." Giants Stadium in New York was divided between a majority of Irish-Americans and an incredible number of Italian-Americans, representatives of the two largest ethnic communities of the region. For the Irish, it was a victorious debut, thanks to a goal by Houghton and an energy which, like four years before, wasn't dazzling, but was good enough to advance them to the next round. For the Italians, it was more of the same: a faltering start, with too much time being spent on fights and internal conflicts about which style of play or which players to use.

Mexico, another of the "home teams," thanks to the large number of its expatriates living in the United States, also started off badly, losing to Norway in a game decided in the last minute. The group would be decided the same way: It would be necessary to wait until the last minute of the last game to determine the position of the teams and who would advance to the next round. Things were so even that the scales were tipped by the smallest goal differences. Mexico, Ireland, Italy, and Norway ended in that order, with the same number of points—four each—by way of an identical number of wins, draws, and losses—one of each—and even the same goal difference—0. Mexico won the group by virtue of having made one more goal than the rest—3. Second place was decided by the direct confrontation between Ireland and Italy: Since they were deadlocked on points, goal difference, and goals scored, Ireland's win in the head-to-head battle gave it the edge over Italy. Norway was eliminated, because it had scored only one goal. A lot of numbers, few standouts.

Because of the teams' reputations and the lack of interest in the matchups, Group F could well have passed unnoticed. But the World Cup was in the United States, so every game was interesting by definition. That's the only explanation for 60,790 fans showing up to see an unimportant Belgium 1–Morocco 0, the opening game in Orlando's Citrus Bowl, which left little to analyze. That said, it was a bit easier to believe that 52,525 saw one of the favorites, Holland, play inexperienced Saudi Arabia. In that first-night game of USA 1994, the team that had to win did, but not before the Arabs had the pleasure of scaring the pants off the Dutch at the outset by scoring their first goal in World Cup history, thanks to Fuad Amin, eighteen minutes in.

Those two games set the stage for what would follow. More was expected from Holland, which narrowly won the group, with intermittent bursts of good play from Bergkamp, Overmars, and Roy, but nothing dazzling. Less was expected from Saudi Arabia, which ended with a surprising second-place finish, after beating Belgium 1–0 on a goal by Said Owairan that was surely the best of the tournament. Owairan had gotten the ball at midfield and dribbled through half the Belgian defense, à la Maradona. Belgium stayed true to form and advanced without showing much.

In those first-round matches, after Wynalda's goal against Switzerland, only two other goals really stood out for me personally, and only later did I understand why: They were the ones that told the great stories of the start of this World Cup.

One was by Diego Armando Maradona against Greece in Boston on June 21. It was important because it signified so much: It was the comeback of the greatest soccer player I had seen in my life, and it was also his retaliation to all the controversy that had surrounded him. My happiness would last only a short while, but it was intense while it lasted. It was his way of showing—unfortunately short-lived, considering what was to come next—that he was still a giant. Besides that, it was simply an extraordinary goal, which I shouted out with passion, allowing me to fulfill a longtime dream:

to announce a goal by the soccer player who has impressed me the most.

The other was Ernie Stewart's goal against Colombia, which qualified the United States team, coached by my friend Bora Milutinovic, for the second round. That scream started in my throat, and, five seconds later, disappeared into the air, overtaken by hoarseness. Instantaneously and instinctively, the "Goooal!" I had started and lost burst out again from the depths of my body. It was a bit more than the end of a hard-day's work: It was the qualifying goal of the only team that could inspire those who believed soccer was boring and useless. I let it all—or at least almost all—out. It was worth it.

I don't really remember when people started to take note of my work. I only know that the doctor had told me to lie down and rest between games, and an ear, nose, and throat specialist had told me not to talk between games. But it was impossible. . . .

I never thought so much attention would be paid to the shout of "goal" that came out of me so naturally, influenced by those unforgettable afternoons in Argentina, with the radio stuck to my ear, listening to play-by-play man José María "*el Gordo*" Muñoz.[1] What I am convinced of is that the passion I put into my work is what set it apart.

Every day, Univision's PR department scheduled me to do at least fifteen interviews a day for newspapers, magazines, other television networks, and radio stations throughout the world. Medicines helped me get over the pain in my body, but it was still hard for me to walk straight. On the door of my office, my coworkers had pasted a picture of me with the words "Sheriff's Office" underneath, referring to my posture while walking, with my legs bent.

They came from all corners of the United States, Argentina, Germany, Italy, and France. . . . They would stay and film me in the studio, observing my routine and my preparation and paying attention to, above all else, my shout of "Goooal!," which was so surprising for them, yet so natural for me. . . .

I remember that one day before the last game of the first round, the head of the PR department came, filled with pride, to tell me that the *Late Show with David Letterman* had called to invite me on

---

[1]*El Gordo:* "the fatman" is endearingly used as a nickname in Argentina for those who are portly.

the show as soon as I got a free day. "No way," I responded, "I've gone more than twenty days without a break. I want to sleep like a normal human being, even if it's for only a few hours." It took them a while to convince me of the importance of going on the show and what could come out of such an appearance. Finally, I agreed to visit Dave as well as *Live with Regis and Kathie Lee*. I remember now, that's when it finally hit me. As I left the Ed Sullivan Theater and ABC's studios, I had to stop and sign autographs for hundreds of new soccer fans.

Meanwhile, I went on with my normal duties. Specifically, my daily participation—by telephone—on the radio show *Fútbol de Primera,*[2] which I had created with my partner and friend, Alejandro Gutman. He moved through all the sites, leaving no stone unturned—our style—to bring the best information to the forty radio stations throughout the country that received our show. In our sixth year on the air, with our own network formed after intense effort, we were on cloud nine.

Then, just as things were really starting to happen, I received very bad news—perhaps the worst of my professional career—news that put my objectivity to the test.

On Wednesday, June 29, as I was preparing for my radio program, in one of my few moments of freedom from the television, my computer began to spit out urgent news. There was a rumor that a player had tested positive for drugs. We reported the news, which still did not include a player's name. Never did it cross my mind that the involved party could be Diego Armando Maradona. But it was quickly confirmed. Even today, I cannot describe the feeling that came over my body and soul, because it was actually many feelings at the same time: frustration, shame, anger, sadness. . . . What is certain is that I felt betrayed, because I, like everyone else, had been inspired by Diego's performance. Those two games of high-quality play had shown that he was still the best, in spite of everything.

I must admit, until that moment I had been harboring a very intimate, personal dream: to see and announce the coronation of the Argentine national team, led by Maradona, in Pasadena's Rose Bowl, a stadium that was "mine." I had seen every game played there, from Johan Cruyff's Los Angeles Aztecs to the 1984

---

[2]*Fútbol de Primera* has a double meaning. It means both "high-quality soccer" and "first division soccer."

Olympics, from every unimportant friendly match played there to even an American college football game between Ohio and Michigan. For me, it was the neighborhood stadium. But my dream was fast shattering before me.

I was crushed. They were destroying Maradona's hopes, and my greatest dream, all at once. Somehow, I was able to gather up my strength and, with my voice shaking, say what I felt: "I'd like to defend the indefensible, but I can't. He made another mistake, I can't deny it, and when we know more about the situation, we'll know why and who was responsible. But for now there is only one responsible party, and his name is Diego Armando Maradona. But I can't hold a grudge. I'd rather think about what he gave me and every one of us who loves soccer. Then, like a movie, it all came flooding back: his incomparable goal against England; Diego lifting the Cup in Mexico 1986; the two *scudetti*[3] and the UEFA Cup he won with Napoli; and the victory lap with Boca Juniors in 1981! And the most recent images, of course: sprinting from the other end of the field to guard a huge Nigerian ninety-two minutes into the game; the cross-legged kick in the same game; the great performance he gave, in spite of everything; and all of it at the age of thirty-four.

In only two games (against Greece and Nigeria), he had shown that he was still hungrier than any of the other players in the World Cup. He made another mistake, it's true, and I don't know what his future will be. I hope that God helps him.

For many, the World Cup ended right there. I couldn't allow myself that luxury. In any case, it was clear that the course of the World Cup had changed.

Argentina, whose morale had been dealt a heavy blow, fell in the last game of the first round, against Bulgaria, and finished third in their group; then landed, all of a sudden, on the other coast of the United States. From its training camp in Boston, from which it had thought that, at worst, it would have to move to New York, the Argentineans went to Los Angeles, a city they thought they wouldn't see until the final. But now, the round of sixteen was in play, and the opponent was Romania, which was again merciless. Just as it had defeated the favored Colombia, it ended Argentina's dreams (3–2), in one of the most exciting games of the World Cup. Alfio

---

[3]*Scudetti:* meaning "badge" in Italian; *scudetto* is the name given to an Italian league championship. *Scudetti* is plural.

Basile's team, now without its captain, was unable to come back. In order to salvage the situation, Basile experimented with systems he had never tried before: a man-to-man defense against the two men in the World Cup who had been most decisive up to that point; but it was not enough. Hagi and Dumitrescu sealed the win in a 3–2 victory that was as entertaining as it was fatal to the South Americans. Without pressure, the Europeans continued their advance.

With the same spirit, Bulgaria took another step forward. Its victim was Mexico which, in spite of playing with only ten men due to the ejection of Luis Garcia, seemed to enter the game's overtime in better shape than its opponent. On the sidelines, conservative Mexican coach Miguel Mejia Baron refused to give in to a bold Hugo Sanchez, who seemed desperate to enter the game, but never did so. Perhaps because of that, the game was decided by penalties. Just as in 1986 in Monterrey, Mexico was again left out of the party. This time around, however, it may have had the maturity necessary to give another jump forward; a jump to where Stoitchkov and his teammates were going.

The round's most awaited game was played on a historic date: July 4. In Stanford stadium in Palo Alto, near San Francisco, filled with 84,147 fans, the United States played its hand against the favorite: Brazil. The fact that the game was played on Independence Day certainly added to the dreams of the Americans. But, beyond this coincidence, the previous games showed that the United States' hopes were not totally quixotic. Only after seventy-four minutes—despite constantly pressuring the U.S. goal—were the Brazilians able to break the deadlock, thanks to a goal by Bebeto. So often criticized for disappearing in the game's important moments, the Brazilian striker responded with the most important goal in his career up to that point. In any case, that wasn't the only repercussion of the game. There was also the sadness of the savage and inexplicable elbow thrown by Leonardo to the head of Tabare Ramos, a blow so strong it kept Ramos off the field for almost six months. Finally, there was the contagious happiness of the Americans, even in defeat, because they proved to themselves and to others that they were capable of playing a good game with the very best. From then on out, names like Alexi Lalas (whose appearance made him stand out), Marcelo Balboa, and Thomas Dooley started to be recognized. The chant of the crowd of "U.S.A.! U.S.A.!" said it all: The World Cup had achieved its first success—the marriage of America to soccer. Bora Milutinovic had been the inspiration behind this un-

precedented achievement, because of his work on one big fundamental: making his players understand tactics down to their very
essence. Unfortunately, not everyone in the United States could appreciate the work of the popular Serb. Six months later, he was
fired. However, others knew what he was worth: Mexico hired him
to face the challenge of France 1998.

At this stage of the Cup, Italy found someone to put its faith in.
Finally, Roberto Baggio lived up to his fame and alone decided the
game against Nigeria, a game that had become very complicated.
The Nigerians had gotten ahead with a goal by Amunike at twenty-
six minutes. Italy's "number ten" turned the game around, leveling
the score only two minutes from the end and scoring the winning
goal from the penalty spot in the first half of overtime, both times
taking advantage of his opponents' errors.

The rest of the games didn't produce many surprises. . . .

Germany beat Belgium narrowly (3–2), aided by Swiss referee
Rothlisberger, who missed a clear penalty against Belguim and
thanks to the aim of its two expert marksmen, Voeller and Klinsmann. The Germans' perennial internal conflicts had already left a
victim—Effenberg, who was sent back home by the team because
of his rude reaction to the public's insults—and had begun to undermine the team's future.

Spain blew out Switzerland (3–0), without breaking a sweat. Sweden woke up Saudi Arabia from its dream (3–1), finally playing to
their full potential and leaving behind one of the tournament's most
pleasant surprises. Holland quietly finished off Ireland (2–0) in a
solid but unremarkable game. And so it went.

The games continued and the articles about me did, too. My
shout of "Goooal!" had taken over the United States, and I, lost in
the daily shuffle, was unaware of the whole thing. Only when I was
given a notebook filled with all the news clippings did I finally realize the impact. All the articles that were gathered were special, but
two in particular touched me deeply: an article published in the Argentine magazine *El Gráfico* and the other in the Argentine newspaper *La Nación*. The acknowledgement by my compatriots was
very special. Everyone wanted to know the secret of how I took
care of my voice. They all were incredulous when I told them there
wasn't any magic formula, only tea with honey.

The quarterfinals once again offered an uneven picture, geo-
graphically speaking: seven European teams, and one South American team. Everyone against Brazil.

For the first game, Old Lobo's team was matched up against a giant: Holland. The game was played in Dallas's Cotton Bowl and didn't turn out to be an easy task, even though it seemed that it would at first. The usual suspects—Romario and Bebeto—put their team ahead in, respectively, fifty-two and sixty-three minutes, unleashing the customary *verdeamarelha* craziness. Just 120 seconds later, the Dutch showed some pride, proving they had made it that far for a reason. Bergkamp scored right away, and Winter equalized shortly afterward, making the game a bit more than a perfunctory exercise and giving the match an unusual ending, making it historic. . . . After eighty minutes, Brazil was given a free kick just outside the penalty area. Branco, a member of the old guard who was rejected by much of the public but staunchly defended by the coach, asked to kick. He hit the ball with his customary class. The ball went toward Romario, just behind the wall of Dutch defenders, but the brilliant striker let the ball pass him. In doing so, he helped the team as much as he would have with a goal of his own. As if it had passed right through him, the ball continued on its way to its fated destination. Obviously, it ended in the net, giving Brazil the win—surely its most important of the tournament up to that point.

In Boston, Italy and Spain took up an old duel, even though the players themselves may not have known it. Back in 1934, they needed two games to decide the battle, and the Spanish were left empty-handed. Destiny would dictate a similar fate for the rematch. The game was tied 1–1 (after goals by Dino Baggio at twenty-five minutes and Caminero at fifty-eight) when Italian defender Mauro Tassotti elbowed Spanish striker Luis Enrique in the face inside the penalty area. With his face bloodied and his nose broken, the Spaniard begged the referee to call what the whole stadium had seen: a penalty as clear as day. Hungarian referee Sandor Puhl changed the course of the game with that blunder (as a "reward" he would be picked to officiate the final). At eighty-five minutes, after a long stretch of not touching the ball, Roberto Baggio showed what made him so special: He dribbled past goalkeeper Zubizarreta and put the ball into the open goal, putting his team in the semifinals.

Joining them in the semifinals would be Bulgaria, which finally showed in the quarterfinals why they had gotten that far. More than anything, it was because of the presence of an extraordinary player, capable of displaying an alarming attitude, yet also capable of the most decisive plays. Leader of his team even in the most important decisions and unpredictable both on and off the field, Hristo Stoitchkov was a long-time star for FC Barcelona in Spain, shining—and making his team shine—for the first time on an international level. He calmed down the rest of the team after they went down 1–0 to Germany. Then, he fired them up, leading them to a surprising 2–1 victory, on his goal and one by Iordan Letchkov, leaving the defending champions no chance to defend their title.

Also in the race was another underdog: Sweden. Its quarterfinal match against Romania had to be decided with penalty kicks—after a dramatic tying goal in the final minutes of overtime by Kenneth Andersson. It was now up to the goalkeepers, and it was Ravelli who came through in the clutch. He stopped Petrescu and Belodedici's tries, putting the Swedes somewhere they hadn't been since 1958, when the party took place in their own country: They were now semifinalists; mission accomplished.

That was the situation right before the semifinals: two big favorites against two big surprises. Brazil and Italy had more on the line than the other two, and the weight of tradition drove them to the final.

For the South Americans, the semifinal game was symbolic of their performances throughout the tournament: not risking too much, measuring each step, even against the Swedes who were happy just to be there rather than worried about winning. After Jonas Thern's controversial expulsion in the sixty-second minute, they were finally able to score nine minutes before the final whistle. A header by Romario (who else?) gave them a 1–0 win and the ticket to the final as if it had been a business transaction.

For the Italians, five minutes of inspiration from Roberto Baggio was all that was needed. Italy's "number ten" had gotten accustomed to making the end of every game more dramatic. This time, he appeared early: He struck twice, at twenty and twenty-five minutes. With his usual class, unleashed conservatively but effectively, he finished off the Bulgarians. At the end of the first half, Stoitchkov provided a glimmer of hope to his squad, which, before USA 1994, had never won a World Cup game and were now amazed to find themselves one step away from playing a World Cup final. In the end, they were blocked by their opponents' greatest strength: a very solid defense, epitomized by the extraordinary Maldini.

At last I got to the Rose Bowl broadcasting after forty-nine games from our studios in Miami. It was for the third-place game, to be played between Sweden and Bulgaria. We did the play-by-play from the stadium, in the open air, and we all had to shade ourselves from the glare with the cardboard that protected the monitors. The heat was stifling, and the only thing that kept me going was the realization that while I was there in the stadium I was becoming a participant in history.

The Swedes and Bulgarians offered a different kind of game, one which once again made clear that the consolation prize was meaningless. They played it only because they were obligated to. It meant a bit more to the Swedes, and that gave them the win.

That night, the eve of the big final, I went on a walk through Pasadena's Old Town. There were people everywhere, and everyone was carrying flags: Italian ones, Brazilian ones, and even American ones. There was an unmistakable feeling of joy in the air, a feeling that only the World Cup can bring about. I had thought before that maybe I was in the wrong city, the wrong country . . . but it was I who was wrong, and the proof was right in front of me: all those people, recognizing and celebrating the power and beauty of soccer. There was only one question to ask: Would they continue to appreciate soccer? But that is a question that is, for the moment, unanswerable.

On the other hand, those who did have to answer the questions that would be put to them on the field were the two finalists: Italy and Brazil. For the Europeans, their advance in this World Cup had remained faithful to their history as discussed earlier: filled with fights and controversy, fueled by their great pride. Their coach—Arrigo Sacchi—had gotten to that lofty position by way of his glorious victories as the head of the revolutionary AC Milan. His reputation gave him the freedom to impose his innovative ideas that diverged so greatly from the traditional Italian style. He proposed a zone defense, aggressive attack soccer, and placed more emphasis on the aesthetic aspect of the game. However, in the end, it was all theory; in practice, the Italians got to the final by taking any road open to them—almost always playing badly—because of the irregular appearances of their crucial star, Roberto Baggio. Whenever the famous *Codino*[4] (so named because of his ponytail) appeared on the brink of collapse, exposing himself to criticism, he reappeared with a life-saving play, giving the Italians a stay of execution. Perhaps that's why the end would be so ironic.

---

[4]*Codino:* "Short tail" or "pigtail" in Italian.

Brazil also arrived by renouncing their traditional principles and set the foundation for a new style. The efforts of Coach Carlos Alberto Parreira were put into words by his assistant, Mario Lobo Zagallo:

The coaching staff decides what a team does on the field. In 1970, I was already talking about opening up spaces on the field without the ball, and those ideas are the same ones we have today. In the 1982 and 1986 World Cup competitions, the Brazilian teams were good, but they played only when they had the ball. The same is true of Argentina this year. Nice teams? Yes. Did they play beautiful soccer? Yes again. But they weren't competitive. One just can't play artistic soccer anymore. A World Cup isn't a show, it's a competition. The one that competes wins, not the one that tries to give an exhibition. I don't want to single out Argentina for criticism, I'm just trying to make a point about today's soccer. This is 1994. Soccer isn't the same as it was in 1970 or in 1958. Things have changed. They've changed! The three top-placed teams of the World Cup—Brazil, Italy, and Sweden—played with a 4–4–2 formation. It's no coincidence. In general, Brazil attacked while their goal was almost never put at risk. There were difficulties because our opponents defended with eight men, but we always tried to go forward anyway. Look, when does a team have space to play the ball? When the opponent attacks, of course. Now, what happens when an opponent doesn't attack? Does one use the long ball? No, one must secure the ball and toss it from right to left and even backward, until an open space is found. That wasn't easy . . . but Brazil always looked for the goal and, by doing so, it was always in its opponents' territory. USA 1994 was a combative, physical, and modern World Cup, in which the winning teams used similar systems. But one must not be confused: One can use the same system and be different. A team can use a 4–4–2 and attack with two men like Italy did, or it can use a 4–4–2 and send five or six men to the attack, including backs and midfielders, taking the game to another level, like Brazil did.

But that strategy, explained and emphatically defended by Zagallo himself, still depended on certain key players, of course.

In the backfield, in spite of any recent changes, were men faithful to traditional Brazilian soccer: a goalkeeper incapable of offering absolute security—Taffarel; right and left backs with the souls of forwards—Jorginho or Cafu on the right, Branco or Leonardo on the left; and central defenders with the skill to play the ball—Marcio Santos and Aldair, who replaced the injured Ricardo Rocha and Ricardo Gomes. In the midfield there were question marks, but also keys to victory like Dunga and Mauro Silva—the leaders who balanced the whole team; Mazinho and Zinho—inconsistent midfielders responsible for the launching of attacks, who were the duo that replaced the traditional "number ten," which didn't exist on this team because of Rai's poor performance. Up front, Bebeto—who had come with a reputation for becoming invisible in big games, but had made important goals, and Romario—the definite key to victory, a fright to any rival defense, even without being the leader of the group.

That's what the Brazilians had to offer when they stepped onto the field on that hot July 17, 1994. There was so much at stake. Not only the chance to lift the sought-after Cup, but also the chance to be the first four-time World Champion. Perhaps because of this, both teams tried hard not to lose and risked little to win. That trophy, the most sought-after in the sporting world, has room for seventeen inscriptions: the year 2038 will therefore be the last time it will be put in play. Italy and Brazil both tried to assure themselves of a spot on it. This is how the battle unfolded. . . .

The Italians' ordered, zone defense neutralized any attempted breakthrough on the part of the Brazilians. Faithful to their plan of defending themselves—even though they did risk a little more than in the old days—they left Brazil with few scoring chances. For the Italians, Daniele Massaro had the only scoring opportunity, but he squandered it when confronted with an inspired Taffarel. The uneventful regulation time ended without score being opened. In the half-hour overtime, only the entrance of young Brazilian striker Viola gave the Italians a fright. But it was too late, nobody was trying anymore.

So they ended regulation time just as they had begun, in a final that certainly won't go down in history as the most memorable. The crucible of the penalty kicks would include the biggest names of this World Cup. In the first kick, the great Baresi—who had had arthroscopic surgery after the first game—failed to convert. In the last kick, the always decisive Roberto Baggio also missed. The Brazilians converted all of their kicks, the glory was theirs. They dedicated the win to the memory of Ayrton Senna—the Formula One driver who had died that very same year, on the way to his promised fourth championship. After twenty-four years filled with disappointments, the Brazilians won the Cup playing a style of soccer nothing like their usual, convinced that it was the only way to victory.

Thus a different kind of World Cup ended; unique in its own way. Played in a country where football is known as "soccer," it was still capable of breaking all sorts of records and filling the stadiums like never before: 3,567,415 fans passed through the gates of the stadiums, surpassing Italy 1990's mark by over one million. An average attendance of 68,604 per game—20,000 more than four years earlier—saw 141 goals scored—every single one of them screamed by yours truly with all my heart and soul—at a promising average of 2.71 per game.

More than mere statistics, these numbers reflect a hope that the soccer party will continue, because, in my opinion, there is nothing else like it anywhere on Earth.

I also hope it continues in the United States, although I once thought the U.S.A. didn't deserve the soccer World Cup. During that unforgettable month in 1994, many people told me I had been one of the stars of that World Cup. The truth is that all I tried to do was convey my passion for the most beautiful game in the world, hoping that more people could understand it and love it the way I do. I think I won that game. And I know that I—and everyone else who loves soccer—will go on playing it, because this story doesn't end here.

ROMARIO
(Brazil)
USA 1994

"I'm getting old," said Romario to some of the friends who visited him at the Hospital de Servidores del Estado, where he was placed under observation in September of 1995, after collapsing in a practice session. According to the Brazilian press, it was not the first time comments like that came from Romario's lips. Even those closest to him assure us that the idea of retiring has been going through the striker's mind since the end of World Cup 1994.

The comment, published in most of the world's newspapers a little more than a year after the end of World Cup USA 1994, portrayed an alarming situation surrounding the last star of international soccer: Romario Souza Faria, better known as simply Romario.

He won himself a place among the greats during the hot afternoons of USA 1994. And even if he didn't quite get to crown himself "king of soccer," a title reserved, for now, for Di Stefano, Pele, Cruyff, and Maradona, he did earn himself the title of "Prince" as the undisputed best player of the moment. He did it with five goals, against Russia, Cameroon, Sweden, Holland (the most spectacular of them all), and Sweden again, all of them done with that magical aura that only Romario could supply.

R.: One can say many things about me, but I live great moments with ease and with more passion than anyone. I never liked friendlies; I prefer games with something on the line. That's why the World Cup was something different for me. I always love going onto a field with the stand full and twenty-two players pumped with adrenaline. It is in those situations that the men stand out from the boys.

A.C.: Even though you played well, you never gave the impression of being completely in shape. . . .

R.: Right, right. I wasn't in good shape before the World Cup. In the days before our first game, I was holed up in Fresno, California, and I didn't train for an entire week. But that's all over now. . . .

A.C.: Were you afraid of being left out of the Cup at any time?

R.: I was very afraid. I had a strong pain in one of my ribs and, because of that, I couldn't practice. A lot of people thought I wasn't practicing with my teammates because of the heat, but that was not the case. They also said I did whatever I wanted, when in fact I was taking care of myself in order to get to each game in the best possible shape.

A.C.: Brazil celebrated a world championship for the first time in twenty-four years. Do they owe it to you?

R.: I was solid, but this one wasn't just me. We had an excellent roster who all came together to make Brazil a great team. Each one of us deserves a bit of credit, but people always make me responsible, not only to praise me, but to criticize me as well. Before the World Cup, I received stacks of faxes asking me, begging me to bring the title back home. Well, here it is, but it was achieved by all of us. The year before the World Cup when I landed in Rio de Janeiro to play the game against Uruguay in the qualifiers, there was an army of reporters waiting to ask me if I was the savior. Even then I said no . . . and even then, in the Maracaná, the entire team won that game, too.

A.C.: But you can't deny that you were the star of the World Cup. . . .

R.: The star, the star . . . who chooses him? I played very well, maybe better than anyone. But I was helped by key men like Dunga and Mauro Silva. Go ask Mario Zagallo, the only person with the authority to say whether I was the star or not, since he has won more Cups than anyone.

A.C.: At any point did it cross your mind that Brazil might not go home with the Cup?

R.: It only crossed my mind that it would be tough to beat Argentina with Maradona. After that, no.

If anyone thinks that Romario wants to renew his waterfall of goals and his title as "Prince of Soccer" in the next World Cup in France, you may be surprised with what he has to say on the subject. In his typical style: "The conquest of the tetracampeonato *was the ultimate. My dream has come true. . . . By the time of the next World Cup, I'll be thirty-two years old. I'm not planning on playing it, in fact the mere possibility hasn't even crossed my mind."*

Appendix:
World Cup Scores

World Cup Uruguay 1930

GROUP 1

France—4   Mexico—1

L. Laurent (F, 19'); Langiller (F, 40'); Maschinot (F, 42', 87'); Careño (M, 70')
Montevideo, 7/13/1930. Referee: D. Lombardi (Uruguay).

Argentina—1   France—0

Monti (A, 81')
Montevideo, 7/15/1930. Referee: G. de Almeida Rego (Brazil).

Chile—3   Mexico—0

Subiabre (C, 4', 50'); Vidal (C, 64')
Montevideo, 7/16/1930. Referee: H. Christophe (Belgium).

Chile—1   France—0

Subiabre (C, 64')
Montevideo, 7/19/1930. Referee: A Tejada (Uruguay).

Argentina—6   Mexico—3

Stabile (A, 8', 17' 80'); Zumelzu (A, 10', 55'); M. Rosas (M, 38' penalty, 65'); Varallo (A, 53'); Gayon (M, 75')
Montevideo, 7/19/1930. Referee: U. Saucedo (Bolivia).

Argentina—3   Chile—1

Stabile (A, 12', 14'); Subiabre (C, 16'); M. Evaristo (A, 51')
Montevideo, 7/22/1930. Referee: J. Langenus (Belgium).

GROUP 2

Yugoslavia—2   Brazil—1

Tirnanic (Y, 21'); Beck (Y, 31'); Nilo (B, 62')
Montevideo, 7/14/1930. Referee: A. Tejada (Uruguay).

Yugoslavia—4   Bolivia—0

Beck (Y, 6', 67'); Marjanovic (Y, 65'); Vujadinovic (Y, 85')
Montevideo, 7/17/1930. Referee: F. Mateucci (Uruguay).

Brazil—4   Bolivia—0

Moderato (Br, 37', 73'); Preguinho
(Br, 57' 83')
Montevideo, 7/20/1930. Referee: G.
Bolway (France).

GROUP 3

Romania—3   Peru—1

Stranciu (R, 1', 35'); Souza (P, 30');
Barbu (R, 80')
Montevideo, 7/14/1930. Referee: A.
Warken (Chile).

Uruguay—1   Peru—0

H. Castro (U, 60')
Montevideo, 7/18/1930. Referee: J.
Langenus (Belgium).

Uruguay—4   Romania—0

Dorado (U, 6'); Scarone (U, 24');
Anselmo (U, 30'); Cea (U, 35')
Montevideo, 7/21/1930. Referee: G.
de Almeida Rego (Brazil).

GROUP 4

USA—3   Belgium—0

McGhee (USA, 10'); Florie (USA,
15'); Brown (USA, 48')
Montevideo, 7/13/1930. Referee J.
Macias (Argentina).

USA—3   Paraguay—0

Patenaude (USA, 10', 50'); R. Gon-
zalez (P, 15' own goal)
Montevideo, 7/17/1930. Referee: J.
Macias (Argentina).

Paraguay—1   Belgium—0

Pena (P, 30')
Montevideo, 7/20/1930. Referee: J.
De Almeida Rego (Brazil).

SEMIFINALS

Argentina—6   USA—1

Monti (A, 20'); Peucelle (A, 56', 80',
85'); Stabile (A, 69', 87'); Brown
(USA 88')
Montevideo, 7/26/1930. Referee: J.
Langenus (Belgium).

Uruguay—6   Yugoslavia—1

Sekulic (Y, 4'); Cea (U, 18', 67', 72');
Anselmo (U, 20', 31'); Iriarte (U,
61')
Montevideo, 7/27/1930. Referee: G.
de Almeida Rego (Brazil).

FINAL

Uruguay—4   Argentina—2

Dorado (U, 12'); Peucelle (A, 20');
Stabile (A, 37'); Cea (U, 57'); Iri-
arte (U, 68'); H. Castro (U, 89')
Montevideo, 7/30/1930. Referee: J.
Langenus (Belgium).
Uruguay: Ballestrero; Nasazzi,
Mascheroni; Andrade, Fernandez,
Gestido; Dorado, Sarcone, Cas-
tro, Cea, Iriarte. Coach: Alberto
Supicci.
Argentina: Botasso; Della Torre, Pa-
ternoster; Evaristo, Monti, Suarez;
Peucelle, Varallo, Stabile, Fer-
reira, Evaristo. Coach: Francisco
Olazar.

World Cup Italy 1934

Austria—3   France—2

Nicolas (F, 19'); Sindelar (A, 44');
  Schall (A, 94'); Bican (A, 96');
  Verriest (F, 114' penalty)
Turin, 5/27/1934. Referee: J. Van
  Moorsel (Holland).
A 30' overtime was played.

Hungary—4   Egypt—2

Teleki (H, 12'); Toldi (H, 31', 52');
  Fawzi (E, 39', 67'); Vincze (H,
  59')
Naples, 5/27/1934. Referee: R. Barlassina (Italy).

Spain—3   Brazil—1

Iraragorri (S, 18' penalty); Langara
  (S, 27', 77'); Leonidas (B, 56')
Genoa, 5/27/1934. Referee: A. Bir-
  lem (Germany).
Brito (Brazil) saved a penalty kick.

Italy—7   USA—1

Schiavio (I, 18', 29', 64'); Orsi (I, 20',
  69'); Donelli (USA, 57'); Ferrari (I,
  63'); Meazza (I, 90')
Rome, 5/27/1934. Referee: R. Mer-
  cet (Switzerland).

Germany—5   Belgium—2

Kobierski (G, 26'); Voorhoof (B,
  31', 43'); Stiffling (G, 47'); Conen
  (G, 67', 70', 86')
Florence, 5/27/1934. Referee: F.
  Mattea (Italy).

Sweden—3   Argentina—2

Belis (A, 3'); Jonasson (S, 8', 67');
  Galateo (A, 47'); Kroon (S, 79')
Bologna, 5/27/1934. Referee: A.
  Braun (Austria).

Switzerland—3   Holland—2

Kielholz (S, 14', 43'); Smit (H, 22');
  Abegglen III (S, 63'); Vente (H,
  87')
Milan, 5/27/1934. Referee: I. Eklind
  (Sweden)

Czech.—2   Romania—1

Dobay (R, 10'); Puc (C, 49'); Nejedly (C, 67')
Trieste, 5/27/1934. Referee: J. Langenus (Belgium)

QUARTERFINALS

Austria—2   Hungary—1

Horvath (A, 5'); Zischek (A, 53');
  Sarosi (H, 67')
Bologna, 5/31/1934. Referee: F.
  Mattea (Italy).

Italy—1   Spain—1

Regueiro (S, 29'); Ferrari (I, 44')
Florence, 5/31/1934. Referee: L.
  Boert (Belgium).
A 30' overtime was played.

Germany—2   Sweden—1

Hohmann (G, 60', 53'); Dunker (S,
  83') Milan, 5/31/1934. Referee: R.
  Barlassina (Italy).

Czech.—3   Switzerland—2

Kielohlz (S, 18'); Svoboda (C, 24');
Sbotka (C, 48'); Abegglen III (S,
71'); Nejedly (C, 83')
Turin, 5/31/1934. Referee: A. Be-
ranek (Germany).

TIE-BREAKER

Italy—1   Spain—0

Meazza (I, 11')
Florence, 6/1/1934. Referee: R. Mer-
cet (Switzerland).

SEMIFINALS

Italy—1   Austria—0

Guaita (I, 21')
Milan, 6/3/1934. Referee: I. Eklind
(Sweden).

Czech.—3   Germany—1

Nejedly (C, 21', 60', 81'); Noack (G,
50')
Rome, 6/3/1934. Referee: R. Barlassina (Italy).

THIRD-PLACE GAME

Germany—3   Austria—2

Leher (G, 1', 42'); Conen (G, 29');
Horvath (A, 30'); Sesta (A, 55')
Naples, 6/7/1934. Referee: A. Car-
raro (Italy).

FINAL

Italy—2   Czechoslovakia—1

Puc (C, 70'); Orsi (I, 80'); Schiavio
(I, 95')
Rome, 6/10/1934. Referee: I. Eklind
(Sweden).

A 30' overtime was played.
Italy: Combi; Monzeglio, Allemandi;
Ferraris IV, Monti, Bertolini;
Guaita, Meazza, Schiavio, Ferrari,
Orsi. Coach: Vittorio Pozzo
Czechoslovakia: Planicka; Zenisek,
Ctyroky; Kostalek, Cambal, Krcil;
Junek, Svoboda, Sobotka, Ne-
jedly, Puc. Coach: Karel Petru

World Cup France 1938

Switzerland—1   Germany—1

Gauchel (G, 29'); Abegglen III (S.
43')
Paris, 6/4/1948. Referee: J. Langenus (Belgium).

Cuba—3   Romania—3

Covaci (R, 38'); Socorro (C, 42');
Baratki (R, 59'); Maquina (C, 88',
101'); Dobay (R, 98')
Toulouse, 6/5/1938. Referee: G.
Scarpi (Italy).
A 30' overtime was played in
which the tie was unbroken,
forcing a new tie-breaker match.

Czech.—3   Holland—0

Kostalek (C, 96'); Nejedly (C, 111');
Zeman (C, 119')
Le Havre, 6/5/1938. Referee: L.
Leclercq (France).
A 30' overtime was played.

France—3   Belgium—1

Veinante (F, 1'); Nicolas (F, 12', 69');
Isemborghs (B, 38')
Paris, 6/5/1938. Referee: H.
Wüthrich (Switzerland).

Hungary—6 Dutch E. Ind.—0

Kohut (H, 18'); Toldi (H, 23', 77');
Sarosi (H, 28'); Zsengeller (H, 35',
52')
Reims, 6/5/1938. Referee: Conrie
(France).

Brazil—6   Poland—5

Leonidas (B, 18', 93', 102'); Wil-
imowski (P, 22' penalty, 59', 88',
107'); Romeu (B, 25'); Peracio (B,
44', 72'); Scherfke (P, 50')
Strasbourg, 6/5/1938. Referee: I. Eklind (Switzerland).
A 30' overtime was played.

Italy—2   Norway—1

Ferraris II (I, 2'); Brustad (N, 83');
Piola (I, 94')
Marseille, 6/5/1938. Referee: A. Be-
ranek (Germany).

TIE-BREAKERS

Switzerland—4 Germany—2

Hahnemann (G, 8'); Lörtscher (S,
22' own goal); Walaschek (S,
41'); Bickel (S, 64'); Abegglen III
(S, 75', 78')
Paris, 6/9/1938. Referee: I Eklind
(Sweden).

Cuba—2   Romania—1

Dobay (R, 9'); Tunis (C, 65'); M.
Sosa (C, 80')
Toulouse, 6/9/1938. Referee: A. Bir-
lem (Germany).

QUARTERFINALS

Italy—3   France—1

Colaussi (I, 9'); Heisserer (F, 10');
Piola (I, 52', 72')
Paris, 6/12/1938. Referee: L. Baert
(Belgium).

Sweden—8   Cuba—0

H. Andersson (S, 15', 54'); Nyberg
(S, 32', 60'); Wetterström (S, 34',
41', 52', 82')
Antibes, 6/12/1938. Referee: Kirst
(Czechoslovakia).

Hungary—2 Switzerland—0

Sarosi (H, 42'); Zsengeller (H, 68')
Lille, 6/12/1938. Referee: R. Borsal-
lina (Italy).

Brazil—1 Czechoslovakia—1

Leonidas (B, 30'); Nejedly (C, 64'
penalty)
Bordeaux, 6/12/1938. Referee: P.
Von Hertzka (Hungary).

TIE-BREAKER

Brazil—2 Czechoslovakia—1

Kopecky (C, 30'); Leonidas (B, 56');
Roberto (B, 63')
Bordeaux, 6/14/1938. Referee: G.
Capdeville (France).

SEMIFINALS

Hungary—5   Sweden—1

Nyberg (S, 4'); Eriksson (S, 18' own
goal); Tikos (H, 26'); Zsengeller
(H, 38', 77'); Sarosi I (H, 61')
Paris, 6/16/1938. Referee: L.
Leclercq (France).

Italy—2   Brazil—1

Colaussi (I, 55'); Meazza (I, 60'
    penalty); Romeu (B, 87')
Marseille, 6/16/1938. Referee: H.
    Wüthrich (Switzerland).

THIRD-PLACE GAME

Brazil—4   Sweden—2

Jonasson (S, 18'); Nyberg (S, 38');
    Romeu (B, 42'); Leonidas (B, 63',
    73'); Peracio (80')
Bordeaux, 6/19/1938. Referee: J.
    Langenus (Belgium).

FINAL

Italy—4   Hungary—2

Colaussi (I, 5', 35'); Titkas (H, 7');
    Piola (I, 16', 82'); Sarosi (H, 70')
Paris, 6/19/1938. Referee: G.
    Capdeville (France).
Italy: Olivieri; Foni, Rava; Serantoni,
    Andreolo, Locatelli; Biavati,
    Meazza, Piola, Ferrari, Colaussi.
    Coach: Vittorio Pozzo.
Hungary: Szabo; Polgar, Biro; Szo-
    lay, Szücs, Lazar; Sas, Vincze,
    Sarosi I, Zsengeller, Titkos.
    Coach: Karl Dietz.

World Cup Brazil 1950

GROUP 1

Brazil—4   Mexico—0

Ademir (B, 32', 81'); Jair (B, 66');
    Baltazar (B, 72')
Rio de Janeiro, 6/25/1950. Referee:
    G. Reader (England).

Yugoslavia—3   Switz.—0

Mitic (Y, 58'); Tomasevic (Y, 64');
    Ognjanov (Y, 82')
Belo Horizonte, 6/25/1950. Referee:
    G. Galeati (Italy).

Brazil—2   Switzerland—2

Alfredo (B, 2'); Falton (S, 16', 88');
    Baltazar (B, 31')
Sao Paulo, 6/28/1950. Referee: R.
    Azon (Spain).

Yugoslavia—4   Mexico—1

Bobek (Y, 19'); Ciaikovski (Y, 22',
    62'); Tomasevic (Y, 81'); L. Ve-
    lazquez (M, 88' penalty)
Porto Alegre, 6/29/1950. Referee:
    Leafe (England).

Brazil—2   Yugoslavia—0

Ademir (B, 3'); Zizinho (B, 69')
Rio de Janeiro, 7/1/1950. Referee:
    B. M. Griffiths (Wales).

Switzerland—2   Mexico—1

Bader (S, 12'); Tamini (S, 45');
    Casarin (M, 88')
Porto Alegre, 7/2/1950. Referee: I.
    Eklind (Sweden).

GROUP 2

England—2   Chile—0

Mortensen (E, 37'); Finney (E, 52')
Porto Alegre, 6/25/1950. Referee:
    K. Van Der Meer (Holland).

Spain—3   USA—1

J. Souza (USA, 18'); Basora (S, 80',
    82'); Zarra (S, 85')
Curitiba, 6/25/1950. Referee: M.
    Viana (Brazil).

Spain—2   Chile—0

Zarra (S, 19', 35')
Rio de Janeiro, 6/29/1950. Referee:
G. Malcher (Brazil).

USA—1   England—0

Gaetjens (USA, 39')
Belo Horizonte, 6/29/1950. Referee:
G. Dattilo (Italy).

Spain—1   England—0

Zarra (S, 49')
Rio de Janeiro, 7/2/1950. Referee:
G. Galeati (Italy).

Chile—5   USA—2

Robeldo (C, 20'); Riera (C, 32');
Wallace (USA, 46'); E. Souza
(USA, 49' penalty); Cremaschi (C,
54', 82'); Prieto (C, 60')
Recife, 7/2/1950. Referee: Gardelli
(Italy).

GROUP 3

Sweden—3   Italy—2

Carapellese (I, 7'); Jeppsson (S, 25',
68'); S. Andersson (S, 33'); Muc-
cinelli (I, 75')
Sao Paulo, 6/25/1950. Referee: Lutz
(Switzerland).

Sweden—2   Paraguay—2

Sundqvist (S, 23'); Palmer (S, 25');
A. Lopez (P, 35', 80')
Curitiba, 6/29/1950. Referee:
Mitchell (Scotland).

Italy—2   Paraguay—0

Carapellese (I, 12'); Pandolfini (I,
62')

Sao Paulo, 7/2/1950. Referee: A.
Ellis (England).

GROUP 4

Uruguay—8   Bolivia—0

Schiaffino (U, 14', 23', 45', 56', 59');
Vidal (U, 18'); J. Perez (U, 73');
Ghiggia (U, 83')
Belo Horizonte, 7/2/1950. Referee:
G. Reader (England).

FINAL ROUND

Brazil—7   Sweden—1

Ademir (B, 17', 36', 52', 54'); Chico
(39', 88'); S. Andersson (S, 67'
penalty); Maneca (B, 85')
Rio de Janeiro, 7/9/1950. Referee:
A. Ellis (England).

Spain—2   Uruguay—2

Ghiggia (U, 29'); Basora (S, 32',
39'); Varela (U, 73')
Sao Paulo, 7/9/1950. Referee: G.
Reader (England).

Brazil—6   Spain—1

Ademir (B, 15', 57'); Jair (B, 21');
Chico (B, 31', 55'); Zizinho (B,
67'); Igoa (S, 71')
Rio de Janeiro, 7/13/1950. Referee:
R. J. Leafe (England).

Uruguay—3   Sweden—2

Palmer (S, 5'); Ghiggia (U, 39');
Sundqvist (S, 40'); Miguez (U, 77',
85')
Sao Paulo, 7/13/1950. Referee: G.
Galeati (Italy).

Sweden—3   Spain—1

Sundqvist (Sw, 15'); Mellberg (Sw, 33'); Palmer (Sw, 80'); Zarra (S, 82')
Sao Paulo, 7/16/1950. Referee: K. Van Der Meer (Holland).

FINAL

Uruguay—2   Brazil—1

Friaça (B, 47'); Schiaffino (U, 66'); Ghiggia (U, 79')
Rio de Janeiro, 7/16/1950. Referee: G. Reader (England).
Uruguay: Maspoli; Gonzales, Tejera; Gambetta, Varela, Rodriguez Andrade; Ghiggia, Julio Perez, Miguez, Schiaffino, Moran. Coach: Juan Lopez.
Brazil: Barbosa; Augusto, Juvenal; Bauer, Danilo, Bigode; Friaça, Zizinho, Ademir, Jair, Chico. Coach: Flavio Costa.

World Cup Switzerland 1954

GROUP 1

Yugoslavia—1   France—0

Milutinovic (Y, 15')
Lausanne, 6/16/1954. Referee: B. M. Griffiths (Wales).

Brazil—5   Mexico—0

Baltazar (B, 23'); Didi (B, 30'); Pinga (B, 34', 43'); Julinho (B, 69')
Geneva, 6/16/1954. Referee: R. Wyssling (Switzerland).

Brazil—1   Yugoslavia—1

Zebec (Y, 48'); Didi (B, 69')
Lausanne, 6/19/1954. Referee: E. C. Faultless (Scotland).

France—3   Mexico—2

J. Vincent (F, 19'); R. Cardenas (M, 49' own goal); Lamadrid (M, 54'); Balcazar (M, 85'); Kopa (F, 88' penalty)
Geneva, 6/19/1954. Referee: M. Asensi (Spain).

GROUP 2

Hungary—9   South Korea—0

Puskas (H, 12', 89'); Lantos (H, 18'); Kocsis (H, 24', 36', 50'); Czibor (H, 59'); Palotas (H, 75', 83')
Zurich, 6/17/1954. Referee: R. Vincenti (France).

West Germany—4   Turkey—1

Suat (T, 2'); Schafer (WG, 14'); Klodt (WG, 52'); O. Walter (WG, 60'); Morlock (WG, 81')
Bern, 6/17/1954. Referee: J. Vieira Da Costa (Portugal).

Hungary—8   W. Germany—3

Kocsis (H, 3', 21' 67', 78'); Puskas (H, 17'); A. Pfaff (WG, 25'); Hidegkuti (H, 50', 54'); J. Toth (H, 73'); Rahn (WG, 77'); Hermann (WG, 81')
Basel, 6/20/1954. Referee: W. H. E. Ling (England).

Turkey—7   South Korea—0

Suat (T, 10', 30'); Lefter (T, 24');
   Burhan (T, 37', 64', 70'); Erol (T,
   76')
Geneva, 6/20/1954. Referee: E.
   Marino (Uruguay).

TIE-BREAKER

West Germany—7 Turkey—2

O. Walter (WG, 10'); Schafer (WG,
   12', 79'); Mustafa (T, 21'); Morlock (WG, 30', 60', 77'); F. Walter
   (WG, 62'); Lefter (T, 82')
Zurich, 6/23/1954. Referee: R. Vincenti (France).

GROUP 3

Austria—1   Scotland—0

Probst (A, 33')
Zurich, 6/16/1954. Referee: L.
   Franken (Belgium).

Uruguay—2   Czech.—0

Miguez (U, 69'); Schiaffino (U, 82')
Bern, 6/16/1954. Referee: A. Ellis
   (England).

Austria—5   Czech.—0

Stojaspal (A, 3', 65'); Probst (A, 4',
   21', 24')
Zurich, 6/19/1954. Referee: V. Stefanovic (Yugoslavia).

Uruguay—7   Scotland—0

Borges (U, 17', 47', 57'); Miguez (U,
   30', 83'); Abbadie (U, 54', 85')
Basel, 6/19/1954. Referee: V. Orlandini (Italy).

GROUP 4

England—4   Belgium—4

Anoul (B, 5', 71'); Broadis (E, 26',
   63'); Lofthouse (E, 36', 91'); Cop-
   pens (B, 78'); Dickinson (E, 94'
   own goal)
Basel, 6/17/1954. Referee: E.
   Schmetzer (West Germany).
The game included a 30' overtime.

Switzerland—2   Italy—1

Ballaman (S, 17'); Boniperti (I, 44');
   Hugi II (S, 78')
Lausanne, 6/17/1954. Referee: M.
   Viana (Brazil).

England—2   Switzerland—0

Mullen (E, 43'); Wilshaw (E, 69')
Bern, 6/20/1954. Referee: I. Zsolt
   (Hungary).

Italy—4   Belgium—1

Pandolfini (I, 44'); C. Galli (I, 48');
   Frignani (I, 58'); Lorenzi (I, 58')
Anoul (B, 81')
Lugano, 6/20/1954. Referee: E.
   Steiner (Austria).

TIE-BREAKER

Switzerland—4   Italy—1

Hugi II (S, 14', 85'); Ballaman (S,
   48'); Nesti (I, 67'); Fatton (S, 90')
Basel, 6/23/1954. Referee: B. M.
   Griffiths (Wales).

QUARTERFINALS

Austria—7   Switzerland—5

Ballaman (S, 16', 39'); Hugi II (S, 17', 23', 58'); Wagner (A, 24', 27', 52'); A. Koerner II (A. 25'); Ocwirck (A, 32'); R. Koerner I (A, 34'); Probst (A, 76')
Lausanne, 6/26/1954. Referee: E. C. Faultless (Scotland).

Uruguay—4   England—2

Borges (U, 4'); Lofthouse (E, 16'); O. J. Varela (U, 39'); Schiaffino (U, 46'); Finney (E, 67'); Ambrois (U, 78')
Basel, 6/26/1954. Referee: E. Steiner (Austria).

Hungary—4   Brazil—2

Hidegkuti (H, 4'); Kocsis (H, 7', 88'); D. Santos (B, 18', penalty); Lantos (H, 60' penalty); Julinho (B, 65')
Bern, 6/27/1954. Referee: A. Ellis (England).

W. Ger.—2   Yugoslavia—0

Horvat (Y, 9', own goal); Kahn (WG, 85')
Geneva, 6/27/1954. Referee: I. Zsolt (Hungary).

SEMIFINALS

Hungary—4   Uruguay—2

Czibor (H, 13'); Hidegkuti (H, 46'); Hohberg (U, 75', 86'); Kocsis (111', 116')
Lausanne, 6/30/1954. Referee: B. M. Griffiths (Wales).
A 30' overtime was played.

West Germany—6 Austria—1

Morlock (WG, 31', 47', 61'); Probst (A, 51'); F. Walter (WG, 54' penalty, 65' penalty); O. Walter (WG, 89')
Basel, 6/30/1954. Referee: V. Orlandini (Italy).

THIRD-PLACE GAME

Austria—3   Uruguay—1

Stojaspal (A, 16' penalty); Hohberg (U, 22'); L. Cruz (U, 59' own goal); Ocwirck (A, 79')
Zurich, 7/3/1954. Referee: B. M. Griffiths (Wales).

FINAL

W. Germany—3 Hungary—2

Puskas (H, 6'); Czibar (H, 8'); Morlock (WG, 10'); Rahn (WG, 18', 84')
Bern, 7/4/1954. Referee: W. H. E. Ling (England).
West Germany: Turek; Posipal, Kohlmeyer; Eckel, Liebrich, Mai; Rahan, Morlock, Otmar Walter, Fritz Walter, Schaefer. Coach: Josef Herberger
Hungary: Grosics; Buzanszky, Lantos; Bozsik, Lorant, Zakariaz; Czibor, Kocsis, Hidegkuti, Puskas, Jozsef Toth. Coach: Gustav Sebes

World Cup Sweden 1958

GROUP 1

N. Ireland—1   Czech.—0

Cush (NI, 16')
Halmstad, 6/8/1958. Referee: R. Seipelt (Austria).

W. Germany—3 Argentina—1

Corbatta (A, 2'); Rahn (WG, 32', 79'); Seeler (WG, 40')
Halmstad, 6/8/1958. Referee: R. Leafe (England).

Argentina—3   N. Ireland—1

McParland (NI, 3'); Corbatta (A, 38' penalty); N. Menendez (A, 55'); Avio (A, 59')
Helsingborg, 6/11/1958. Referee: Alhner (Sweden).

Czech.—2   W. Germany—2

Dvorak (C, 24' penalty); Zikan (C, 43'); Schaefer (WG, 59'); Rahn (WG, 70')
Malmö, 6/11/1958. Referee: A. Ellis (England).

W. Ger.—2   N. Ireland—2

McParland (NI, 17', 58'); Rahn (WG, 20'); Seeler (WG, 79')
Helsingborg, 6/15/1958. Referee: J. Campos (Portugal).

Czech.—6   Argentina—1

Dvorak (C, 8'); Zikan (C, 17', 40'); Corbatta (A, 65' penalty); Feureisl (C, 69'); Hovorka (C, 82' 89')
Malmö, 6/17/1958. Referee: A. Ellis (England).

TIE-BREAKER

N. Ireland—2   Czech.—1

Ziken (C, 19'); McFarland (NI, 44', 89')
Malmö, 6/17/1958. Referee: M. Guigue (France).

GROUP 2

Yugoslavia—1   Scotland—1

Petakovic (Y, 6'); Murray (S, 49')
Västerås, 6/8/1958. Referee: P. Wyssling (Switzerland).

France—7   Paraguay—3

Amarilla (P, 20', 44'); Fontaine (F, 24', 30', 67'); J. Romero (P, 50'); Piantoni (F, 52'); Wisnieski (F, 61'); Kopa (F, 68'); Vincent (F. 83')
Norrköping, 6/8/1958. Referee: J. Gardeazabal (Spain).

Paraguay—3   Scotland—2

Agüero (P, 4'); Mudie (S, 24'); Re (P, 45'); J. Parodi (P, 71'); Collins (S, 72')
Norrköping, 6/11/1958. Referee: V. Orlandini (Italy).

Yugoslavia—3   France—2

Fontaine (F, 4', 85'); Petakovic (Y, 16'); Veselinovic (Y, 61', 88')
Västerås, 6/11/1958. Referee: B. M. Griffiths (Wales).

France—2   Scotland—1

Piantoni (F, 22'); Fontaine (F, 44'); Baird (S, 58')
Örebro, 6/15/1958. Referee: J. Brozzi (Argentina).

Yugoslavia—3   Paraguay—3

Ognjanovic (Y, 12'); J. Parodi (P,
  20'); Veselinovic (Y, 28'); Agüero
  (P, 52'); Rajkov (Y, 73'); J.
  Romero (P, 80')
Eskilstuna, 6/15/1958. Referee:
  Marko (Czechoslovakia).

GROUP 3

Sweden—3   Mexico—0

Simonsson (S, 17', 64'); Liedholm
  (S, 57' penalty)
Stockholm, 6/8/1958. Referee: N.
  Latishev (Soviet Union).

Wales—1   Hungary—1

Bozsik (H, 5'); J. Charles (W, 27')
Sandviken, 6/8/1958. Referee: J. M.
  Codesal (Uruguay).

Mexico—1   Wales—1

Allchurch (W, 32'); Belmonte (M,
  89')
Stockholm, 6/11/1958. Referee:
  Lemesic (Yugoslavia).

Sweden—2   Hungary—1

Hamrin (S, 34', 55'); Tichy H, 77')
Stockholm, 6/12/1958. Referee:
  Mawatt (Scotland).

Sweden—0   Wales—0

Stockholm, 6/15/1958. Referee: Van
  Nuffel (Belgium).

Hungary—4   Mexico—0

Tichy (H, 19', 46'); Sandor (H, 54');
  Bencsics (H, 69')
Sandviken, 6/15/1958. Referee:
  Eriksson (Finland).

TIE-BREAKER

Wales—2   Hungary—1

Tichy (H, 33'); Allchurch (W, 55');
  Medwin (G, 76')
Stockholm, 6/17/1958. Referee: N.
  Latishev (Soviet Union).

GROUP 4

Brazil—3   Austria—0

Altafini (B, 38', 89'); Nilton Santos
  (B, 49')
Uddevalla, 6/8/1958. Referee: M.
  Guigue (France).

England—2   USSR—2

Simonjan (USSR, 13'); A. Ivanov
  (USSR, 55'); Kevan (E, 66');
  Finney (E. 85' penalty)
Göteborg, 6/8/1958. Referee: I.
  Zsalt (Hungary).

USSR—2   Austria—0

Iljin (USSR, 15'); V. Ivanov (USSR,
  62')
Borås, 6/11/1958. Referee: J. F. Jor-
  gensen (Denmark).

Brazil—0   England—0

Göteborg, 6/11/1958. Referee: A.
  Dusch (West Germany).

Austria—2   England—2

Koller (A, 16'); Haynes (E, 61'); Koerner (A, 70'); Kevan (E, 78')
Borås, 6/15/1958. Referee: As-
  mussen (Denmark).

Brazil—2   USSR—0

Vava (B, 2', 77')
Göteborg, 6/15/1958. Referee: M.
Guigue (France).

TIE-BREAKER

USSR—1   England—0

Iljin (USSR, 78')
Göteborg, 6/17/1958. Referee: A.
Dusch (West Germany).

QUARTERFINALS

W. Ger.—1   Yugoslavia—0

Rahn (WG, 12')
Malmö, 6/19/1958. Referee: P.
Wyssling (Switzerland).

Sweden—2   USSR—0

Hamrin (S, 4'); Simonsson (S, 88')
Stockholm, 6/19/1958. Referee: R.
Leafe (England).

France—4   N. Ireland—0

Wisnieski (F, 22'); Fontaine (F, 55',
63'); Piantoni (F, 68')
Norrköping, 6/19/1958. Referee: J.
Gardeazabal (Spain).

Brazil—1   Wales—0

Pele (B, 66')
Göteborg, 6/19/1958. Referee: E.
Seipelt (Austria).

SEMIFINALS

Sweden—3   W. Germany—1

Schaefer (WG, 23'); Skoglund (S,
32'); Gren (S, 81'); Hamrin (S,
88')
Göteborg, 6/24/1958. Referee: I.
Zsalt (Hungary).

Brazil—5   France—2

Vava (B, 2'); Fontaine (F, 9'); Didi
(B, 39'); Pele (B, 52', 64', 75');
Piantoni (F, 83')
Stockholm, 6/24/1958. Referee: B.
M. Griffiths (Wales).

THIRD-PLACE GAME

France—6   West Germany—3

Fontaine (F, 14', 36', 78', 90');
Cleslarczyk (WG, 17'); Kopa (F,
26' penalty); Douis (F, 49'); Rahn
(WG, 51'); Schaefer (WG, 84')
Göteborg, 6/28/1958. Referee: J.
Brozzi (Argentina).

FINAL

Brazil—5   Sweden—2

Liedholm (S, 3'); Vava (B, 9', 32');
Pele (B, 55', 90'); Zagallo (B, 68');
Simonsson (S, 80')
Stockholm, 6/29/1958. Referee: M.
Guigue (France).
Brazil: Gilmar; Djalma Santos, Nil-
ton Santos; Zito, Bellini, Orlando;
Garrincha, Didi, Vava, Pele, Za-
gallo. Coach: Vicente Feola.
Sweden: Svensson; Bergmark,
Axbom; Boerjesson, Gustavsson,
Parling; Gren, Simonsson, Lied-
holm, Hamrin, Skoglund. Coach:
George Raynor.

World Cup Chile 1962

GROUP 1

Uruguay—2   Colombia—1

Zuluaga (C, 28' penalty); Sasia (U, 57'); Cubilla (U, 73')
Arica, 5/30/1962. Referee: A. Dorogy (Hungary).

USSR—2   Yugoslavia—0

V. Ivanov (USSR, 60'); Ponedelnik (USSR, 85')
Arica, 5/31/1962. Referee: A. Dusch (West Germany).

Yugoslavia—3   Uruguay—1

R. Cabrera (U, 18'); Skoblar (Y, 27' penalty); Galic (Y, 38'); Jerkovic (Y, 47')
Arica, 6/2/1962. Referee: J. Etzel Filho (Brazil).

USSR—4   Colombia—4

V. Ivanov (USSR, 9', 14'); Cislenko (USSR, 11'); Aceros (C, 20'); Ponedelnik (USSR, 51'); Coll (C, 67'); Rada (C, 71'); Kilinger (C, 77')
Arica, 6/3/1962. Referee: J. Etzel Filho (Brazil).

USSR—2   Uruguay—1

Mamykin (USSR, 37'); Sasia (Ur, 53'); V. Ivanov (USSR, 89')
Arica, 6/6/1962. Referee: C. Jonni (Italy).

Yugoslavia—5   Colombia—0

Galic (Y, 20', 52'); Jerkovic (Y, 25', 87'); Melic (Y, 73')
Arica, 6/7/1962. Referee: C. Robles (Chile).

GROUP 2

Chile—3   Switzerland—1

Wütrich (S, 8'); L. Sanchez (C, 43', 56'); J. Ramirez (C, 51')
Santiago, 5/30/1962. Referee: K. Aston (England).

Italy—0   West Germany—0

Santiago, 5/31/1962. Referee: R. Holley Davidson (Scotland).

Chile—2   Italy—0

J. Ramirez (C, 74'); Toro (C, 87')
Santiago, 6/2/1962. Referee: K. Aston (England).

W. Germany—2   Switz.—1

Brülls (WG, 44'); Seeler (WG, 61'); Antenen (S, 75')
Santiago, 6/3/1962. Referee: L. Horn (Holland).

West Germany—2   Chile—0

Szymaniak (WG, 22' penalty); Seeler (WG, 82')
Santiago, 6/6/1962. Referee: R. Holley Davidson (Scotland).

Italy—3   Switzerland—0

Mora (I, 3'); Bulgarelli (I, 65', 68')
Santiago, 6/7/1962. Referee: N. Latyshev (Soviet Union).

GROUP 3

Brazil—2   **Mexico—0**

Zagallo (B, 56'); Pele (B, 72')
Viña del Mar, 5/30/1962. Referee:
   G. Dienst (Switzerland).

Czechoslovakia—1 Spain—0

Stibranyi (C, 78')
Viña del Mar, 5/31/1962. Referee: E.
   Steiner (Austria).

Brazil—0 Czechoslovakia—0

Viña del Mar, 6/2/1962. Referee: P.
   Schwinte (France).

Spain—1   **Mexico—0**

Peiro (S, 88')
Viña del Mar, 6/3/1962. Referee: B.
   Tesanic (Yugoslavia).

Brazil—2   **Spain—1**

Adelardo (S, 34'); Amarildo (B, 71',
   89')
Viña del Mar, 6/6/1962. Referee: S.
   Bustamante (Chile).

Mexico—3   **Czech.—1**

Masek (C, 1'); I. Diaz (M, 10'); Del
   Aguila (M, 29'); H. Hernandez
   (M, 89' penalty)
Viña del Mar, 6/7/1962. Referee: G.
   Dienst (Switzerland).

GROUP 4

Argentina—1   **Bulgaria—0**

Facundo (A, 4')
Rancagua, 5/30/1962. Referee: J.
   Gardeazabal (Spain).

Hungary—2   **England—1**

Tichy (H, 15'); Flowers (E, 60'
   penalty); Albert (H, 75')
Rancagua, 5/31/1962. Referee: L.
   Horn (Holland).

England—3   **Argentina—1**

Flowers (E, 14' penalty); B. Charlton (E, 42'); Greaves (E, 57'); San-
   filippo (A, 83')
Rancagua, 6/2/1962. Referee: N.
   Latichev (Soviet Union).

Hungary—6   **Bulgaria—1**

Albert (H, 1', 6', 53'); Tichy (8', 70');
   Salymasi (12'); Sokolov (B, 64')
Rancagua, 6/3/1962. Referee: J.
   Gardeazabal (Spain).

Hungary—0   **Argentina—0**

Rancagua, 6/6/1962. Referee: A.Ya-
   masaki (Peru).

Bulgaria—0   **England—0**

Rancagua, 6/7/1962. Referee: A.
   Blavier (Belgium).

QUARTERFINALS

Chile—2   **USSR—1**

L. Sanchez (C, 10'); Cislenko (USSR,
   72'); E. Rojas (C, 73')
Arica, 6/10/1962. Referee: L. Horn
   (Holland).

Yugoslavia—1   **W. Ger.—0**

Radakovis (Y, 87')
Santiago, 6/10/1962. Referee: A. Yamasaki (Peru.)

Brazil—3   England—1

Garrincha (B, 29', 59'); Hitchens (E, 38'); Vava (B, 53')
Viña del Mar, 6/10/1962. Referee: P. Schwinte (France).

Czech.—1   Hungary—0

Scherer (C, 13')
Rancagua, 6/10/1962. Referee: N. Latishev (Soviet Union).

Brazil—4   Chile—2

Garrincha (B, 9', 31'); Toro (C, 41'); Vava (48', 77'); L. Sanchez (C, 61' penalty)
Santiago, 6/13/1962. Referee: A. Yamasaki (Peru).

Czech.—3   Yugoslavia—1

Kadraba (C, 49'); Jerkovic (Y, 69'); Scherer (C, 81', 89')
Viña del Mar, 6/13/1962. Referee: G. Dienst (Switzerland).

THIRD-PLACE GAME

Chile—1   Yugoslavia—0

E. Rojas (C, 90')
Santiago, 6/16/1962. Referee: J. Gardeazabal (Spain).

FINAL

Brazil—3 Czechoslovakia—1

Masopust (C, 15'); Amarildo (B, 17'); Zito (B, 68'); Vava (B, 77')
Santiago, 6/17/1962. Referee: N. Latishev (Soviet Union).
Brazil: Gilmar; Djalma Santos, Nilton Santos; Zito, Mauro, Zozimo; Garrincha, Didi, Vava, Amarildo, Zagallo, Coach: Aimore Moreira.

Czechoslovakia: Schrojf; Tichy, Novak; Pluskal, Popluhar, Masopust; Pospichal, Scherer, Kvasnak, Kadrabo, Jelinek. Coach: Rudolf Vytlacil.

World Cup England 1966

England—0   Uruguay—0

London, 7/11/1966. Referee: I. Zsolt (Hungary).

France—1   Mexico—1

Borja (M, 48'); Hausser (F, 52') London, 7/13/1966. Referee: M. Ashkenazi (Israel).

Uruguay—2   France—1

De Bourgoing (F, 15' penalty); Rocha (U, 27'); Cortes (U, 32')
London, 7/15/1966. Referee: K. Galba (Czechoslovakia).

England—2   Mexico—0

B. Charlton (E, 37;); Hunt (E, 75')
London, 7/16/1966. Referee: C. Lo Bello (Italy).

Mexico—0   Uruguay—0

London, 7/19/1966. Referee: B. Lööw (Sweden).

England—2   France—0

Hunt (E, 38', 75')
London, 7/20/1966. Referee: A Yamasaski (Peru).

GROUP 2

West Germany—5   Switz.—0

Held (WG, 15'); Haller (WG, 21', 77'
    penalty); Beckenbauer (WG, 40',
    52')
Sheffield, 7/12/1966. Referee:
    Phillips (Scotland).

Argentina—2   Spain—1

Artime (A, 64', 80'); Pirri (S, 72')
Birmingham, 7/13/1966. Referee:
    Rumentchev (Romania).

Spain—2   Switzerland—1

Quentin (Sw, 29'); Sanchis (Sp, 57');
    Amancio (Sp, 75')
Sheffield, 7/15/1966. Referee: T.
    Bakhramov (Soviet Union).

W. Ger.—0   Argentina—0

Birmingham, 7/16/1966. Referee: K.
    Zecevic (Yugoslavia).

Argentina—2 Switzerland—0

Artime (A, 52'); E. Onega (A, 80')
Birmingham, 7/20/1966. Referee: J.
    Campos (Portugal).

West Germany—2   Spain—1

Fuste (S, 22'); Emmerich (WG, 38');
    Seeler (WG, 89')
Birmingham, 7/20/1966. Referee: A.
    Marquez

GROUP 3

Brazil—2   Bulgaria—0

Pele (Br, 15'); Garrincha (Br, 63')
Liverpool, 7/12/1966. Referee:
    Tschenscher (Germany).

Portugal—3   Hungary—1

Jose Augusto (P, 1', 67'); Bene (H,
    60'); J. Torres (P, 90')
Manchester, 7/13/1966. Referee:
    Callaghan (Wales).

Hungary—3   Brazil—1

Bene (H, 2'); Tostao (B, 14'); Farkas
    (H, 64'); Meszöly (H, 73' penalty)
Liverpool, 7/15/1966. Referee: K.
    Dagnall (England).

Portugal—3   Bulgaria—0

Kutzov (B, 5' own goal); Eusebio
    (P, 36'); J. Torres (P, 75')
Manchester, 7/16/1966. Referee: J.
    M. Codesal (Uruguay).

Portugal—3   Brazil—1

Simoes (P, 15'); Eusebio (P, 26', 85');
    Rildo (B, 73')
Liverpool, 7/19/1966. Referee: Mc-
    Cobe (England).

Hungary—3   Bulgaria—1

Asparukov (B, 15'); Davidov (B, 43'
    own goal); Meszöly (H, 47');
    Bene (H, 54')
Manchester, 7/20/1966. Referee: R.
    Goycochea (Argentina).

GROUP 4

USSR—3   North Korea—0

Malafeev (USSR, 32', 88');
    Banichevski (USSR, 33')
Middlesbrough, 7/12/1966. Referee:
    J. Gardeazabal (Spain).

Italy—2   **Chile—0**

Mazzola (I, 10')' Barison (I, 80')
Sunderland, 7/13/1966. Referee: G.
Diens (Switzerland).

Chile—1   North Korea—1

Marcos (C, 20'); Pak Sung Jin (NK,
88' penalty)
Middlesbrough, 7/15/1966. Referee:
A. Kandil (Egypt).

USSR—1   Italy—0

Cislenko (USSR, 58')
Sunderland, 7/16/1966. Referee: R.
Kreitlen (West Germany).

North Korea—1   Italy—0

Pak Dook Ik (NK, 41')
Middlesbrough, 7/19/1966. Referee:
P. Schwinte (France).

USSR—2   Chile—1

Porkujan (USSR, 28', 85'); Marcos
(C, 42')
Sunderland, 7/20/1966. Referee: J.
Adair (Northern Ireland).

QUARTERFINALS

England—1   Argentina—0

Hurst (E, 76')
London, 7/23/1966. Referee: R. Kreitlen (West Germany).

W. Germany—4   Uruguay—0

Haller (WG, 11', 84'); Beckenbauer
(WG, 71'); Seeler (WG, 76')
Sheffield, 7/23/1966. Referee: J.
Finney (England).

Portugal—5 North Korea—3

Pak Sun Jin (NK, 1', 24'); Sing Yong
Gyu (NK, 22'); Eusebio (P, 27',
42' penalty, 53' 56' penalty); Jose
Augusto (P, 77')
Liverpool, 7/23/1966.

USSR—2   Hungary—1

Cislenko (USSR, 5'); Porkujan
(USSR, 47'); Bene (H, 58')
Sunderland, 7/23/1966. Referee: J.
Gardeazabal (Spain).

SEMIFINALS

England—2   Portugal—1

B. Charlton (E, 30', 79'); Eusebio (P,
82' penalty)
London, 7/26/1966. Referee: P.
Schwine (France).

West Germany—2   USSR—1

Haller (WG, 43'); Beckenbauer
(WG, 69'); Porkujan (USSR, 88')
Liverpool, 7/25/1966. Referee: C. Lo
Bello (Italy).

THIRD-PLACE GAME

Portugal—2   USSR—1

Eusebio (P, 12' penalty);
Banichevski (USSR, 43'); J. Torres
(P, 88')
London, 7/28/1966. Referee: K.
Dognalf (England).

FINAL

England—4   W. Germany—2

Haller (WG, 12'); Hurst (E, 18', 101',
120'); Peters (E, 78'); Weber (WG,
90')

London, 7/30/1966. Referee: G. Dienst (Switzerland).

A 30' overtime was played.

England: Banks; Cohen, Wilson; Stiles, Jack Charlton, Moore; Ball, Hunt, Bobby Charlton, Hurst, Peters. Coach: Alf Ramsey.

West Germany: Tilkowski; Höttges, Schnellinger; Beckenbauer, Schulz, Weber; Held, Haller, Seeler, Overath, Emmerich. Coach: Helmut Schön.

World Cup Mexico 1970

GROUP 1

Mexico—0   USSR—0

Mexico City, 5/31/1970. Referee: K. Tsechenscher (West Germany).

Belgium—3   El Salvador—0

Van Moer (B, 12', 54'); Lambert (B 76' penalty)

Mexico City, 6/1/1970. Referee: Radulescu (Romania).

USSR—4   Belgium—1

Byscevetz (USSR, 15', 63'); Asatiani (USSR, 56'); Hmelnistski (USSR, 76'); Lambert (B, 86')

Mexico City, 6/6/1970. Referee: R. Scheurer (Switzerland).

Mexico—4   El Salvador—0

Valdivia (M, 45'); J. L. Gonzalez (M, 46'); Fragoso (M, 54'); Basaguern (M, 83')

Mexico City, 6/7/1970. Referee: A. Husein Kandil (Egypt).

USSR—2   El Salvador—0

Byscevetz (USSR, 51', 74')

Mexico City, 6/10/1970. Referee: R. Hormazabal (Chile).

Mexico—1   Belgium—0

Peña (M, 15' penalty)

Mexico City, 6/11/1970. Referee: A. N. Coerezza (Argentina).

GROUP 2

Uruguay—2   Israel—0

Maneiro (U, 23'); Mujica (U, 50')

Puebla, 6/2/1970. Referee: R. Holley Davidson (Scotland).

Italy—1   Sweden—0

Domenghini (I, 10')

Toluca, 6/3/1970. Referee: J. K. Taylor (England).

Italy—0   Uruguay—0

Puebla, 6/6/1970. Referee: R. Glöckner (East Germany).

Sweden—1   Israel—1

Turesson (S, 54'); Spiegler (I, 56')

Toluca, 6/7/1970. Referee: Tarrekegn (Egypt).

Sweden—1   Uruguay—0

Grahn (S, 90')

Puebla, 6/10/1970. Referee: Landauer (United States).

Italy—0   Israel—0

Toluca, 6/11/1970. Referee: A. de Maraes (Brazil).

GROUP 3

England—1   Romania—0

Hurst (E, 65')
Guadalajara, 6/2/1970. Referee: V. Louraux (Belgium).

Brazil—4 Czechoslovakia—1

Petras (C, 11'); Rivelino (B, 24'); Pele (B, 59'); Jairzinho (B, 61', 81')
Guadalajara, 6/3/1970. Referee: R. Barreto (Uruguay).

Romania—2   Czech.—1

Petras (C, 5'); Neagu (R, 52'); Dumitrache (R, 75' penalty)
Guadalajara, 6/6/1970. Referee: D. de Leo (Mexico).

Brazil—1   England—0

Jairzinho (B, 59')
Guadalajara, 6/7/1970. Referee: A. Klein (Israel).

Brazil—3   Romania—2

Pele (B, 19', 67'); Jairzinho (B, 22'); Dumitrache (R, 34'); Dembrovski (R, 84')
Guadalajara, 6/10/1970. Referee: Marschall (Austria).

England—1   Czech.—0

Clarke (E, 50' penalty)
Guadalajara, 6/11/1970. Referee: R. Machin (France).

GROUP 4

Peru—3   Bulgaria—2

Dermendjev (B, 13'); Bonev (B, 49'); Gallardo (P, 50'); Chumpitaz (P, 55'); Cubillas (P, 73')
Leon, 6/2/1970. Referee: A. Sbardella (Italy).

W. Germany—2 Morocco—1

Human (M, 21'); Seeler (WG, 56'); Müller (WG, 78')
Leon, 6/3/1970. Referee: L. Van Ravens (Holland).

Peru—3   Morocco—0

Cubillas (P, 65', 75'); Challe (P, 67')
Leon, 6/6/1970. Referee: T. Bakhramov (Soviet Union).

W. Germany—3 Bulgaria—2

Nikodimov (B, 12'); Libuda (WG, 20'); Müller (WG, 27' penalty, 52', 88' penalty); Seeler (WG, 69'); Kolev (B, 89')
Leon, 6/7/1970. Referee: Ortiz de Mendivil (Spain).

West Germany—3   Peru—1

Müller (WG, 19', 23', 39'); Cubillas (P, 44')
Leon, 6/10/1970. Referee: A. Aguilar (Mexico).

Bulgaria—1   Morocco—1

Zecev (B, 40'); Ghazuani (M, 61')
Leon, 6/11/1970. Referee: Saldanha (Portugal).

QUARTERFINALS

Italy—4   Mexico—1

J. L. Gutierrez (M, 13'); Peña (M, 25'
own goal); Riva (I, 64', 76');
Rivera (I, 69')
Toluca, 6/14/1970. Referee: R.
Scheurer (Switzerland).

Uruguay—1   USSR—0

Esparrago (U, 117')
Mexico City, 6/14/1970. Referee: L.
Van Ravens (Holland).
A 30' overtime was played.

W. Germany—3   England—2

Mullery (E, 31'); Peters (E, 49');
Beckenbauer (WG, 68'); Seeler
(WG, 76'); Müller (WG, 108')
Leon, 6/14/1970. Referee: A. N. Co-
erezza (Argentina).
A 30' overtime was played.

Brazil—4   Peru—2

Rivelino (B, 11'); Tostao (B, 15',
52'); Gallardo (P, 28'); Cubillas (P,
70'); Jairzinho, (B, 75')
Guadalajara, 6/14/1970. Referee: V.
Loraux (Belgium).

SEMIFINALS

Italy—4   West Germany—3

Boninsegna (I, 7'); Schnellinger
(WG, 82'); Müller (WG, 94', 109');
Burgnich (I, 98'); Riva (I, 103');
Rivera (I, 110')
Mexico City, 6/17/1970. Referee:
Yamasaki (Peru).

Brazil—3   Uruguay—1

Cubilla (U, 19'); Clodoaldo (B, 44');
Jairzinho (B, 76'); Rivelino (B,
89')
Guadalajara, 6/17/1970. Referee:
Ortiz de Mendivil (Spain).

THIRD-PLACE GAME

W. Germany—1   Uruguay—0

Overath (WG, 26')
Mexico City, 6/20/1970. Referee: A.
Shardella (Italy).

FINAL

Brazil—4   Italy—1

Pele (B, 18'); Boninsegna (I, 37');
Gerson (B, 65'); Jairzinho (B,
70'); Carlos Alberto (B, 86')
Mexico City, 6/21/1970. Referee: R.
Glöckner (East Germany).
Brazil: Felix; Carlos Alberto, Ever-
aldo; Clodoaldo, Piazza, Brito;
Jairzinho, Gerson, Tostão, Pele,
Rivelino. Coach: Mario Zagallo.
Italy: Albertosi; Rosato, Burgnich;
Cera, Facchetti, De Sisti; Bertini
(replaced by Juliano at 73'),
Mazzola, Domenghini, Bonin-
segna (replaced by Rivera at
84'), Riva. Coach: Ferruccio Val-
careggi.

World Cup Germany 1974

GROUP 1

West Germany—1   Chile—0

Breitner (WG, 16')
Berlin, 6/16/1974. Referee: D. Babacon (Turkey).

E. Germany—2   Australia—0

Curran (A, 57' own goal); Strich (EG, 69')
Hamburg, 6/18/1974. Referee: Y. N'Diaye (Senegal).

W. Germany—3   Australia—0

Overath (WG, 12'); Cullmann (WG, 34'); Müller (WG, 53')
Hamburg, 6/20/1974. Referee: M. Kamel (Egypt).

Chile—1   East Germany—1

Hoffmann (EG, 55'); Ahumada (C, 69')
Berlin, 6/18/1974. Referee: A. Angonese (Italy).

Australia—0   Chile—0

Berlin, 6/22/1974. Referee: J. Namdor (Iran).

E. Ger.—1   W. Ger.—0

Sparwasser (EG, 77')
Hamburg, 6/22/1974. Referee: R. Barreto Rujz (Uruguay).

GROUP 2

Brazil—0   Yugoslavia—0

Frankfurt, 6/13/1974. Referee: L. Pestarino (Argentina).

Scotland—2   Zaire—0

Lorimer (S, 26'); Jordan (S, 33')
Dortmund, 6/14/1974. Referee: K. Schulenburg (West Germany).

Yugoslavia—9   Zaire—0

Bajevic (Y, 7', 29', 70'); Dzaijc (Y, 13'); Surjak (Y, 18'); Katalinski (Y, 21'); Bogicevic (Y, 34'); Oblak (Y, 60'); Petkovic (Y, 62')
Gelsenkirchen, 6/18/1974. Referee: O. Delgado (Colombia).

Scotland—0   Brazil—0

Frankfurt, 6/18/1974. Referee: A. Van Gemert (Holland).

Brazil—3   Zaire—0

Jairzinho (B, 13'); Rivelino (B, 67'); Valdomiro (B, 79')
Gelsenkirchen, 6/22/1974. Referee: N. Rainea (Romania).

Yugoslavia—1   Scotland—1

Karasi (Y, 81'); Jordan (S, 89')
Frankfurt, 6/22/1974. Referee: A. Archundia (Mexico).

GROUP 3

Bulgaria—0   Sweden—0

Dusseldorf, 6/15/1974. Referee: E. Nuñez (Peru).

Holland—2   Uruguay—0

Rep (H, 7', 87')
Hannover, 6/15/1974. Referee: K. Palotai (Hungary).

Holland—0   Sweden—0

Dortmund, 6/19/1974. Referee: W. Winsemann (Canada).

Bulgaria—1   Uruguay—1

Banev (B, 75'); Pavoni (U, 87')
Hannover, 6/19/1974. Referee: J.
Taylor (England).

Sweden—3   Uruguay—0

Edstroem (S, 46', 78'); Sandberg (S, 74')
Dusseldorf, 6/23/1974. Referee: E.
Linemayr (Austria).

Holland—4   Bulgaria—1

Neeskens (H, 6' penalty, 45'
penalty); Rep (H, 71'); Krol (H,
78' own goal); De Jong (H, 86')
Dortmund, 6/23/1974. Referee: A.
Boskovic (Australia).

GROUP 4

Italy—3   Haiti—1

Sanon (H, 46'); Rivera (I, 53');
Benetti (I, 66'); Anastasi (I, 79')
Munich, 6/15/1974. Referee: V. Llo-
bregot (Venezuela).

Poland—3   Argentina—2

Lato (P, 6', 62'); Szarmach (P, 8');
Heredia (A, 61'); Babington (A, 66')
Stuttgart, 6/15/1974. Referee: C.
Thomas (Wales).

Poland—7   Haiti—0

Lato (P, 17', 87'); Deyna (P, 19');
Szarmach (P, 30', 34', 51'); Gor-
gon (P, 32')
Munich, 6/19/1974. Referee: S.
Covindasamy (Singapore).

Argentina—1   Italy—1

Houseman (A, 19'); Perfumo (A, 25'
own goal)
Stuttgart, 6/19/1974. Referee: N.
Rainea (Romania).

Argentina—4   Haiti—1

Yazalde (A, 15', 67'); Houseman (A,
18'); Ayala (A, 56'); Sanon (H,
63')
Munich, 6/23/1974. Referee: P.
Sanchez Ibañez (Spain).

Poland—2   Italy—1

Szarmach (P, 38'); Deyna (P, 44');
Capello (I, 86')
Stuttgart, 6/23/1974. Referee: H.
Weyland (West Germany).

SECOND ROUND

GROUP A

Holland—4   Argentina—0

Cruyff (H, 11', 89'); Krol (H, 25');
Rep (H, 72')
Gelsenkirchen, 6/26/1974. Referee:
R. Davidson (Scotland).

Brazil—1   East Germany—0

Rivelino (B, 61')
Hannover, 6/26/1974. Referee: C.
Thomas (Wales)

Holland—3 East Germany—0

Neeskens (H, 8'); Rensenbrink (H,
59')
Gelsenkirchen, 6/30/1974. Referee:
R. Scheurer (Switzerland).

Brazil—2   Argentina—1

Rivelino (B, 32'); Brindisi (A, 34');
Jairzinho (B, 48')
Hannover, 6/30/1974. Referee: V.
Loraux (Belgium).

Holland—2   Brazil—0

Neeskens (H, 50'); Cruyff (H, 65')
Dortmund, 7/3/1974. Referee: K.
Tschenscher (West Germany).

Argentina—1 E. Germany—1

Streich (EG 14'); Houseman (Ar,
22')
Gelsenkirchen, 7/3/1974. Referee:
J. Taylor (England).

GROUP B

W. Ger.—2   Yugoslavia—0

Breitner (WG, 38'); Müller (WG,
77')
Dusseldorf, 6/26/1974. Referee: A.
Marques (Brazil).

Poland—1   Sweden—0

Lato (P, 42')
Stuttgart, 6/26/1974. Referee: R.
Barreto (Uruguay).

Poland—2   Yugoslavia—1

Deyna (P, 26' penalty); Karasi (Y,
44'); Lato (P, 64')
Frankfurt, 6/30/1974. Referee: R.
Gloeckner (East Germany).

W. Germany—4 Sweden—2

Edstroem (S, 26'); Overath (WG,
50'); Ronhof (WG, 51'); Sandberg
(S, 53'); Grabowski (WG, 89');
Hoeness (WG, 90' penalty)
Dusseldorf, 6/30/1974. Referee: P.
Kasakov (Soviet Union).

West Germany—1 Poland—0

Müller (WG, 75')
Frankfurt, 7/3/1974. Referee: E.
Linemayr (Austria).

Sweden—2   Yugoslavia—1

Surjak (Y, 27'); Edstroem (S, 30');
Tortensson (S, 85')
Dusseldorf, 7/3/1974. Referee: L.
Pestarino (Argentina).

THIRD-PLACE GAME

Poland—1   Brazil—0

Lato (P, 75')
Munich, 7/6/1974. Referee: A. Angonese (Italy).

FINAL

W. Germany—2 Holland—1

Neeskens (H, 1' penalty); Breitner
(WG, 26' penalty); Müller (WG,
44')
Munich, 7/7/1974. Referee: J. K.
Taylor (England).
West Germany: Maier; Vogts, Breit-
ner, Schwarzenbeck, Becken-
bauer, Bonhof, Grabowski,
Hoennes, Müller, Overath, Hol-
lzenbein. Coach: Helmut Schon.
Holland: Jongbloed; Suurbier, Krol,
Haan, Rijsbergen (replaced by
De Jong at 68'), Jansen, Rep,

Neeskens, Cruyff, Van Hanegem, Rensenbrink (replaced by Rene Van der Kerkhof at 45'). Coach: Rinus Michels.

World Cup Argentina 1978

GROUP 1

Italy—2   France—1

P. Rossi (I, 29'); Lacombe (F, 40'); Zaccarelli (I, 52')
Mar del Plata, 6/2/1978. Referee: N. Rainea (Romania).

Argentina—2   Hungary—1

Csapo (H, 10'); Luque (A, 15'); Bertoni (A, 83')
Monumental Stadium, Buenos Aires, 6/2/1978. Referee: A. Garrido (Portugal).

Italy—3   Hungary—1

P. Rossi (I, 34'); Bettega (I, 36'); Benetti (I, 61'); A. Toth (H, 81' penalty)
Mar del Plata, 6/6/1978. Referee: R. Barreto (Uruguay).

Argentina—2   France—1

Passarella (A, 45' penalty); Platini (F, 60'); Luque (A, 73')
Monumental Stadium, Buenos Aires, 6/6/1978. Referee: J. Dubach (Switzerland).

Italy—1   Argentina—0

Bettega (I, 67')
Monumental Stadium, Buenos Aires, 6/10/1978. Referee: A. Klein (Israel).

France—3   Hungary—1

C. Lopez (F, 22'); Berdoll (F, 37'); Zambari (H, 41'); Rocheteau (F, 42')
Mar del Plata, 6/10/1978. Referee: A. C. Coelho (Brazil).

GROUP 2

West Germany—0 Poland—0

Monumental Stadium, Buenos Aires, 6/1/1978. Referee: A. N. Coerezza (Argentina).

Tunisia—3   Mexico—1

Vazquez Ayala (M, 45' penalty); Kaabi (T, 53'); Gommidh (T, 80'); Dhouib (T, 87')
Rosario, 6/2/1978. Referee: J. Gordon (Scotland).

Poland—1   Tunisia—0

Lato (P, 42')
Rosario, 6/6/1978. Referee: A. Martinez (Spain).

West Germany—6 Mexico—0

D. Müller (WG, 14'); H. Müller (WG, 29'); Rummenigge (WG, 37', 72'); Flohe (WG, 44', 89')
Cordoba, 6/6/1978. Referee: F. Bouza (Syria).

Tunisia—0 West Germany—0

Cordoba, 6/10/1978. Referee: C. Orosco (Peru).

Poland—3   Mexico—1

Deyna (P, 56'); Boniek (P, 42', 83'); Rangel (M, 52')
Rosario, 6/10/1978. Referee: J. Namdar (Iran).

GROUP 3

Austria—1   **Sweden—0**

Krankl (A, 42' penalty)
Jose Amalfitani Stadium, Buenos
 Aires, 6/2/1978. Referee: C.
 Corver (Holland).

Brazil—1   **Sweden—1**

Sjöberg (S, 38'); Reinaldo (B, 44')
Mar del Plata, 6/3/1978. Referee: C.
 Thomas (Wales).

Austria—2   **Spain—1**

Schachner (A, 9'); Dani (S, 21');
 Krankl (A, 76')
Jose Amalfitani Stadium, Buenos
 Aires, 6/3/1978. Referee: K.
 Palotai (Hungary).

Brazil—0   **Spain—0**

Mar del Plata, 6/7/1978. Referee: S.
 Gonella (Italy).

Brazil—1   **Austria—0**

Roberto (B, 40')
Mar del Plata, 6/11/1978. Referee:
 R. Wurtz (France).

Spain—1   **Sweden—0**

Asensi (S, 67')
Jose Amalfitani Stadium, Buenos
 Aires, 6/11/1978. Referee: F. Biw-
 ersi (West Germany).

GROUP 4

Holland—3   **Iran—0**

Rensenbrink (H, 37' penalty, 62',
 77' penalty)
Mendoza, 6/3/1978. Referee: A.
 Gonzalez Archundia (Mexico).

Peru—3   **Scotland—1**

Jordan (S, 14'); Cueto (P, 43'); Cu-
 billas (P, 71', 77')
Cordoba, 6/3/1978. Referee: U.
 Eriksson (Sweden).

Holland—0   **Peru—0**

Mendoza, 6/7/1978. Referee: A.
 Prokop (East Germany).

Scotland—1   **Iran—1**

Danaifar (I, 60'); Eskandarian (I, 63'
 own goal)
Cordoba, 6/7/1978. Referee: Y.
 N'Dlaye (Senegal).

Scotland—3   **Holland—2**

Rensenbrink (H, 34' penalty);
 Dalglish (S, 44'); Gemmill (S, 46',
 68'); Rep (H, 71')
Mendoza, 6/11/1978. Referee: E.
 Linemayer (Austria).

Peru—4   **Iran—1**

Velazquez (P, 2'); Cubillas (P, 36'
 penalty, 39' penalty, 78'); Row-
 shan (I, 40')
Cordoba, 6/11/1978. Referee: A.
 Jarguz (Poland).

SECOND ROUND

GROUP A

Italy—0   West Germany—0

Monumental Stadium, Buenos
 Aires, 6/14/1978. Referee: D.
 Maksimovic (Yugoslavia).

Holland—5 Austria—1

Brandts (H, 6'); Rensenbrink (H, 35'
  penalty); Rep (H, 36', 53'); Ober-
  mayer (A, 79'); Willy Van der
  Kerkhof (H, 82')
Cordoba, 6/14/1978. Referee: J.
  Gordon (Scotland).

W. Germany—2 Holland—2

Abramczik (WG, 2'); Haan (H, 26');
  D. Müller (WG, 69'); Rene Van
  der Kerkhof (H, 83')
Cordoba, 6/18/1978. Referee: R.
  Barreto (Uruguay).

Italy—1 Austria—0

P. Rossi (I, 13')
Monumental Stadium, Buenos
  Aires, 6/18/1978. Referee: F. Rion
  (Belgium).

Holland—2 Italy—1

Brandts (H, 18' own goal); Brandts
  (H, 50'); Haan (H, 75')
Monumental Stadium, Buenos
  Aires, 6/21/1978. Referee: A. Mar-
  tinez (Spain).

Austria—3 West Germany—2

Rummenigge (WG, 18'); Vogts
  (WG, 59' own goal); Krankl (A,
  65', 88'); Hölzeinbein (WG, 67')
Cordoba, 6/21/1978. Referee: A.
  Klein (Israel).

GROUP B

Brazil—3 Peru—0

Dirceu (B, 14', 27'); Zico (B, 71'
  penalty)
Mendoza, 6/14/1978. Referee: N.
  Rainea (Romania).

Argentina—2 Poland—0

Kempes (A, 15', 71')
Rosario, 6/14/1978. Referee: U.
  Eriksson (Sweden).

Poland—1 Peru—0

Szarmach (Po, 65')
Mendoza, 6/18/1978. Referee: P.
  Partridge (England).

Argentina—0 Brazil—0

Rosario, 6/18/1978. Referee: K.
  Palotai (Hungary).

Brazil—3 Poland—1

Nelinho (B, 12'); Lato (P, 44');
  Roberto (B, 57', 63')
Mendoza, 6/21/1978. Referee: J.
  Ambrosio Silvagna (Chile).

Argentina—6 Peru—0

Kempes (A, 20', 48'); Tarantini (A,
  42'); Luque (A, 50', 72'); Houseman (A, 66')
Rosario, 6/21/1978. Referee: R.
  Wurtz (France).

THIRD-PLACE GAME

Brazil—2 Italy—1

Causio (I, 39'); Nelinho (B, 64');
  Dirceu (B, 71')
Monumental Stadium, Buenos
  Aires, 6/24/1978. Referee: A.
  Klein (Israel).

FINAL

Argentina—3   Holland—1

Kempes (A, 37', 103'); Naninga (H, 81'); Bertoni (A, 114')

Monumental Stadium, Buenos Aires, 6/25/1978. Referee: S. Gonella (Italy).

A 30' overtime was played.

Argentina: Fillol; Olguin, Luis Galvan, Passarella, Tarantini; Ardiles (replaced by Larrosa at 66'), Gallego, Kempes; Bertoni, Luque, Ortiz (replaced by Houseman at 74'). Coach: Cesar Luis Menotti.

Holland: Jongbloed; Jansen (replaced by Suurbier at 72'), Brandts, Krol, Poortvliet; Willy Van der Kerkhof, Neeskens, Haan; Rep (replaced by Naninga at 78'), Rensenbrink, Rene Van der Kerkhof. Coach: Wiener Ernst Happel.

World Cup Spain 1982

GROUP 1

Italy—0   Poland—0

Vigo, 6/14/1982. Referee: M. Vautrot (France).

Peru—0   Cameroon—0

La Coruña, 6/15/1982. Referee: F. Wöhrer (Austria).

Italy—1   Peru—1

Conti (I, 19'); Scirea (I, 84' own goal)

Vigo, 6/18/1982. Referee: W. Eschweiler (West Germany).

Poland—0   Cameroon—0

La Coruña, 6/19/1982. Referee: A. Ponnet (Belgium).

Poland—5   Peru—1

Smolareck (Po, 57'); Lato (Po, 60'); Boniek (Po, 62'); Buncol (Po, 70'); Ciolek (Po, 78'); La Rosa (Pe, 85')

La Coruña, 6/22/1982. Referee: M. Rubio (Mexico).

Italy—1   Cameroon—1

Graziani (I, 62'); M'Bida (C, 63')

Vigo, 6/23/1982. Referee: B. Dotchev (Bulgaria).

GROUP 2

Algeria—2 West Germany—1

Madjer (A, 52'); Rummenigge (WG, 68'); Belluomi (A, 69')

Gijon, 6/16/1982. Referee: E. Labo (Peru).

Austria—1   Chile—0

Schachner (A, 68')

Oviedo, 6/17/1982. Referee: J. Cardellino (Uruguay).

West Germany—4   Chile—1

Rummenigge (WG, 9', 55', 65'); Reinders (WG, 82'); Moscoso (C, 89')

Gijon, 6/20/1982. Referee: B. Galler (Switzerland).

Austria—2   Algeria—0

Schachner (Au, 56'); Krankl (Au, 67')

Oviedo, 6/21/1982. Referee: T. Boskovic (Australia).

Algeria—3   Chile—2

Assad (A, 7', 31'); Neira (C, 60'
   penalty); Bensaoula (A, 74');
   Letelier (C, 74')
Oviedo, 6/24/1982. Referee: R.
   Mendez (Guatemala).

West Germany—1 Austria—0

Hrubesch (WG, 10')
Gijon, 6/25/1982. Referee: R. Valentine (Scotland).

GROUP 3

Belgium—1   Argentina—0

Vanderbergh (B, 61')
Barcelona, 6/13/1982. Referee: V.
   Christov (Czechoslovakia).

Hungary—10   El Salvador—1

Nylasi (H, 3', 38'); Poloskei (H, 11');
   Fazekas (H, 23', 54'); Toth (H,
   51'); Ramirez Zapata (ES, 65');
   Kiss (H, 70', 73', 78'); Sallai (H,
   71')
Elche, 6/15/1982. Referee: A. Doy
   (Bahrein).

Argentina—4   Hungary—1

Bertoni (A, 27'); Maradona (A, 29',
   57'); Ardiles (A, 61'); Poloskei (H,
   76')
Alicante, 6/17/1982. Referee: B. La-
   cairne (Algeria).

Belgium—1   El Salvador—0

Coeck (B, 17')
Elche, 6/19/1982. Referee: M. Mof-
   fat (Northern Ireland).

Belgium—1   Hungary—1

Varga (H, 27'); Czerniatynski (B,
   75')
Elche, 6/22/1982. Referee: C. Withe
   (England).

Argentina—2   El Salvador—0

Passarella (A, 22' penalty); Bertoni
   (A, 55')
Alicante, 6/23/1982. Referee: L. Bar-
   rancos (Bolivia).

GROUP 4

England—3   France—1

Robson (E, 1', 66'); Soler (F, 24');
   Mariner (I, 82')
Bilbao, 6/16/1982. Referee: A. Gar-
   rido (Portugal).

Czech.—1   Kuwait—1

Panenka (C, 22' penalty); Al Dokhil
   (K, 58')
Valladolid, 6/17/1982. Referee: B.
   Dwamoh (Ghana).

England—2   Czech.—0

Francis (E, 63'); Barmos (C, 66' own
   goal)
Bilbao, 6/20/1982. Referee: C.
   Corver (Holland).

France—4   Kuwait—1

Genghini (F, 30'); Platini (F, 43'); Six
   (F, 47'); Al Boloushi (K, 75');
   Bossis (F, 89')
Valladolid, 6/21/1982. Referee: M.
   Stupar (Soviet Union).

France—1   Czech.—1

Six (F, 67'); Panenka (C, 86')
Valladolid, 6/24/1982. Referee: P.
Casarin (Italy).

England—1   Kuwait—0

Francis (E, 27')
Bilbao, 6/25/1982. Referee: G. Ariztizabal (Colombia).

GROUP 5

Spain—1   Honduras—1

Zelaya (H, 7'); Lopez Uriarte (S, 66'
penalty)
Valencia, 6/16/1982. Referee: A. Andres Iturralde (Argentina).

Yugoslavia—0   N. Ireland—0

Zaragoza, 6/16/1982. Referee: E.
Fredriksson (Sweden).

Spain—2   Yugoslavia—1

Gudelj (Y, 10'); Juanito (S, 12'
penalty); Saura (S, 66')
Valencia, 6/20/1982. Referee: L.
Sörensen (Denmark).

Honduras—1   N. Ireland—1

Armstrong (NI, 9'); Laing (H, 61')
Zaragoza, 6/21/1982. Referee: C.
Ram Sun (Hong Kong).

Yugoslavia—1   Honduras—0

Petrovic (Y, 87' penalty)
Zaragoza, 6/24/1982. Referee: G.
Castro (Chile).

N. Ireland—1   Spain—0

Armstrong (NI, 47')
Valencia, 6/25/1982. Referee: H.
Ortiz (Paraguay).

GROUP 6

Brazil—2   USSR—1

Bal (USSR, 36'); Socrates (B, 74');
Eder (B, 87')
Sevilla, 6/14/1982. Referee: A.
Lomo Castillo (Spain).

Scotland—5 New Zealand—2

Dalglish (S, 17'); Wark (S, 29', 32');
Sumner (NZ, 54'); Wooddin (NZ,
64'); Robertson (S, 73'); Archibald
(S, 79')
Malaga, 6/15/1982. Referee: D.
Socha (United States).

Brazil—4   Scotland—1

Narey (S, 18'); Zico (B, 32'); Oscar
(B, 48'); Eder (B, 64'); Falcao (B,
87')
Sevilla, 6/18/1982. Referee: L.
Calderon (Costa Rica).

USSR—3   New Zealand—0

Gavrilov (USSR, 28'); Blokhin
(USSR, 48'); Baltacha (USSR, 69')
Malaga, 6/19/1982. Referee: Y. El
Ghoul (Libya).

USSR—2   Scotland—2

Jordan (S, 15'); Chivadze (USSR,
59'); Shengelia (USSR, 84');
Sauness (S, 86')
Malaga, 6/22/1982. Referee: N.
Rainea (Romania).

Brazil—4   New Zealand—0

Zico (B, 28', 31'); Falcao (B, 55');
Serginho (B, 69')
Sevilla, 6/23/1982. Referee: D. Matovinovic (Yugoslavia).

QUARTERFINAL ROUND

GROUP A

Poland—3   Belgium—0

Boniek (P, 3', 26', 50')
Barcelona, 6/28/1982. Referee: L.
Calderon (Costa Rica).

USSR—1   Belgium—0

Oganesian (USSR, 48')
Barcelona, 7/1/1982. Referee: M.
Vautrot (France).

USSR—0   Poland—0

Barcelona, 7/4/1982. Referee: R.
Valentine (Scotland).

GROUP B

W. Germany—0   England—0

Madrid, 6/29/1982. Referee: A.
Coelho (Brazil).

West Germany—2   Spain—1

Littbarski (WG, 49'); K. Fischer
(WG, 75'); Zamora (S, 81')
Madrid, 7/2/1982. Referee: P.
Casarin (Italy).

England—0   Spain—0

Madrid, 7/5/1982. Referee: A. Ponnet (Belgium).

GROUP C

Italy—2   Argentina—1

Tardelli (I, 56'); Cabrini (I, 67'); Pas-
sarella (A, 83')
Barcelona, 6/29/1982. Referee: N.
Rainea (Romania).

Brazil—3   Argentina—1

Zico (B, 11'); Serginho (B, 67'); Ju-
nior (B, 74'); R. A. Diaz (A, 89')
Barcelona, 7/2/1982. Referee: M.
Rubio (Mexico).

Italy—3   Brazil—2

P. Rossi (I, 5', 25', 75'); Socrates (B,
12'); Falcao (B, 68')
Barcelona, 7/5/1982. Referee: A.
Klein (Israel).

GROUP D

France—1   Austria—0

Genghini (F, 38')
Madrid, 6/28/1982. Referee: K.
Palotai (Hungary).

N. Ireland—2   Austria—2

Hamilton (NI, 27', 74'); Pezzey (A,
61'); Hintermayer (A, 68')
Madrid, 7/1/1982. Referee: A.
Prokop (East Germany).

France—4   N. Ireland—1

Giresse (F, 34', 80'); Rocheteau (F,
47', 68'); Armstrong (NI, 75')
Madrid, 7/4/1982. Referee: A. Jarguz (Poland).

SEMIFINALS

Italy—2   Poland—0

P. Rossi (I, 22', 72')
Barcelona, 7/8/1982. Referee: J.
Cardellino (Uruguay).

W. Ger.—3 (5)   France—3 (4)

Littbarski (WG, 17'); Platini (F, 27'
penalty); Tresor (F, 92'); Giresse
(F, 99'); Rummenigge (WG, 102');
K. Fischer (WG, 107')
Sevilla, 7/8/1982. Referee: C. Corver
(Holland).
Game decided by penalty-kick tie-
breaker.

THIRD-PLACE GAME

Poland—3   France—2

Girard (F, 13'); Szarmach (P, 40');
Majewski (P, 44'); Kupcewicz (P,
46'); Couriol (F, 73')
Alicante, 7/10/1982. Referee: A.
Garrido (Portugal).

FINAL

Italy—3   West Germany—1

P. Rossi (I, 56'); Tardelli (I, 68'); Al-
tobelli (I, 81'); Breitner (A, 83'
penalty)
Madrid, 7/11/1982. Referee: A. C.
Coelho (Brazil).
Cabrini (Italy) saved a penalty
kick.
Italy: Zoff; Scirea, Gentile, Collo-
vatti, Bergomi, Cabrini; Oriali,
Tardelli, Conti; Graziani (re-
placed by Altobelli at 7' [re-
placed by Causio at 89']), Paolo
Rossi. Coach: Enzo Bearzot.
West Germany: Schumacher; Kaltz,
Karl Heinz Förster, Sthelike,
Briegel; Breitner, Bernd Förster,
Dremmler (replaced by
Hrubesch at 62'); Littbarski, Klaus
Fischer, Rummenigge (replaced
by Hans Müller at 69'). Coach:
Jupp Derwall.

World Cup Mexico 1986

GROUP A

Bulgaria—1   Italy—1

Altobelli (I, 43'); Sirakov (B, 85')
Mexico City, 5/31/1986. Referee: E.
Fredrikksson (Sweden).

Argentina—3   S. Korea—1

Valdano (A, 5', 46'); Ruggeri (A,
18'); Park Chang Sun (SK, 74')
Mexico City, 6/2/1986. Referee:
Sanchez Arminio (Spain).

Italy—1   Argentina—1

Altobelli (I, 7' penalty); Maradona
(A, 33')
Puebla, 6/13/1986. Referee: I.
Keizer (Holland).

South Korea—1 Bulgaria—1

Getov (B, 11'); Dimitrov (B, 69'
own goal)
Mexico City, 6/5/1986. Referee: F.
Khuzam Al-Shanar (Saudi Arabia).

Argentina—2   Bulgaria—0

Valdano (A, 3'); Burruchaga (A, 76')
Mexico City, 6/10/1986. Referee: B.
Ulloa (Costa Rica).

Italy—3   South Korea—2

Altobelli (I, 17', 73'); Choi Soon Ho
(SK, 62'); Jung Yong-Hwan (SK,
77' own goal); H. Jung-Moo (SK,
88')
Puebla, 6/10/1986. Referee: David
Socha (United States).

GROUP B

Mexico—2   Belgium—1

Quirarte (M, 23'); H. Sanchez (M, 38'); Vandenbergh (B, 45')
Mexico City, 6/3/1986. Referee: C. Esposito (Argentina).

Paraguay—1   Iraq—0

J. C. Romero (P, 35')
Toluca, 6/4/1986. Referee: S. Picon (Mauritius).

Mexico—1   Paraguay—1

L. Flores (M, 2'); J. C. Romero (P, 80')
Mexico City, 6/7/1986. Referee: G. Courtney (England).

Belgium—2   Iraq—1

Scifo (B, 15'); Claesen (B, 20' penalty); Amaiesh (I, 57')
Toluca, 6/8/1986. Referee: J. Diaz (Colombia).

Mexico—1   Iraq—0

Quirarte (M, 54')
Mexico City, 6/11/1986. Referee: Z. Petrovic (Yugoslavia).

Paraguay—2   Belgium—2

Vercauteren (B, 30'); Cabañas (P, 50', 75'); Veyt (B, 60')
Toluca, 6/11/1986. Referee: B. Dotschev (Bulgaria).

GROUP C

France—1   Canada—0

Papin (F, 79')
Leon, 6/1/1986. Referee: H. Silva (Chile).

USSR—6   Hungary—0

Yakovenko (USSR, 2'); Aleinikov (USSR, 4'); Belanov (USSR, 21' penalty); Varemchuk (USSR, 66'); Dajka (H, 74' own goal); Rodionov (USSR, 80')
Irapuato, 6/2/1986. Referee: L. Agnolin (Italy).

France—1   USSR—1

Rats (USSR, 34'); L. Fernandez (F. 61')
Leon, 6/5/1986. Referee: R. Arppi (Brazil).

Hungary—2   Canada—0

Esterhazy (H, 2'); Detari (H, 75')
Irapuato, 6/6/1986. Referee: J. Al-Sharif (Syria).

France—3   Hungary—0

Stopyra (F, 29'); Tigana (F, 63'); Rocheteau (F, 83')
Leon, 6/9/1986. Referee: C. Da Silva (Portugal).

USSR—2   Canada—0

Biokhin (USSR, 58'); Zavarov (USSR, 74')
Irapuato, 6/9/1986. Referee: I. Traare (Mali).

GROUP D

Brazil—1   Spain—0

Socrates (B, 61')
Guadalajara, 6/1/1986. Referee: C. Bambridge (Australia).

Algeria—1   N. Ireland—1

Whiteside (NI, 5'); Zidane (A, 59')
Guadalajara, 6/3/1986. Referee: V.
  Butenko (Soviet Union).

Brazil—1   Algeria—0

Careca (B, 71')
Guadalajara, 6/6/1986. Referee: R.
  Mendez Molina (Guatemala).

Spain—2   N. Ireland—1

Butragueño (S, 1'); Julio Salinas (S,
  18'); Clarke (NI, 47')
Guadalajara, 6/7/1986. Referee: H.
  Brummeier (Austria).

Brazil—3   N. Ireland—0

Careca (B, 16', 88'); Josimar (B, 42')
Guadalajara, 6/12/1986. Referee: S.
  Kirschen (East Germany).

Spain—3   Algeria—0

Caldere (S, 15', 68'); Eloy (S, 70')
Monterrey, 6/12/1986. Referee: S.
  Takada (Japan).

GROUP E

Uruguay—1   W. Germany—1

Alzamendi (U, 4'); Allofs (WG, 84')
Queretaro, 6/4/1986. Referee: V.
  Christov (Czechoslovakia).

Denmark—1   Scotland—0

Eikjaer (D, 57')
Nezahualcoyotl, 6/4/1986. Referee:
  Lajos Nemeth (Hungary).

W. Germany—2 Scotland—1

Strachan (S, 18'); Völler (WG, 22');
  Allofs (WG, 50')
Queretaro, 6/8/1986. Referee: I.
  Igna (Romania).

Denmark—6   Uruguay—1

Eikjaer (D, 10', 68', 79'); Lerby (D,
  40'); Francescoli (U, 44' penalty);
  Laudrup (D, 51'); J. Olsen (D,
  88')
Nezahualcoyotl, 6/8/1986. Referee:
  A. Marquez (Mexico).

Denmark—2 W. Germany—0

J. Olsen (D, 43' penalty); Eriksen
  (D, 63')
Queretaro, 6/13/1986. Referee: A.
  Ponnet (Belgium).

Scotland—0   Uruguay—0

Nezahualcoyotl, 6/13/1986. Referee: J. Quiniou (France).

GROUP F

Morocco—0   Poland—0

Monterrey, 6/2/1986. Referee: J.
  Martinez Bazan (Uruguay).

Portugal—1   England—0

Carlos Manuel (P, 74')
Monterrey, 6/3/1986. Referee: V.
  Roth (West Germany).

England—0   Morocco—0

Monterrey, 6/6/1986. Referee: G.
  Gonzalez (Paraguay).

Poland—1   Portugal—0

Smolareck (Pol, 57')
Monterrey, 6/7/1986. Referee: A.
Bennaceur (Tunisia).

Morocco—3   Portugal—1

Khairi (M, 19', 27'); Krimau (M, 61');
Diamantino (P, 79')
Guadalajara, 6/11/1986. Referee: A.
Snoody (Northern Ireland).

England—3   Poland—0

Lineker (E 7', 13', 35')
Monterrey, 6/11/1986. Referee: A.
Daina (Switzerland).

SECOND ROUND

Belgium—4   USSR—3

Belanov (USSR, 27', 70', 109'
penalty); Scifo (B, 55'); Ceule-
mans (B, 79'); De Mol (B, 101');
Claesen (B, 108')
Leon, 6/15/1986. Referee: E.
Fredriksson (Sweden).

Argentina—1   Uruguay—0

Pasculli (A, 41')
Puebla, 6/16/1986. Referee: L. Agnolin (Italy).

Brazil—4   Poland—0

Socrates (B, 30' penalty); Josimar
(B, 55'); Edinho (B, 77'); Careca
(B, 81' penalty)
Guadalajara, 6/16/1986. Referee: V.
Roth (West Germany).

France—2   Italy—0

Platini (F, 14'); Stopyra (F, 57')
Mexico City, 6/17/1986. Referee: C.
Esposito (Argentina).

W. Germany—1   Morocco—0

Matthäus (WG, 87')
Monterrey, 6/17/1986. Referee: Z.
Petrovic (Yugoslavia).

England—3   Paraguay—0

Lineker (E 31', 72'); Beardsley (E,
55')
Mexico City, 6/18/1986. Referee: J.
Al-Sharif (Syria).

Spain—5   Denmark—1

J. Olsen (D, 31' penalty); Butragueño (S, 43', 56', 80', 89'
penalty); Goicochea (S, 69'
penalty)
Queretaro, 6/18/1986. Referee: J.
Keizer (Holland).

QUARTERFINALS

Brazil—1 (4)   France—1 (3)

Careca (B, 16'); Platini (B, 41')
Guadalajara, 6/21/1986. Referee: I.
Igna (Romania).
Game decided by penalty-kick tie-
breaker.

W. Ger.—0 (4)   Mexico—0 (1)

Monterrey, 6/21/1986. Referee: J.
Diaz (Colombia).
Game decided by penalty-kick tie-
breaker.

Belgium—1 (5)   Spain—1 (4)

Ceulemans (B, 35'); Señor (S, 84')
Puebla, 6/22/1986. Referee: S.
Kirschen (West Germany).
Game decided by penalty-kick tie-
breaker.

Argentina—2   England—1

Maradona (A, 51', 55'); Lineker (E, 81')
Mexico City, 6/22/1986. Referee: A. Bennaceur (Tunisia).

SEMIFINALS

Argentina—2   Belgium—0

Maradona (A, 51', 62')
Mexico City, 6/25/1986. Referee: A. Marquez (Mexico).

W. Germany—2   France—0

Brehme; Völler (WG, 89')
Guadalajara, 6/25/1986. Referee: L. Agnolin (Italy)

THIRD-PLACE GAME

France—4   Belgium—2

Ceulemans (B, 11'); Ferreri (F, 27'); Papin (F, 42'); Claesen (B, 72'); Genghini (F, 103'); Amoros (F, 109' penalty)
Puebla, 6/27/1986.
A 30' overtime was played.

FINAL

Argentina—3   W. Ger.—2

Brown (A, 22'); Valdano (A, 56'); Rummenigge (WG, 74'); Völler (WG, 81'); Burruchaga (A, 84')
Mexico City, 6/29/1986. Referee: R. Arppi (Brazil).
Argentina: Pumpido; Brown; Cucciuffo, Ruggeri, Olarticoechea; Giusti, Batista, Enrique; Burruchaga (replaced by Trobbiani at 89'), Maradona; Valdano.
Coach: Carlos Salvador Bilardo.

West Germany: Schumacher; Brehme, Jakobs, Karl Heniz Föster, Briegel; Matthäus, Berthold, Eder, Magath (replaced by Hoeness at 61'); Allofs (replaced by Völler at 45'), Rummenigge. Coach: Franz Beckenbauer.

World Cup Italy 1990

GROUP A

Italy—1   Austria—0

Schillaci (I, 77')
Rome, 6/9/1990. Referee: J. R. Wright (Brazil).

Czechoslovakia—5   USA—1

Skuhravy (C, 26', 78'); Bilek (C, 40' penalty); Hasek (C, 50'); Caligiuri (USA, 60'); Luhovy (C, 90')
Florence, 6/10/1990. Referee: K. Röthlisberger (Switzerland).

Italy—1   USA—0

Giannini (I, 11')
Rome, 6/14/1990. Referee: E. Codesal (Mexico).

Czech.—1   Austria—0

Bilek (C, 40' penalty)
Florence, 6/15/1990. Referee: G. Smith (Scotland).

Italy—2   Czechoslovakia—0

Schillaci (I, 9'); Baggio (I, 77')
Rome, 6/19/1990. Referee: J. Quiniou (France).

Austria—2   USA—1

Ogris (A, 49'); Rodax (A, 63'); Murray (USA, 83')
Florence, 6/19/1990. Referee: J. Al-Sharif (Syria).

GROUP B

Argentina—0   Cameroon—1

O. Biyik (C, 67')
Milan, 6/8/1990. Referee: M. Vautrot (France).

Romania—2   USSR—0

Lacatus (R, 40', 54')
Bari, 6/9/1990. Referee: J. D. Cardelino (Uruguay).

Argentina—2   USSR—0

Troglio (A, 27'); Burruchaga (A, 79')
Naples, 6/13/1990. Referee: E. Fredriksson (Sweden).

Cameroon—2   Romania—1

Milla (C, 76', 86'); Balint (R, 88')
Bari, 6/14/1990. Referee: H. Silva (Chile).

USSR—4   Cameroon—0

Protasov (USSR, 20'); Zygmantovic (USSR, 29'); Zavarov (USSR, 52'); Dobrovolski (USSR, 62')
Bari, 6/18/1990. Referee: J. R. Wright (Brazil).

Argentina—1   Romania—1

Monzon (A, 61'); Balint (R, 68')
Naples, 6/18/1990. Referee: C. Silva Valente (Portugal).

GROUP C

Brazil—2   Sweden—1

Careca (B, 40', 62'); Brolin (S, 74')
Turin, 6/10/1990. Referee: T. Lanese (Italy).

Costa Rica—1   Scotland—0

Cayasso (CR, 50')
Genoa, 6/11/1990. Referee: J. C. Loustau (Argentina).

Brazil—1   Costa Rica—0

Müller (B, 33')
Turin, 6/16/1990. Referee: N. Jouini (Tunisia).

Scotland—2   Sweden—1

McCall (Sc, 10'); Johnston (Sc, 81' penalty); Strömberg (Sw, 85')
Genoa, 6/16/1990. Referee: C. Maciel (Paraguay).

Brazil—1   Scotland—0

Müller (B, 81')
Turin, 6/20/1990. Referee: H. Köhl (Austria).

Costa Rica—2   Sweden—1

Ekström (S, 34'); R. Flores (CR, 74'); Medford (CR, 86')
Genoa, 6/20/1990. Referee: Z. Petrovic (Yugoslavia).

GROUP D

Colombia—2   U.A.E.—0

Redin (C, 51'); Valderrama (C, 85')
Bologna, 6/9/1990. Referee: G. Courtney (England).

W. Ger.—4   Yugoslavia—1

Matthäus (A, 28', 63'); Jozic (Y, 55');
  Klinsmann (A, 39'); Brehme (A,
  71')
Milan, 6/10/1990. Referee: P. Mik-
  lelsen (Denmark).

Yugoslavia—1   Colombia—0

Jozic (Y, 74')
Bologna, 6/14/1990. Referee: L. Agnolin (Italy).

W. Germany—5   U.A.E.—1

Völler (WG, 35', 74'); Klinsmann
  (WG, 37'); Khalid Ismail (UAE,
  46'); Matthäus (WG, 47'); Bein
  (WG, 58')
Milan, 6/15/1990. Referee: A. Spirin
  (Soviet Union).

W. Germany—1 Colombia—1

Littbarski (WG, 87'); Rincon (C, 89')
Milan, 6/19/1990. Referee: A.
  Snoody (Northern Ireland).

Yugoslavia—4   U.A.E.—1

Susic (Y, 4'); Pancev (Y, 9', 46'); Ali
  Thani (UAE, 21'); Prosinecki (Y,
  90')
Bologna, 6/19/1990. Referee: S.
  Takada (Japan).

GROUP E

Belgium—2   South Korea—0

De Grijse (B, 52'); De Wolf (B, 63')
Verona, 6/12/1990. Referee: V.
  Mauro (United States).

Spain—0   Uruguay—0

Udine, 6/13/1990. Referee: H. Köhl
  (Austria).

Belgium—3   Uruguay—1

Clijster (B, 15'); Scifo (B, 24');
  Ceulemans (B, 46'); Bengoechea
  (U, 71')
Verona, 6/17/1990. Referee: S.
  Kirschen (East Germany).

Spain—3   South Korea—1

Michel (S, 23', 60', 80'); Hwangbo
  (SK, 43')
Udine, 6/17/1990. Referee: E. Ja-
  come (Ecuador).

Spain—2   Belgium—1

Michel (S, 26' penalty); Vervoort (B,
  29'); Gorriz (S, 38')
Verona, 6/21/1990. Referee: J. C.
  Loustau (Argentina).

Uruguay—1   South Korea—0

Fonseca (U, 89')
Udine, 6/21/1990. Referee: T.
  Lanese (Italy).

GROUP F

England—1   Ireland—1

Lineker (E, 9'); Sheedy (I, 73')
Cagliari, 6/11/1990. Referee: A.
  Schmidhuber (West Germany).

Holland—1   Egypt—1

Kieft (H, 52'); Abed El Ghany (E,
  83' penalty)
Palermo, 6/12/1990. Referee: E. Al-
  adren Soriano (Spain).

Holland—0   England—0

Cagliari, 6/16/1990. Referee: Z.
  Petrovic (Yugoslavia).

Ireland—0 **Egypt—0**

Palermo, 6/17/1990. Referee: M.
Van Langenhove (Belgium).

England—1 **Egypt—0**

Wright (E, 59')
Cagliari, 6/21/1990. Referee: K.
Roethlisberger (Switzerland).

Holland—1 **Ireland—1**

Gullit (H, 11'); Quinn (I, 71')
Palermo, 6/21/1990. Referee: M.
Vautrot (France).

SECOND ROUND

Cameroon—2 **Colombia—1**

Milla (Ca, 106', 109'); Redin (Co,
115')
Naples, 6/23/1990. Referee: T.
Lanese (Italy).
A 30' overtime was played.

Czech.—4 **Costa Rica—1**

Skhuravy (Cz, 12', 64', 83'); R. Gon-
zalez (CR, 55'); Kubik (Cz, 76')
Bari, 6/23/1990. Referee: S.
Kirschen (East Germany).

Argentina—1 **Brazil—0**

Caniggia (A, 79')
Turin, 6/24/1990. Referee: J. Quiniou (France).

W. Germany—2 **Holland—1**

Klinsmann (WG, 51'); Brehme
(WG, 85'); R. Koeman (H, 88'
penalty)
Milan, 6/24/1990. Referee: J. C.
Loustau (Argentina).

Ire.—0 (5) **Romania—0 (4)**

Genoa, 6/25/1990. Referee: J. R.
Wright (Brazil).
Game decided by penalty-kick tie-
breaker.

Italy—2 **Uruguay—0**

Schillaci (I, 69'); Serena (I, 83')
Rome, 6/25/1990. Referee: G.
Courtney (England).

Yugoslavia—2 **Spain—1**

Stojkovic (Y, 77', 92'); Salinas (S,
84')
Verona, 6/26/1990. Referee: A.
Schmidhuber (West Germany).
A 30' overtime was played.

England—1 **Belgium—0**

Platt (E, 119')
Bologna, 6/26/1990. Referee: P.
Mikkelsen (Denmark).
A 30' overtime was played.

QUARTERFINALS

Argentina—0 (3) **Yug.—0 (2)**

Florence, 6/30/1990. Referee: K.
Roethlisberger (Switzerland).
Game decided by a penalty-kick
tie-breaker.

Italy—1 **Ireland—0**

Schillaci (I, 38')
Rome, 6/30/1990. Referee: C. Silva
Valente (Portugal).

W. Germany—1 **Czech.—0**

Matthäus (WG, 24' penalty)
Milan, 7/1/1990. Referee: H. Köhl
(Austria).

England—3   Cameroon—2

Platt (E, 25'); Kunde (C, 61'
  penalty); Ekeke (C, 66'); Lineker
  (E, 82' penalty, 104' penalty).
Naples, 7/1/1990. Referee: E. Code-
  sal (Mexico).
A 30' overtime was played.

SEMIFINALS

Argentina—1 (4) Italy—1 (3)

Schillaci (I, 17'); Caniggia (A, 67')
Naples, 7/3/1990. Referee: M.
  Vautrot (France).
Game decided by a penalty-kick
  tie-breaker.

W. Ger.—1 (4) England—1 (3)

Brehme (WG, 60'); Lineker (E, 80')
Milan, 7/5/1990. Referee: J. R.
  Wright (Brazil).
Game decided by penalty-kick tie-
  breaker.

THIRD-PLACE GAME

Italy—2   England—1

Baggio (I, 70'); Platt (E, 80');
  Schillaci (I, 85' penalty)
Bari, 7/7/1990. Referee: J. Quiniou
  (France).

FINAL

W. Germany—1 Argentina—0

Brehme (WG, 85' penalty)
Rome, 7/8/1990. Referee: E. Codesal (Mexico).
West Germany: Illgner; Augen-
  thaler; Kohler, Buchwald;
  Berthold (replaced by Reuter at
  73'); Littbraski, Matthäus, Hässler,

Brehme; Klinsmann, Völler.
Coach: Franz Beckenbauer.
Argentina: Goycochea; Simon; Ruggeri [replaced by Monzon at 45'
  (ejected at 63')], Serrizuela,
  Sensini; Troglio, Basualdo, Burruchaga (replaced by Calderon
  at 52'), Lorenzo; Dezotti (ejected
  at 86'), Maradona. Coach: Carlos
  Salvador Bilardo.

World Cup USA 1994

GROUP A

USA—1   Switzerland—1

Bregy (S, 39'); Wynalda (USA, 44')
Detroit, 6/18/1994. Referee: F. Lamolina (Argentina).

Romania—3   Colombia—1

Raducioiu (R, 16', 89'); Hagi (R,
  34'); Valencia (C, 43')
Los Angeles, 6/18/1994. Referee: J.
  Al-Sharif (Syria).

Switzerland—4 Romania—1

Sutter (S, 16'); Hagi (R, 36'); Cha-
  puisat (S, 51'); Knup (S, 65', 72')
Detroit, 6/22/1994. Referee: N.
  Jouini (Tunisia).

USA—2   Colombia—1

Escobar (C, 32' own goal); Stewart
  (USA, 51'); Valencia (C, 89')
Los Angeles, 6/22/1994. Referee: F.
  Baldas (Italy).

Romania—1   USA—0

Petrescu (R, 17')
Los Angeles, 6/26/1994. Referee: M.
  Van Der Ende (Holland).

Colombia—2 Switzerland—0

Gaviria (C, 44'); Lozano (C, 89')
San Francisco, 6/26/1994. Referee:
P. Mikkelsen (Denmark).

GROUP B

Cameroon—2   Sweden—2

Ljung (S, 7'); Embe (C, 30'); O.
Biyik (C, 46'); Dahlin (S, 74')
Los Angeles, 6/19/1994. Referee: A.
Tejada (Peru).

Brazil—2   Russia—0

Romario (B, 26'); Rai (B, 52'
penalty)
San Francisco, 6/20/1994. Referee:
L. Kee Chong (Mauritius).

Brazil—3   Cameroon—0

Romario (B, 38'); Marcio Santos (B,
65'); Bebeto (B, 73')
San Francisco, 6/24/1994. Referee:
A. Brizio (Mexico).

Sweden—3   Russia—1

Salenko (R, 4' penalty); Brolin (S,
38' penalty); Dahlin (S, 59', 81')
Detroit, 6/24/1994. Referee: J.
Quiniou (France).

Russia—6   Cameroon—1

Salenko (R, 15', 40', 44' penalty, 72'
74'); Milla (C, 46'); Radchenko (R,
82')
San Francisco, 6/28/1994. Referee:
J. Al-Sharif (Syria).

Brazil—1   Sweden—1

K. Andersson (S, 23'); Romario (B,
47')

Detroit, 6/28/1994. Referee: S. Puhl
(Hungary).

GROUP C

Germany—1   Bolivia—0

Klinsmann (G, 61')
Chicago, 6/17/1994. Referee: A.
Brizio (Mexico).

Spain—2   South Korea—2

Salinas (Sp, 50'); Goikoetxea (Sp,
55'); Hong Myong Bo (SK, 84');
Seo Jung Won (SK, 89')
Dallas, 6/17/1994. Referee: P.
Mikkelsen (Denmark).

Germany—1   Spain—1

Goikoetxea (S, 14'); Klinsmann (G,
48')
Chicago, 6/21/1994. Referee: E. Fil-
ippi (Uruguay).

Bolivia—0   South Korea—0

Boston, 6/23/1994. Referee: L. Mottram (Scotland).

Spain—3   Bolivia—1

Guardiola (S, 9' penalty); Caminero
(S, 66', 71'); E. Sanchez (B, 67')
Chicago, 6/27/1994. Referee: R.
Badilla (Costa Rica).

Germany—3 South Korea—2

Klinsmann (G, 12', 37'); Riedle (G,
19'); Hwang Sun Hong (SK, 52');
Hong Myong Bo (SK, 58')
Dallas, 6/27/1994. Referee: J. Quiniou (France).

GROUP D

Argentina—4   Greece—0

Batistuta (A, 2', 43', 88' penalty);
   Maradona (A, 60')
Boston, 6/21/1994. Referee: A. Angeles (United States).

Nigeria—3   Bulgaria—0

Yekini (N, 21'); Amokachi (N, 42');
   Amunike (N, 54')
Dallas, 6/21/1994. Referee: R.
   Badilla (Costa Rica).

Argentina—2   Nigeria—1

Siasia (N, 8'); Caniggia (A, 21', 29')
Boston, 6/25/1994. Referee: B.
   Karlsson (Sweden).

Bulgaria—4   Greece—0

Stoitchkov (B, 5' penalty, 55'
   penalty); Letchkov (B, 66');
   Borimirov (B, 90')
Chicago, 6/25/1994. Referee: A. M.
   Bujsaim (United Arab Emirates).

Nigeria—2   Greece—0

Finidi (N, 43'); Amokachi (N, 89')
Boston, 6/30/1994. Referee: L. Mottram (Scotland).

Bulgaria—2   Argentina—0

Stoitchkov (B, 60'); Sirakov (B, 90')
Dallas, 6/30/1994. Referee: N.
   Jouini (Tunisia).

GROUP E

Ireland—1   Italy—0

Houghton (Ir, 11')
New York, 6/18/1994. Referee: M.
   Van Der Ende (Holland).

Norway—1   Mexico—0

Rekdal (N, 84')
Washington, 6/19/1994. Referee: S.
   Puhl (Hungary).

Italy—1   Norway—0

D. Baggio (I, 69')
New York, 6/23/1994. Referee: H.
   Krug (Germany).

Mexico—2   Ireland—1

L. Garcia (M, 44', 66'); Aldridge (I,
   84')
Orlando, 6/24/1994. Referee: K.
   Roethlisberger (Switzerland).

Ireland—0   Norway—0

New York, 6/28/1994. Referee: J.
   Torres (Colombia).

Italy—1   Mexico—1

Massaro (I, 48'); Bernal (M, 57')
Washington, 6/28/1994. Referee: F.
   Lamolina (Argentina).

GROUP F

Belgium—1   Morocco—0

Degryse (B, 11')
Orlando, 6/19/1994. Referee: J. Torres (Colombia).

Holland—2   Saudi Arabia—1

Amin (SA, 18'); Jonk (H, 49'); Tament (H, 86')
Washington, 6/20/1994. Referee: M.
   Diaz Vega (Spain).

Saudi Arabia—2 Morocco—1

Al Jaber (SA, 7' penalty); Chaouch (M, 26'); Amin (SA, 45')
New York, 6/25/1994. Referee: P. Don (England).

Belgium—1   Holland—0

Albert (B, 66')
Orlando, 6/25/1994. Referee: R. Marsiglia (Brazil).

Holland—2   Morocco—1

Bergkamp (H, 42'); Nader (M, 47'); Roy (H, 78')
Orlando, 6/29/1994. Referee: A. Tejada (Peru).

Saudi Arabia—1 Belgium—0

Owa Iran (SA, 8')
Washington, 6/29/1994. Referee: H. Krug (Germany).

SECOND ROUND

Germany—3   Belgium—2

Völler (G, 5', 39'); Grun (B, 7'); Klinsmann (G, 10'); Albert (B, 87')
Chicago, 7/2/1994. Referee: K. Roethlisberger (Switzerland).

Spain—3   Switzerland—0

Hierro (S, 15'); Luis Enrique (S, 74'); Beguiristain (S, 86' penalty)
Washington, 7/2/1994. Referee: M. Van Der Ende (Holland).

Sweden—3 Saudi Arabia—1

Dahlin (Sw, 5'); K. Andersson (Sw, 50', 86'); Al Ghashiyan (SA, 85')
Dallas, 7/3/1994. Referee: R. Marsiglia (Brazil).

Romania—3   Argentina—2

Dumitrescu (R, 11', 17'); Batistuta (A, 14' penalty); Hagi (R, 57'); Balbo (A, 74')
Los Angeles, 7/3/1994. Referee: P. Pairetto (Italy).

Holland—2   Ireland—0

Bergkamp (H, 11'); Jonk (H, 41')
Orlando, 7/4/1994. Referee: P. Mikkelsen (Denmark).

Brazil—1   USA—0

Bebeto (B, 74')
San Francisco, 7/4/1994. Referee: J. Quiniou (France).

Italy—2   Nigeria—1

Amunike (N, 26'); R. Baggio (I, 88', 112' penalty)
Boston, 7/5/1994. Referee: A. Brizio (Mexico)
A 30' overtime was played.

Bulgaria—1 (3)   Mex.—1 (1)

Stoitchkov (B, 6'); Garcia Aspe (M, 16' penalty)
New York, 7/5/1994. Referee: J. Al-Sharif (Syria).
Game decided by penalty-kick tie-breaker.

QUARTERFINALS

Italy—2   Spain—1

D. Baggio (I, 25'); Caminero (S, 58'); R. Baggio (I, 85')
Boston, 7/9/1994. Referee: S. Puhl (Hungary).

Brazil—3   Holland—2

Romario (B, 52'); Bebeto (B, 63');
Bergkamp (H, 65'); Winter (H,
75'); Branco (B, 80')
Dallas, 7/9/1994. Referee: R. Badilla
(Costa Rica).

Bulgaria—2   Germany—1

Matthäus (G, 50' penalty);
Stoitchkov (B, 75'); Letchkov (B,
80')
New York, 7/10/1994. Referee: J.
Torres (Colombia).

Sweden—2 (5)   Rom.—2 (4)

Brolin (S, 79'); Raducioiu (R, 89',
101'); K. Andersson (S, 115')
San Francisco, 7/10/1994. Referee:
P. Don (England)
Game decided by penalty-kick tie-
breaker.

SEMIFINALS

Italy—2   Bulgaria—1

R. Baggio (I, 20', 25'); Stoitchkov
(B, 44' penalty)
New York, 7/13/1994. Referee: J.
Quiniou (France).

Brazil—1   Sweden—0

Romario (B, 81')
Los Angeles, 7/13/1994. Referee: J.
Torres (Colombia).

THIRD-PLACE GAME

Sweden—4   Bulgaria—0

Brolin (S, 8'); Mild (S, 30'); H. Lars-
son (S, 37'); K. Andersson (S, 39')
Los Angeles, 7/16/1994. Referee: A.
Mohamed Bujsaim (United Arab
Emirates).

FINAL

Brazil—0 (3)   Italy—0 (2)

Los Angeles, 7/17/1994. Referee: S.
Puhl (Hungary).
Game decided by penalty-kick tie-
breaker: Baresi (missed), Marcio
Santos (saved), Albertini, Ro-
mario, Evani, Branco, Massaro
(saved), Dunga, R. Baggio
(missed).
Brazil: Taffarel; Jorginho (replaced
by Cafu), Aldair, Marcio Santos,
Branco; Mauro Silva, Dunga,
Mazinho, Zinho (replaced by
Viola); Bebeto, Romario. Coach:
Carlos Alberto Parreira.
Italy: Pagliuca; Mussi (replaced by
Apolloni), Maldini, Baresi, Benar-
rivo; Donadoni, D. Baggio (re-
placed by Evani), Albertini, Berti;
R. Baggio, Massaro. Coach: Ar-
rigo Sacchi.

Acknowledgments

Ignacio Matus
Jorge Ventura
Carlos Bonelli
Matteo Dotto
Manuel Epelbaum
Jose Felix Suarez
Roger Lindse
Alberto Cantore
Tony Signore
Daniel Gutman
Becky Cabaza
Dan Lane
Guillermo Gorroño

Bibliography

Books

Beha, Oliveriero, and Roberto Chiod. *MundialGate*. Tulio Pironti Editore, 1984.

Bilardo, Carlos. *Asi Ganamos*. Sudamericana-Planeta, 1986.

Cien Años con el Fútbol: AFA 1893–1993 Centenario. AFA 1993.

Confederación Sudamericana de Fútbol, *Fútbol 75 años*. *1916– 1991*. (Confederación Sudamericana de Fútbol, 1991).

Duarte, Orlando. *Todas as copas do mundo*. Makron Books du Brasil, 1994.

Enciclopedia Mundial del Fútbol. Ediciones Oceano S.A., 1984.

FIFA. *1904–1984: Historical Publication of the Federation Internale de Football Association*. FIFA, 1984.

FIFA. *World Cup Italia 90* (Official Report). FIFA 1990.

Gardner, Paul. *The Simplest Game*. Collier Books, 1993.

Glanville, Brian. *The Story of the World Cup*. Faber and Faber, 1993.

Le Goulven, Francis, and Dellamarre Gilles. *Les grandes heures de La Coupe de Monde*. Editions PAC, 1981.

Libro del Fútbol. Abril Educativa Cultural, 1974.

Lucero, Diego. *Siento ruido de pelota*. Editorial Freeland, 1975.

Nunes, Marus Vinícius Bucar. *Zico, uma liçao de vida*. Offset Editoria Grafica y Jornalistica Ltda, 1986.

Pelé. *My Life and the Beautiful Game*. Warner Books, 1977.

Pippo, Antonio. *Obdulio desde el Alma*. Editorial Fin de Siglo, 1993.

Poveda Marquez, Fabio. *Dioses de carne y hueso*. Calveria S.A., 1990.

Real Federación Española de Fútbol. *75 aniversario* 1913–1988. Real Federación Española de Fútbol, 1988.

Robinson, John. *Soccer, The World Cup*. Soccer Book Publishing Limited, 1990.

Roland, Thierry. *La fabuleuse Histoire de la coupe du monde*. Editions Odil, 1986.

Rollin, Jack. *The World Cup 1930–1990*. Facts on File, 1990.

Publications:

France Football, France
El Grafico, Argentina
Guerin Sportivo, Italy
Placar, Brasil
Special editions of *El Grafico* and *Guerin Sportivo*

Index of Players